Developing Effective Assessment in Higher Education: a practical guide

Sue Bloxham
Pete Boyd

Open University Press

Open University Press
McGraw-Hill Education
McGraw-Hill House
Shoppenhangers Road
Maidenhead
Berkshire
England
SL6 2QL

email: enquiries@openup.co.uk
world wide web: www.openup.co.uk

and Two Penn Plaza, New York, NY 10121–2289, USA

First published 2007

Copyright © Sue Bloxham and Pete Boyd 2007

A catalogue record of this book is available from the British Library

ISBN 13: 9780 335 221073 (pb) 9780 335 221080 (hb)
ISBN 10: 0335 221 076 (pb) 0335 221 084 (hb)

Library of Congress Cataloguing-in-Publication Data
CIP data applied for

Typeset by YHT Ltd, London
Printed and bound by CPI Group (UK) Ltd, Croydon, CR0 4YY

The **McGraw·Hill** Companies

Developing Effective Assessment in Higher Education: a practical guide

Contents

Contributors

Sue Bloxham is Professor of Academic Practice and Head of the Centre for Development of Learning and Teaching at the University of Cumbria, England. She has been experimenting with and researching improvements to assessment in higher education for twenty years both as a lecturer, and more recently, as an educational developer. Her research interests are also in the area of supporting student transition.

Peter Boyd is Senior Lecturer in the Centre for Development of Learning and Teaching at the University of Cumbria. His background is in Education and his current teaching role is mainly within a postgraduate course for newly appointed lecturers. Peter's research interests are in the area of induction and workplace learning of newly appointed academics in professional subject disciplines and also in peer review of teaching among academics.

Sarah Chesney is Senior Lecturer in E-learning in the Centre for Development of Learning and Teaching at the University of Cumbria. Sarah's background is in using the internet to enhance education. Her MEd from University of Sheffield in e-learning cultivated her interest in networked communication. Her research and development interests are in e-portfolios for CPD, and the enhancement of teaching and learning through web tools and new technologies.

Andrew Ginty is currently Director of the Human Anatomy Learning and Research Centre within the School of Dentistry at the University of Central Lancashire. Andrew previously worked at the University of Manchester and at Liverpool Hope University teaching in the life sciences. He also worked at St. Martin's College, Lancaster, where he contributed particularly to the development of learning through use of technology. His interests are in computer aided learning and their dimensional modelling.

Marion Nuttall is the Academic Enhancement Manager at the University of Cumbria and is an experienced lecturer and manager in higher education. She has taught and assessed students on a wide range of courses and has led professional development for staff on assessment, marking and moderating, and management of assessment at departmental level. She is particularly interested in students' engagement with assessment feedback to enhance their learning.

Acknowledgements

The authors would like to thank the following friends and colleagues for assistance in writing this book: Tim Barry, Penny Bradshaw, Matthew Brown, Christine Colcomb, Richard Lording, Caroline Marcangelo, Nicky Metcalfe-Meer, Kay Sambell and her colleagues at the Centre for Excellence in Teaching & Learning in Assessment for Learning at Northumbria University, Elliott Shaw and Bobbie Smith. In particular, we would like to thank all members of the Centre for the Development of Learning and Teaching at the University of Cumbria who gave us the space to write.

PART 1
INTRODUCTION AND CONTEXT

1   Introduction

The primacy of assessment

Research and experience tell us very forcefully about the importance of assessment in higher education. It shapes the experience of students and influences their behaviour more than the teaching they receive. The influence of assessment means that 'there is more leverage to improve teaching through changing assessment than there is in changing anything else' (Gibbs and Simpson 2004–5: 22). Tutors implicitly know the importance of assessment. Anecdotal experience tells us that, to a large extent, assessment activity in higher education is the learning activity. Students may take notes in lectures, seminars or from their reading, they may have been through the prescribed activities in laboratories or on field trips, but it is only when faced with assessment tasks that the majority seriously engage with that material. Tutors despair of trying to persuade students to undertake study which does not contribute in some way to their grades.

Sadly, though, university assessment practice lags well behind its equivalent in the school sector (Murphy 2006), relying largely on a limited range of tried (but not always tested) methods. It is dealt with in an *ad hoc* way (Swann and Ecclestone 1999a) and the situation is not mitigated by the 'amateur' status of many academics regarding assessment (Ramsden 2003: 177). We learn the craft of assessment informally through being assessed ourselves and through being part of a community of practice, but lack scholarship regarding assessment (Price 2005). Undoubtedly, most of us have survived this approach to professional learning reasonably unscathed but it is not a recipe for enhancement; it provides no reliable route for ensuring that research on assessment reaches those doing the assessing.

Assessment pressures and influences

The contemporary environment of higher education means that assessment cannot carry on unaltered; it is subject to too many pressures and influences which create a force for change. Increasing cohort size and the shrinking unit of resource creates pressure for more cost-effective assessment methods especially as assessment is very expensive and, in today's mass classrooms, can use more resources than teaching (Gibbs 2006b). This problem is exacerbated by **modularisation**, which has increased the volume of assessment as each small block of learning must be formally assessed and graded.

In addition, the student body is changing. Reliance on part-time work and other commitments appear to be turning students into very strategic learners (Kneale 1997) unwilling to devote effort to study which does not contribute to **summative assessment**. Tutors are increasingly teaching a much more diverse student body who challenge existing assumptions about what can be expected from new students (Northedge 2003a), with many non-traditional students needing greater support in making the transition to higher education. Poor early experience of assessment is associated with high student **attrition** rates (Krause 2001).

Moreover, the employability and graduate skills agenda is placing pressure on tutors to design assignments and examinations which assess a much broader range of achievement than in the past. Assessment is now expected to assess subject knowledge and a wide range of intellectual, professional and generic skills in a quality-assurance climate that stresses reliability with robust marking and **moderation** methods. Tutors are also facing pressure to modify assessment so that it supports learning through student involvement in assessment, prompt **feedback**, flexible and formative approaches and a wide variety of assessment methods.

In addition, assessment practices are being influenced by advances in technology. While computers afford the opportunity for online assessment, immediate feedback and computer-marked assignments, they also provide the breeding ground for the increase in **plagiarism**.

Within individual universities the mediation of regulations and the assessment process by departments, programme teams and individual tutors may be influenced, possibly constrained, by locally based, taken-for-granted assumptions, and even myths. Effective communication and academic development work may often be required to support programme teams in enhancing their assessment design and practice.

Finally, student evaluation through the National Student Survey (2006) has made student reactions to our programmes public for the first time, and assessment is proving to be the weakest area in the analysis. Competition in the new consumer market in higher education will mean that departments cannot neglect the student perspective for too long.

Policy

Perhaps the most obvious recent influence on assessment has been the policy climate in relation to quality assurance and enhancement. The quality assurance and accountability climate differs from nation to nation. In the UK, institutional autonomy and self-regulation are now constrained by unambiguous public policy (Jackson 2000), largely in the guise of the 'academic infrastructure' of the Quality Assurance Agency (QAA 2006d). This includes a set of guidelines designed to create greater confidence in standards across British higher education, including the Framework for Higher Education Qualifications (**FHEQ**) which indicates the types of learning outcomes expected from different awards, **subject benchmark statements** for individual disciplines, various codes of practice, including one for assessment, and programme specifications. A key feature of external review of institutions (institutional audit) by the **QAA** is the extent to which the quality assurance procedures for any university comply with these guidelines.

At the heart of the QAA approach is the notion of constructive alignment between 'learning outcomes' and assessment. Assessment practice is judged primarily on whether it effectively measures the intended outcomes of a course of study in a valid, reliable and transparent way. This book acknowledges the centrality of this approach and its pervading influence on so much day-to-day institutional practice, and therefore an outcome-based method has been adopted throughout the text. However, such a philosophy is not accepted unquestioningly. Outcome-based course design represents a set of ideas which are currently fashionable in higher education quality assurance and educational development circles, but the approach is also open to criticism. Box 2.3 in Chapter 2 summarises the debate.

A further policy imperative emerged in the late 1990s in the UK. The Dearing Report (National Committee of Inquiry into Higher Education 1997), followed by various initiatives and the 2003 Higher Education White Paper (Department for Education and Skills 2003), placed considerable emphasis on raising standards of teaching and assessment in higher education. This included requirements for institutional learning and teaching strategies and strong encouragement for the professionalisation of academic staff in relation to learning, teaching and assessment. Some form of initial training for higher education lecturers is now widespread in British universities.

Research evidence

Publications now abound with tips for improving assessment and case study accounts of assessment practice. However, Knight and Yorke (2003: 209) argue that they largely represent a 'cottage industry' lacking a systematic theoretical basis for understanding judgements of achievement, and thus 'attempts to enhance assessment practices are built on sand'. This book attempts to distil the consistent elements of research findings to provide well-informed but intensely practical advice. In doing this, it is recognised that academics are by definition sceptical and will wish to see an acknowledgement of conflicting ideas and alternative perspectives, with any subsequent recommendations emerging from persuasive evidence.

Despite the evidence-based approach, we have attempted to write in an accessible way that does not require the reader to have prior knowledge of educational theory. *Leads into Literature* boxes will be used to provide routes into further reading or summarise areas of debate in relation to conflicting theories or controversial policies. In this manner, the book aims to provide strong guidelines explicitly supported by research.

Why another assessment book?

The dominance of assessment in the student experience and the social, economic and policy climate have led to a situation where assessment is in a state of flux, facing pressures for enhancement while simultaneously coping with demands to restrict its burden on students and staff. It is a demanding agenda but one which this book endeavours to embrace. The book recognises and welcomes the challenges presented above of assessment for learning, quality assurance, student numbers and diversity, modularisation, workload, plagiarism and technology. It also aims to provide a guide which focuses on all stages of the assessment cycle (see Figure 1.1). In this sense, the book is unique and comprehensive.

The book attempts to translate what is implied from research into the day-to-day demands of *doing* assessment in higher education. Our approach is informed by many years of experience struggling to improve assessment and use it creatively to influence students' learning. The poverty of assessment in higher education has made it tempting for assessment texts to advocate major institutional change; in our view this is an ideal rather than a realistic approach. Our experience and knowledge of the sector have persuaded us towards a more pragmatic approach recognising the limited appetite for change among academics facing huge pressures for productivity in other aspects of their role. Potential frustration for staff attempting change but constrained by institutional structures (Cuban 1988) is also acknowledged, so the book advocates practices which can have significant impact on the student experience yet have the potential to work within existing structures.

Thus, although we do not gainsay many of the conclusions of other scholars in the assessment field, they are not developed here. As Boud (2000: 159) suggests, 'one of the traps in arguing for a shift in assessment practice is to propose an unrealistic ideal that can never be attained'. In its place, we have attempted to write this guide within the bounds of what is possible in most university departments. The book focuses on discussion of issues, offering pragmatic solutions, and does not spend too much time advocating

Box 1.1 Code of Practice

The text below sets out Appendix 1 of the *Code of Practice for the Assurance of Academic Quality and Standards in Higher Education*, Section 6: Assessment of Students (© The Quality Assurance Agency for Higher Education 2006) and identifies which chapters address each specific principle.

<u>**The Precepts**</u>

General principles

1. As bodies responsible for the academic standards of awards made in their name, institutions have effective procedures for:

i   designing, approving, monitoring and reviewing the assessment strategies for programmes and awards
    Chapter 11

ii implementing rigorous assessment policies and practices that ensure the standard for each award and award element is set and maintained at the appropriate level, and that student performance is properly judged against this
    Chapter 12

iii evaluating how academic standards are maintained through assessment practice that also encourages effective learning.
    Chapter 9

2. Institutions publicise and implement principles and procedures for, and processes of, assessment that are explicit, valid and reliable.
Chapters 2 and 4

Contribution to student learning

3. Institutions encourage assessment practice that promotes effective learning.
Chapters 2, 4, 7, 10, 11, 12, 13, 14.

Assessment panels and examination boards

4. Institutions publicise and implement effective, clear and consistent policies for the membership, procedures, powers and accountability of assessment panels and boards of examiners.
Chapters 8 and 9

Conduct of assessment

5. Institutions ensure that assessment is conducted with rigour, probity and fairness and with due regard for security.
Chapters 6, 8 and 9

Amount and timing of assessment

6. Institutions ensure that the amount and timing of assessment enables effective and appropriate measurement of students' achievement of intended learning outcomes.
Chapters 4, 11 and 12

Marking and grading

7. Institutions have transparent and fair mechanisms for marking and for moderating marks.
Chapters 6 and 8

8. Institutions publicise and implement clear rules and regulations for progressing from one stage of a programme to another and for qualifying for an award.
Chapter 9

Feedback to students on their performance

9. Institutions provide appropriate and timely feedback to students on assessed work in a way that promotes learning and facilitates improvement but does not increase the burden of assessment.
Chapter 7

Staff development and training

10. Institutions ensure that everyone involved in the assessment of students is competent to undertake their roles and responsibilities.
Chapters 9 and 15

Language of study and assessment

11. The languages used in teaching and assessment are normally the same. If, for any reason, this is not possible, institutions ensure that their academic standards are not consequently put at risk.

Professional, statutory and regulatory bodies' requirements

12. Institutions provide clear information to staff and students about specific assessment outcomes or other criteria that must be met to fulfil the requirements of PSRBs.
Chapter 11

Assessment regulations

13. Institutions review and amend assessment regulations periodically, as appropriate, to assure themselves that the regulations remain fit for purpose.
Chapter 9

Student conduct in assessment

14. Institutions encourage students to adopt good academic conduct in respect of assessment and seek to ensure they are aware of their responsibilities.
Chapters 3, 4, 5 and 14

Recording, documenting and communicating assessment decisions

15. Institutions ensure that assessment decisions are recorded and documented accurately and systematically and that the decisions of relevant assessment panels and examination boards are communicated as quickly as possible.
Chapter 9

programme assessment strategy. Module leaders are encouraged to read Chapter 12 as a first step in rethinking the assessment of their modules.

- Staff developers could use the text as a resource in designing staff development workshops, for example by using the case study approach in Chapter 3 to analyse how well diverse types of assignment provide for the different principles of assessment or using Chapter 6 as the pre-reading for a workshop on marking for postgraduate teaching assistants.
- Practitioner researchers could use the references in the *Leads into Literature* boxes as a stimulus for further investigation of aspects of assessment.
- Quality assurance teams could use Chapter 11 in the training for validation or accreditation panels. It can help them identify the questions they might want to ask in testing the merit of a new programme assessment strategy.

Cross-references are used throughout the book to assist readers in finding broader information of relevance to the topic of a particular chapter.

A note about terminology

Various different terms are used to refer to the same entity in higher education across English-speaking countries. Therefore, in order to avoid considerable confusion and repetition in the book, we have adopted certain terms as follows:

Assessment task – any item of assessment whether examination, test, coursework or direct observation.
Assignment – coursework usually undertaken by a student or students in their own time and not under controlled conditions.
Examination – an assessment task undertaken under controlled conditions.
Test – an assessment task taken in semi-controlled conditions such as an in-class or online test, usually of a relatively short duration.
Assessment strategy – the procedures adopted to assess student learning in a given module or programme.
Module – a specific unit of study or block of learning which is separately assessed. Combinations of modules form a programme of study.
Programme – the overall curriculum followed by an individual student, normally comprising a specified set of modules or option choices.
Course – unlike programme and module, which are used very specifically, the term *course* is used generally, to refer to any organised scheme of teaching.

Curriculum – like 'course', used generally to refer to all aspects of the student learning experience. It includes both the syllabus (content) and the teaching, learning and assessment methods.

Year – many staff in higher education have replaced the term 'year' with 'level' to represent the stage of learning, because the diversity in modes of study means that students are often spending more than a year on a programme level. Thus, level 1 is equal to year 1 of a full-time undergraduate programme. We have chosen to use 'year' as the indicator of level of study because it is readily understood and because various labels exist for different levels. For example, level 1 is also referred to as foundation or level 4 depending on the framework in use. The use of the term 'year' implies no assumption that all students are full-time. (See Box 11.3 for a discussion of levels.)

Attribution/attributable – we have selected these terms to refer to the extent to which an assignment can be reliably attributed as the work of an individual student. The word 'authenticity' is frequently used in this way, but we have rejected that term because it is also commonly used to mean an assignment which mirrors realistic demands outside the university. Using the term for both meanings would be confusing.

A full glossary of terms and acronyms used in this text is set out in the Appendix.

Conclusion

This text is offered as a comprehensive resource based on research, public policy and experience. As with most things educational, there are no right or simple answers that can be employed across the messy business of providing programmes of learning for adults. There are only more or less likely solutions to problems and they will be affected by you, your students, the learning environment, and the **subject discipline** in many different ways. The temptation might be to hold back from advice in such unpredictable circumstances, yet that is a recipe for leaving things as they are in an environment which is hardly static. The pressures discussed in the opening paragraphs emphasise the importance of taking action, and that action should at least be as well informed as possible. Having said that, we have had to be fairly sparing in our use of evidence in order to balance background information with practical advice. We realise it is presumptuous to claim this as a guide to good practice, and indeed we would prefer our advice to provoke you, even enrage you, rather than leave you untouched. If we wish for anything, it is that tutors and teaching teams seriously engage in debate about assessment and decide for themselves what constitutes good practice.

2 The evidence base for assessment practice in higher education

There is a growing body of research into higher education assessment on which we can begin to build robust policy and practice decisions. This book has drawn on that evidence as a basis for its advice on 'good practice'. Therefore, in advance of our discussions on dealing with and developing assessment in Parts 2 and 3, respectively, this chapter summarises what the research evidence tells us about assessment practice in higher education. Of course, a methodical appraisal of the field would constitute a substantive book in its own right, whereas for the purposes of this text we shall limit ourselves to summarising the main conclusions of research in an accessible way. The *Leads into Literature* boxes will direct readers seeking more information to appropriate research literature. Box 2.1 introduces four useful systematic reviews of the assessment literature.

Assessment purposes have been categorised usefully as assessment *of* learning, assessment *for* learning and assessment *as* learning (Earl 2003). Assessment *of* learning characterises how we may traditionally view assessment. It involves making judgements about students' summative achievement for purposes of selection and certification, and it also acts as a focus for institutional accountability and quality assurance – for example, the number of 'good' degrees awarded is used as a key variable in university league tables. On the other hand, assessment *for* learning is **formative** and **diagnostic**. It provides information about student achievement which allows teaching and learning activities to be changed in response to the needs of the learner and recognises the huge benefit that feedback can have on learning (Black and Wiliam 1998a). Finally, assessment *as* learning can be defined in two interlinked ways. First, at a very straightforward level, tackling assignments and **revision** is when higher education students *do* much of their learning. Second, assessment *as* learning is a subset of assessment *for* learning and sees student involvement in assessment, using feedback, participating in peer assessment, and self-monitoring of progress as moments of learning in themselves (Black and Wiliam 1998a). Students come to have a better understanding of the subject matter and their own learning through their close involvement with assessment.

This summary of relevant literature focuses primarily on what the

---

Box 2.1   Leads into literature: systematic reviews of assessment literature in higher education.

Gibbs and Simpson (2004–5) have conducted a thorough review of research studies which they have drawn upon to develop a set of eleven 'conditions under which assessment supports learning' which are offered as a useful reference point for developing assessment practice.

An earlier comprehensive review of formative assessment by Black and Wiliam (1998a) includes research from both school and university settings with consistent findings regarding the significance of feedback on learning compared with other elements of teaching, and the distinctive benefits for learning accruing from peer and self-assessment.

Struyven *et al.* (2002) have also conducted a useful review of the research into students' perceptions of assessment in higher education although they conclude that the literature and research on this area are relatively limited, particularly in relation to students' perceptions of specific types of assessment.

Finally, Elton and Johnston (2002) have drawn on a wide range of studies in their critical review of research on assessment in higher education, with particular emphasis on challenging some of the underlying assumptions in our assessment traditions.

These publications will provide the reader with extensive lists of further reading across the range of assessment topics.

---

literature tells us about assessment *for* learning and *as* learning, but will also briefly address assessment *of* learning. Chapter 3, which debates the major tensions in contemporary assessment practice, will discuss assessment *of* learning in more detail.

The relationship between assessment and learning

The assessment strategy of a particular course has a major impact on student activity (Snyder 1971). It influences the approach students adopt towards their learning, how much time they spend on their studies, how widely they study the curriculum, and whether they grasp the key concepts of the subject. There is also evidence of a significant, negative 'backwash' effect (Biggs 2003) on student learning and achievement from poorly conceived assessment strategies. Therefore, tutors who neglect to pay attention to their assessment practices are ignoring an important opportunity to enhance students' effort, approach and outcomes.

Approaches to learning

The concept of student approaches to learning has developed from the initial work of Marton (1976), with findings replicated in many other studies using a phenomenographic approach. Prosser and Trigwell (1999: 88) provide an excellent overview of the history of the seminal studies in this field, concluding that the 'approaches to study' work has 'resulted in an approach to research in student learning which has played a major role in bridging the gap between educational research and the practice of university learning and teaching'.

In the research, two approaches to learning by students which consistently emerge are a **surface** approach and a **deep** approach (Marton and Saljo 1997; Ramsden 2003). The student's conception of learning and their *intention* when studying are central to the approach they take. Students adopt a surface approach when their intention is to cope with the requirements of the task but with little personal engagement or aim to understand the material. Such students want to get by with minimum effort and tend to focus on the detail of the knowledge, memorising the information or procedures, for example rote learning for an examination. As a result, students do not grasp the overall meaning of their studies, develop limited conceptual understanding of the material and have poor-quality learning outcomes (Entwistle 1997).

In contrast, students who adopt a deep approach aim to understand ideas and are intrinsically interested in their studies. The learning strategies they use include relating information and ideas together and to their own experience and looking for patterns, principles and meaning in the texts. This approach leads to higher-quality learning outcomes for the student.

An approach to learning is not a fixed characteristic of an individual but is influenced by their perception of the learning environment, most particularly the assessment task (Morgan and Beatty 1997; Biggs 2003). Appropriate assessment can encourage students to adopt a deep approach to learning, and the contrary is true for poorly designed assessment. If students perceive that a task requires memorisation and reproduction of facts, then that is what they will do. The link between assessment method and student approach to learning is vital for the design of assessment in higher education, and later chapters on teaching a module (Chapter 4) and developing programme and module assessment strategies (Chapters 11 and 12) will discuss the practical implications.

Biggs and Moore (1993) have argued that a range of course characteristics encourage students to take a deep approach. These include a clear structure to the knowledge base of the course, so that the content is integrated and new topics relate to previous knowledge. Moreover, courses should encourage students' intrinsic interest in the subject matter. Finally, they should involve learner activity and interaction with others. Other features in the context are also important, such as using 'teaching and assessment methods that foster active and long term engagement with learning tasks [and] ... opportunities to exercise responsible choice in the method and content of study' (Ramsden 2003: 80). These criteria are helpful in thinking through the design of assessments.

In summary, the research evidence suggests that if the nature of the learning context is changed, and assessment is the most influential element of that context (Elton and Johnston 2002), there is a likelihood that students' approach to learning will change (Prosser and Trigwell 1999). Chapters 11–13 will concentrate on how programme and module design can use this pattern of student response to develop effective programme and module assessment strategies.

Students' perceptions of assessment

Changing student approaches is a complex business, with evidence from some studies that it appears relatively easy to induce a surface approach (Struyven *et al.* 2002) but less straightforward to encourage a deep approach. A key explanation for this difficulty appears to lie in the research on students' conceptions of learning and their perceptions of assessment. Prosser and Trigwell (1999) draw on research studies to show how student learning is a result of an interaction between a student and the learning situation and this is unique for every student in every different learning context. It will vary between modules because aspects of the situation will differ. Various factors contribute to this, including students' prior experience of education, their perception of the current situation and their approach to learning. In relation to assessment, the students' perception of what the assessment requires affects the approach they take (Prosser and Trigwell 1999). Students behave differently because they perceive tasks differently. Changing the assessment may change the approach of some students who perceive the new requirements appropriately, but will not necessarily change every student's approach to learning. As Ramsden (2003: 66) says of a group of students who did not change in response to assessment encouraging a deep approach: such students 'have brought with them a predisposition to use a surface approach which they had previously developed in response to similar situations. Like all of us, they carried their history of learning along with them'. Entwistle and Tait (1990) discovered a relationship between students' approaches to study and their assessment preferences, with students who take a surface approach preferring teaching and assessment procedures that supported that approach and vice-versa. These habitual tendencies (Ramsden 2003) may work against students engaging in effective learning in higher education. The implications for preparing students for assessment will be discussed in Chapter 5.

While students' 'approaches to learning' and 'conceptions of learning' are key factors in understanding the relationship between assessment and learning, research has also identified a range of related features of assessment which impact on student behaviour and the student learning experience, and these are discussed below.

Strategic approaches and cue seeking

A feature of modern modular course structures means that most assessment has a summative function, and this places a pressure on students throughout their programmes to focus on assessment rather than learning (Heywood 2000). Evidence suggests that students are increasingly taking a strategic approach to their studies, focusing their effort on assessment-related tasks (Kneale 1997; Gibbs 2006b). Students become 'cue-conscious' (Miller and Parlett 1974), concentrating on passing the assessment. The latter activity may, unintentionally, be at the expense of understanding the subject matter (Gibbs 2006a). This cue-seeking behaviour, where students are determined to work out what the tutor is looking for rather than developing an understanding of the subject matter of the assignment, has been identified in other studies (Bloxham and West 2007). As Ramsden (2003: 67) asserts, much of student activity is about adjusting to the perceived requirements of the tutor – the 'hidden curriculum'. Research suggests that students who fail to pick up on such cues are not likely to do well (Miller and Parlett 1974). This has major implications for the choice of assessment and the guidance provided for students in order to direct their efforts towards appropriate activity: 'unless assessment tasks mirror the official curriculum, they will erode it. Assessing outside, or below, the curriculum gives irrelevant or counter-productive tasks a false value' (Biggs, 2003: 63).

Time devoted to studying

Different assessment regimes are also related to different amounts of time devoted by students to their out-of-class studies. Gibbs and Simpson (2004–5) draw on a range of research to show that time spent studying increases achievement, although it can be wasted by ineffective surface learning. In addition, more frequent assessment tasks are associated with greater time allocated to study. Moreover, there is evidence that students will work harder in preparation for some modes of assessment than for others. Traub and MacRury (1990), in a review of research on multiple choice and free response tests over the previous 20 years, found that students appear to prepare better for free response (that is, where the student must construct the answer rather than select from a given set of answers).

In addition to assessment influencing the amount of time spent studying, it can also affect when students study. For example, infrequent examinations and coursework tasks encourage students to bunch all their **learning hours** together in the time immediately preceding the examination or submission date (Gibbs and Simpson 2004–5). Overloading of students through excessive amounts of content is also associated with a surface approach to learning (Ramsden 2003).

Student reactions to assessment

Most students undergo some stress in relation to assessment, but few suffer from severe psychological difficulty (Heywood 2000). Indeed, as Heywood (2000: 149) asserts, a level of stress 'would appear to be essential for learning'. Nevertheless anxiety provoked by assessment can encourage students to adopt surface approaches to learning (Rust 2002) and make them less likely to take a deep approach (Fransson 1977). There is particular evidence of stress associated with examinations (Falchikov 2005), with students generally preferring coursework (Gibbs and Simpson 2004–5), although there is support for the view that size and volume of tasks can act as stress factors (Sarros and Densten 1989). Heywood (2000) argues that preparation for assessment is a necessary response to reducing anxiety, supported by research showing that improving students' understanding of goals and standards is associated with enhanced achievement (Rust *et al.* 2003), particularly with unfamiliar forms of assessment (Hounsell *et al.* 2006). Chapter 5 provides practical ideas to help students understand the criteria and standards of their assignments and examinations.

The relationship between feedback and learning

The most important aspect of the assessment process in raising achievement is the provision of feedback (Black and Wiliam 1998a; Gibbs and Simpson 2004–5). Research indicates that students value feedback (Hartley *et al.* 2002; Weaver 2006) despite anecdotal staff views and contrary research evidence regarding how students fail to engage with it (Gibbs and Simpson 2004–5). However, not all feedback is perceived as useful by students (Black and Wiliam 1998a; Hounsell *et al.* 2006), and concerns over feedback have been strongly reflected in the first two years of the UK National Student Survey (2006). Entwistle *et al.* (1989), studying engineering students, showed that early failure was related to students gaining no feedback at all in their first term. According to Hounsell (2003), this combination of students choosing not to or being unable to use feedback, and staff cynicism that their efforts are wasted, creates a vicious 'downward spiral' in relation to the potential gains from feedback.

Feedback has little value unless it is timely and students pay attention to it, understand it, and act on it (Gibbs and Simpson 2004–5), and various studies suggest or investigate practical activities to help students engage with it (Nicol and Macfarlane-Dick 2004). Black and Wiliam (1998a), in an extensive review of literature on formative assessment, concluded that feedback in the form of comments can have a significantly greater effect on future improvement than feedback that is limited to a grade or mark. Knight and Yorke (2003) argue that feedback is mostly likely to be useful to learners if they are willing and able to expose their areas of weakness and confusion with a topic. This is supported by Black *et al.*'s (2003) work on formative assessment with school teachers, where students found that revealing their problems was worthwhile and led to gaining help. Reflective assignments such as learning journals attempt to tackle this dilemma by providing students with an opportunity to reflect on their strengths and weaknesses as learners without losing marks, but these provide their own problems for assessment (Gibbs, 1995; see also Chapter 13). Recent studies have placed greater importance on the notion of **feed forward** (Torrance 1993; Hounsell 2006), which focuses on what a student should pay attention to in future assessment tasks, and ensuring that feedback is embedded in day-to-day learning activities as well as provided in response to formal assignments, for example as in-class and online activities (Laurillard 2002).

Using feedback to adjust teaching

It is not just students who need to act on feedback. For assessment to function in a formative way that supports students' future learning, the findings have to be used to adjust teaching (Black and Wiliam 1998a; Prosser and Trigwell 1999; Nicol and Macfarlane-Dick 2006). Difficulties with a particular concept or problem may signal that further or different tuition is needed. Angelo and Cross (1993) and Nicol and MacFarlane-Dick (2004) provide a range of 'classroom assessment techniques' designed to assist staff in gaining immediate feedback from students which can be used to revise teaching strategies. However, course structures with short modules can make it difficult for individual tutors to respond to the information about student learning emerging from summative assessment. Chapter 4 on 'teaching a module' will provide practical advice on embedding formative assessment in your teaching and being responsive to what you find out.

Students as assessors

Recent work in the field of feedback is focusing on the importance of the student as self-assessor: someone who is able to provide their own feedback because they understand the standard they are aiming for and can judge and change their own performance (that is, self-regulate) in relation to that standard (Nicol and Macfarlane-Dick 2006). This is assessment *as* learning (Klenowski 2002; Earl 2003) and is firmly located in Sadler's (1989) view that improvement involves three key elements:

- students must know what the standard or goal is that they are trying to achieve (assessment guidance);
- they should know how their current achievement compares to those goals (feedback);
- they must take action to reduce the gap between the first two (applying feedback to future assignments).

As Black and Wiliam (1998a: 15) assert, 'self-assessment is a sine qua non for effective learning', and certainly systematic reviews of research (Black and Wiliam 1998a; Falchikov 2005) indicate strong positive benefits to students of being involved in their own assessment.

If students are to become specialists within a subject discipline, they need to develop the capacity to assess quality in that field. Involving students in assessment provides an authentic opportunity for them to learn what 'quality' is in a given context and apply that judgement to their own work (Black *et al.* 2003). The context might be solving a problem, doing an experiment, creating a design, or writing an essay. Thereby the student becomes aware of what the goals or standards of the subject are (Earl 2003), a precondition of taking responsibility for their work (Swann and Ecclestone 1999a). Feedback allows the student to see their performance against those goals. This view is supported by Black and Wiliam (1998a) when they stress that peer and self-assessment are the key to learning from formative assessment. It is not enough for a tutor to tell a student what they need to do to improve ('your writing is too descriptive', 'you have mistaken correlation for cause') if the student does not understand what these comments mean in relation to the subject or their writing. They cannot do anything about it until they begin to share the tutor's conception of the subject (Sadler 1989). Box 2.2 develops this topic in relation to peer and self-assessment.

The assessment *as* learning approach is challenging prior ideas about the separation of formative assessment (assessment *for* learning) and summative assessment (assessment *of* learning) (Carless *et al.* 2006; Hounsell 2006) and replacing it with the notion of 'learning-oriented assessment' characterised as 'when tasks are "fit for purpose"; when students are involved in the assessment process in ways which support the development of evaluative expertise; and when feedback is forward-looking and can be acted upon' (Carless *et al.* 2006: 396). It is argued that assessment and feedback activity of this nature does not just contribute to learning at university but develops learning and evaluative skills essential for employment and lifelong learning (Boud and

---

Box 2.2   Leads into literature: peer and self-assessment

Peer and self-assessment involve students in assessing themselves and other students and are widespread in higher education today, often linked to wider innovation in learning and teaching (Stefani 1998). Numerous studies of peer assessment exist with considerable agreement about the benefits (Bostock 2000; Topping 2000; Falchikov 2005), including a greater sense of accountability, motivation and responsibility, and an increase in the speed of feedback (Black *et al.* 2003). In particular, peer assessment increases understanding of the subject matter, standards required and students' own achievement; it involves using disciplinary knowledge and skills in order to make judgements (Bostock 2000).

Peer and self-assessment are also seen as valuable in helping students develop important skills for lifelong learning (Authur 1995; Boud 2000), such as self-evaluation, giving feedback, justifying a point of view and negotiation skills. 'If assessment processes are intended to enhance student learning then it follows that students must be enabled to reflect on their current attainment' (Stefani 1998: 346). Black *et al.* (2003), working with secondary school teachers, found that peer assessment helped students develop the objectivity required for self-assessment and thus the capacity to direct their own work and thereby become autonomous learners. They conclude that peer and self-assessment 'make unique contributions to the development of students' learning – they secure aims that cannot be achieved in any other way' (2003: 53).

Concerns about peer assessment, such as imprecise marking, are not supported by the research, which generally finds good levels of agreement between staff and students where students are working with criteria (Falchikov and Goldfinch 2000) and have been trained (Falchikov 2005). Various other strategies have been successfully developed to address student and staff concerns, such as use of **double anonymous** peer marking (Bostock 2000). Falchikov (2005) presents evidence that the greatest degree of agreement between student and tutor scores in self-assessment occurred with more detailed grading scales. In general, research on peer assessment has tended to focus on agreement between tutor and student grades, whereas if it is used at the formative stage with the emphasis on feedback, many of the worries regarding grading can be discounted (Falchikov 2005). In addition, feedback from students may be superior in some ways to teacher feedback. Black *et al.* (2003: 77) found that peer feedback is not as 'emotionally loaded', students will accept criticism more readily from peers, and the language used by peers may be easier for students to understand (Bloxham and West 2004).

Studies consistently report positive responses to peer marking from students (Bostock 2000; Orsmond *et al.* 2000; Black *et al.* 2003) who claim it has made them think more, become more critical, learn more and gain in confidence. This positive response is reflected in Falchikov's (2005) substantive summary of research, although she notes some areas of difficulty and the improvement that comes from familiarity with the method. Even where students were negative about the experience, researchers continued to find evidence of benefits in terms of motivation and critical thinking (Oliver and Omari 1999).

In summary, peer and self-assessment have emerged as important tools in the tutor's repertoire for their many potential benefits. For practical advice on implementing peer assessment, including training students, see Chapter four, and for advice on peer marking of group assessments, see Chapter 7.

Falchikov 2006), characterised as 'sustainable assessment' (Boud 2000; Hounsell 2006).

While the latter ideas are in early stages of development in terms of practice-based research, they do underpin the growing acknowledgement of the importance of involving students in assessment. This attention has stimulated a range of empirical and theoretical studies, practical projects, innovations and action research which are used extensively in the following chapters of this book.

The validity of assessment tasks

While much of the research evidence discussed earlier has focused on assessment *for* and *as* learning, there is extensive research on the effectiveness of assessment practices as measurement *of* learning, including a focus on the validity of assessment tools. Here validity means that assessment tasks are assessing the stated learning outcomes. Prosser and Trigwell (1999) point out that assessment does not always test what we think it does and sometimes cannot reveal the qualitative differences in understanding between different students. Knight and Yorke (2003) argue that assessing higher-order learning in any discipline is not uncomplicated and judging the products (essay, exam script) of student learning has its limitations. For example, Entwistle and Entwistle (1997) show that where students are able to reproduce in their examination answer the structure of the topic as given by the tutor, they can give the impression of well-structured understanding. Similarly, Knight (2000) found that if a student has been given considerable support and direction, they may produce an assignment of similar quality to one produced in another context where the questions are not closely aligned to the teaching and the student has to work unsupported. Although the products look the same, they do not represent the same achievement.

In other words, our assessment tasks may be assessing learning at a lower level than that intended. In order to develop this idea, we need to think about what we mean by different 'levels' of achievement.

A confusing number of taxonomies or frameworks of thinking have been developed to assist instructional design (Moseley *et al.* 2005). Brown *et al.*

(1997: 38) argue that while not all lecturers may find such taxonomies suitable for their programmes, 'a classification of the kinds of skills and capabilities that one wants students to develop is a necessary first step in developing an assessment system'. Biggs and Collis's (1982) structure of observed learning outcomes (SOLO) taxonomy (see Figure 2.1) provides such a framework to discriminate between different stages of achievement. The learning is described not just in relation to the content the students should learn, but also what they are able to do with the knowledge. Thus, in the SOLO taxonomy, the selection of appropriate verbs to describe student capabilities is fundamental.

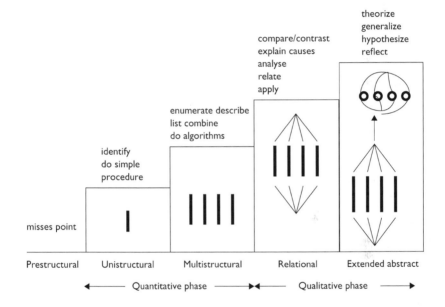

Figure 2.1   A hierarchy of verbs that may be used to form curriculum objectives
Source: Biggs (2003: 48).

This is not dissimilar to Anderson and Krathwohl's (2001) approach in revising Bloom's taxonomy of educational objectives. However, their taxonomy (Table 2.1) has two dimensions, the *knowledge* dimension and the *cognitive process* dimension. In a similar way to the SOLO taxonomy, the *cognitive process* dimension enables the tutor to identify an appropriate verb which should be used to express the learning outcome. The other dimension determines what knowledge (the noun) the verb is describing, and delineates between the facts a student needs to be familiar with the discipline; conceptual knowledge such as knowledge of classifications, principles, theories, models and structures; procedural knowledge, that is, knowing how to do something, including techniques, skills and methods of inquiry; and meta-cognitive knowledge, knowledge of self and cognitive tasks, and methods of learning and organising ideas (Anderson 2003).

Table 2.1   The taxonomy table (Anderson and Krathwohl, 2001)

Knowledge dimension	Cognitive process dimension					
	1. Remember	2. Understand	3. Apply	4. Analyse	5. Evaluate	6. Create
A. Factual	X				Z	
B. Conceptual		X			Z	
C. Procedural			Y			
D. Metacognitive						

Source: adapted from Anderson (2003: 29).

Anderson (2003) argues that this taxonomy table helps teachers design appropriate assessment because it enables them to work out prototypical ways of assessing objectives that fall within the relevant cells. For example, it is easy to see that a multiple-choice exam could assess memory of factual knowledge or possibly understanding of conceptual knowledge (the cells marked X in Table 2.1). However, application of procedural knowledge (cell marked Y) will need an assessment task, for example problem solving or case study analysis, which requires students to demonstrate not just that they can remember or understand something, but that they can use it.

Such a taxonomy is helpful in thinking about what different assessment tasks are testing. Here are two religious studies essays:

- Outline one of the five pillars of faith and explain why it is important for Muslims (Year 1)
- Critically assess the claim that British society has not adequately provided for the needs of its Muslim population (Year 3)

The first example appears to demand recall of factual information and understanding of conceptual knowledge, again in the cells marked X in Table 2.1. The second essay appears to be demanding 'evaluation', the cells marked Z in Table 2.1, a relatively high-level cognitive skill requiring good command of the subject matter. Unfortunately, the questions alone are insufficient to determine whether they measure qualitatively different achievements. For example, if the issues in the year 3 question have been carefully rehearsed in a lecture, the student may be largely engaged in reproducing the tutor's notes – a low-level skill. Likewise, if the year 1 question topic has not been 'taught', the process of researching the answer may be at least as, if not more, demanding. It is for this reason that Knight (2006) asserts that we can only ensure validity at the local level where we are able to judge the quality of the learning processes behind the assessment products. This discussion alerts us to the potential limitations of what may appear to be demanding assessment tasks. A useful review of taxonomies of thinking skills can be found in Moseley *et al.* (2005), and Chapters 11 and 12 of this book discuss the relevance for designing assessment of the different 'levels' in the UK Framework for Qualifications in Higher Education (Quality Assurance Agency 2006d).

Constructive alignment

The notion of matching course objectives with assessment underpins the concept of 'constructive alignment' (Biggs 1996). It is a course design methodology which emphasises the centrality of intended learning outcomes. These should determine the teaching and assessment such that they are compatible and act to support one another. 'You wouldn't lecture students on how to teach using small groups, and give them a written test. You would get them to participate in small groups, then run their own and see how well they did it' (Biggs 2003: 27).

Constructive alignment, and the taxonomies discussed earlier, assume we can devise learning outcomes in a meaningful way (see Box 2.3. for an introduction to the debate). Although this is a contested proposition, this book has adopted an outcome-based approach to assessment design, on a pragmatic basis, because such an approach is widely employed.

Overall, the research suggests that tutors do need to be mindful that their assessment methods may not be as discriminating as they hope they are and may permit students to pass with 'conceptions of subject matter that teachers wished to change' (Ramsden 2003: 72) or to avoid large sections of the curriculum (Struyven *et al.* 2002). Chapter 13 on diversifying assessment provides practical ideas for increasing assessment validity, particularly in relation to examinations.

Authentic assessment

In addition, as discussed earlier, intrinsic interest in the learning activity is associated with deep approaches to learning. Students value assessment activities which appear worthwhile in themselves; they appear to have value beyond completing the task (Struyven *et al.* 2002). This notion has prompted the idea of 'authentic' assessment which is seen as 'more practical, realistic and challenging' (Torrance 1995). In reality, much of the move towards diversifying higher education assessment is based on the implicit notion of

Box 2.3 Leads into literature: the learning outcome debate

An outcome-based approach to specifying the curriculum has gained currency internationally in recent years. It aims to improve transparency by stating what achievements are represented by individual academic awards. It also provides for flexibility, for example by facilitating credit transfer and accreditation of prior learning (Gosling and Moon 2002).

Unfortunately, the term 'learning outcome' (LO) is often interchangeable with other educational constructs such as 'objectives', 'competencies', 'achievements' and 'skills', and this causes some confusion for educators (McGourty et al. 1999). In an attempt to clarify the term, McGourty et al. (1999: 4) define LOs as 'observable and measurable manifestations of applied knowledge', something which is 'reflected through the action and behaviour of the individual' rather than their ability to write about it. This is why some form of taxonomy of learning outcomes is useful; it lays out the types of cognitive skills students should be performing at different levels.

Hussey and Smith (2002) consider the specification of LOs to be part of a new regime of accountability. Outcome-based descriptions of academic awards notionally allow scrutiny of the appropriateness of the curriculum, how it reflects the subject benchmark statements and the standards being set. It allows comparison within and between institutions (Gosling and Moon 2002). This leads to one of the central criticisms of LOs, that they imply that the 'fuzzy' business of learning and teaching can be clearly specified (Hussey and Smith 2003). On the contrary, it is argued that they are difficult to write in a meaningful way (Knight and Yorke 2003) and have to be interpreted in relation to the context, which can only be done by those who are already familiar with that context (Hussey and Smith 2002). Thus they are not 'objective' or easily understandable by other stakeholders such as students.

Learning outcomes are also criticised for ignoring the unpredictable and indefinable aspects of learning, the 'emergent outcomes' (Hussey and Smith 2003: 362), and for reducing the value of subject content compared with skills. They may restrict learning as students focus on what is needed to pass. Jackson (2000) points to further criticisms, some more practical than educational, such as the time needed to prepare staff for the LO approach to course design and teaching, the bureaucracy, and the threat to professional autonomy contained in the requirement to make explicit what has been implicit.

However, there are strong arguments in favour of the outcome-based approach as opposed to former methods. Gosling and Moon contend that undefined learning is difficult to assess fairly, and students should know what is expected of them. Many academics associate such transparency with fairness, better communication and avoiding confusion between staff and students as the rules and structures are made clear (Orr 2005). Indeed Hussey and Smith (2003) do not reject the concept of LOs but urge that they are only written in general terms so that modules can embrace outcomes that emerge during the messy business of learning.

> Gosling and Moon accept that we should avoid detailed lists of competences in higher education and use a broader description of outcomes, including skills, knowledge and understanding. In addition, Biggs (2003) suggests that the nature of higher-order outcomes means that they do not discourage unforeseen or unforeseeable outcomes because they tend to specify the process the student should demonstrate, rather than the detailed content.
>
> Whatever your views, the learning outcome approach to documenting higher education is here to stay, at least for the foreseeable future. However, it may be wise to accept that learning outcomes can only be described in fairly general terms and must be interpreted in the light of the specific programme or module context.

authentic assessment, and higher education has a tradition of using it in various ways, for example on vocational awards. Nevertheless Knight and Yorke (2003) provide a convincing critique of authentic assessment both in terms of how it is being interpreted and in the pragmatic and economic costs of doing it well in the current regulatory framework of higher education. They do, however, recognise that the relative freedom of higher education gives more scope for authentic assessment than exists in schools.

Conclusion

This chapter has attempted to digest key themes in assessment research as a basis for the enhancement of practice. Essentially, they are as follows:

- Assessment strongly influences students' learning, including what they study, when they study, how much work they do and the approach they take to their learning.
- The type of assessment influences the quality and amount of learning achieved by students.
- Poorly designed assessment can lead to students developing limited conceptual understanding of the material, although the limitations of the assessment tool and process may mask this failure.
- Well-designed assessment is likely to be intrinsically motivating for students and lead to better retention of material which the students can apply in other settings.
- Students' prior experience of learning and perceptions of assessment may override attempts by lecturers to change their approach to learning, and they should be helped to a better understanding of assessment tasks.
- Assessment tasks may not be assessing what we think they are assessing, they may be assessing lower-level understanding of the

material, and may be failing to assess the stated outcomes of a programme of study.

- Anxiety-provoking assessment is associated with a surface approach to learning by students.
- Feedback is the most important aspect of the assessment process for raising achievement, yet currently students express considerable dissatisfaction with much feedback and it does not always impact on their learning.
- Self- and peer assessment are crucial elements of helping students to learn from their assessment and become more autonomous learners.
- Feedback should inform tutors' teaching and support strategies as well as student activity.

3 The conflicting purposes of assessment

The purpose of this chapter is to discuss the various purposes of assessment. This may seem a rather academic debate, of little practical use to staff wishing to develop their module and programme assessment strategies. Nonetheless, once tutors attempt to seriously evaluate and enhance assessment methods, it becomes clear that there is a constant need to juggle these different intentions and the concentration on some purposes over others can distort the value of assessment in universities. Paying attention to neglected purposes helps pinpoint where our enhancement efforts should lie. Box 3.1 illustrates the sort of dilemma that the different purposes of assessment create.

The lecturer in case study 1 has designed an assessment which is assessment *as* learning (the students are doing the learning as they work on the assessment), assessment *for* learning (the peer and group learning encourages formative discussion and feedback) and assessment *of* learning in that the task attempts to be a valid measurement of the learning outcomes in terms of understanding and application of the law (see discussion of these terms in Chapter 2).

The moderator, on the other hand, emphasises her responsibility to focus entirely on the assessment *of* learning: whether this assignment is generating evidence of individual student achievement at the appropriate standard. Can she, with integrity, report to the institution that the marks awarded reflect the students' work and are comparable with standards on equivalent courses in other institutions? There is a tension between these different purposes of assessment which needs to be resolved.

First, let us consider four purposes of assessment:

1. **Certification**: providing the means to identify and discriminate between different levels of achievement, and between students, providing a licence to practise in the case of professional programmes, enabling selection of students for further study and employment – assessment *of* learning.
2. **Student learning**: promoting learning by motivating students, steering their approach to learning and giving the teacher useful information to inform changes in teaching strategies – assessment *for* and *as* learning.
3. **Quality assurance**: providing evidence for relevant stakeholders

(for example employers, inspectors, external examiners) to enable them to judge the appropriateness of standards on the programme (Gibbs 1999) – assessment *of* learning.

4. **Lifelong learning capacity**: encouraging students to develop 'knowledge, skills and predispositions to underpin lifelong learning' (Boud 2000: 151) – assessment *as* learning.

Although each of these purposes appears entirely proper, they often conflict with one another. Boxes 3.2 and 3.3 illustrate this problem. While some assessment methods give confidence that the work is the student's own, other techniques promote higher-level learning. Some techniques provide reliable scores while others produce widely varying grades from different markers. In effect, the different purposes emphasise different principles of assessment.

The fourth purpose of 'lifelong learning capacity' does not always feature in lists of assessment purposes. However, it has been included here in recognition of the fact that assessment may also be important for developing

---

Box 3.1 Case study 1

A law tutor has introduced a simulation of an aspect of legal practice where student teams negotiate towards settlement of a dispute as if they were partners in a law firm. They spend three weeks working on these cases, posting their claims or defence against the claims on a group discussion page on the module's site within a virtual learning environment. The tutor e-moderates the discussion, responding with comments, questions and sources for further investigation. At the end of the period, each group presents the legal basis for their claim or defence in a classroom session. The student audience, working in threes, is asked to discuss the claim or defence and identify two strengths and two weaknesses of the legal argument adopted which are fed back to the presenting group. Each group assesses individual members' contribution to the team's work. The module tutor gives the presentation a mark which is altered for each member of the group depending on their peer assessment. The latter often, but not always, indicates that everyone should get the same mark.

However, the colleague moderating the module is not happy with the allocation of marks for two reasons. First, she feels that she has not been able to view the presentations and therefore cannot confirm that the marks given reflect the standard of work. Second, and most importantly, she thinks that it is impossible to guarantee that each student deserves the mark they gained. How does the tutor know that they didn't just turn up at the presentation and persuade the rest of the group to allocate them the same mark? She would prefer that the element of this exercise that counts towards the final mark is limited to individual students' written accounts of the legal negotiations.

Box 3.2   Case study 2

The summative assessment of a year 2 undergraduate philosophy module is a three-hour unseen examination, with a rubric requiring four answers, three from section A and one from Section B. Section A has a choice of eight questions and section B has a choice of three questions. The questions in section A require knowledge of the main topics on the course curriculum, whereas the questions in section B require students to draw learning from all topics of the course in order to analyse new material.

The students sit the examination in controlled conditions. Work is marked by the module tutor, with a sample moderated by a second tutor and marks adjusted accordingly. A sample of examination scripts is then sent to an external examiner who reports to the examination board on the comparability of marking standards.

In analysing the module results, the external moderator reports that standards are comparable, but he has asked why the students tend to achieve significantly lower marks in the section B essays compared with section A. Moreover, the tutor is concerned that section A tends to lead to regurgitation of his lecture material in a fairly undigested form.

Box 3.3   Case study 3

A year 1 undergraduate engineering module involves students in completing four on-line multiple choice question (MCQ) tests. The test questions have been developed and scrutinised for validity and accuracy by the course team. These tests must be taken during four one-week periods evenly distributed across the semester and each counts 10% towards the final module marks. The students sit the tests by making appointments to attend a controlled PC lab. The topics in the tests are also examined in the final unseen written examination. The students have access to paper and pens to use while doing the tests but they cannot remove any paper from the examination room.

The students get immediate feedback on their performance online at the end of the test, with the correct answer explained.

The tutor has seen an improvement in the end-of-course examination results, although he finds it difficult to write MCQs which test procedural rather than factual knowledge.

---

students' evaluative and self-assessment skills in preparation for employment and a future of learning (Jacques 2000; Boud and Falchikov 2006). This links to 'student learning' as a purpose of assessment, but stresses the active engagement of students in aspects of assessment, not just for the current course, but to help them develop the capacity to determine appropriate standards, discern the critical aspects of tasks, monitor their own progress, use feedback and other skills for lifelong learning (Boud 2000). Boud refers to this purpose as 'sustainable' assessment.

In order to analyse the conflicts illustrated by the case studies, it is necessary to examine them against a set of principles of assessment. There are varying views on what the principles of assessment should be (Jonsson and Baartman 2006; Quality Assurance Agency 2006c), and we have selected those which we see as particularly significant and which reflect the four different purposes listed earlier. Table 3.1 lists the different principles and evaluates each case study against them. It identifies how the assignments in the different case studies are robust in relation to certain principles and unconvincing in relation to others. The case studies also illustrate that achieving all of the principles is enormously difficult or impracticable. The remainder of this chapter discusses the implementation of each principle, followed at the end of the chapter (see Table 3.2) by suggested ways to resolve some of the weaknesses identified in the cases studies.

Validity

There is extensive debate in the educational literature about validity which we do not have the scope to review here. A range of different types of validity exist (Elton and Johnston 2002), many of which overlap with other principles such as effectiveness, reliability and transparency. For the purposes of this guide, we are focusing on 'intrinsic validity' (Brown *et al.* 1997), which means that **assessment tasks are assessing the stated learning outcomes** for the module, and this principle clearly underpins the notion of constructive alignment (see Chapter 2).

The traditional range of assessment tasks in higher education does not cope well with a wide range of learning outcomes – for example, those involving professional, subject-specific or **key skills** (Elton and Johnston 2002). Falchikov (2005) discusses the concept of 'predictive validity', the notion that an assessment tells us something about future behaviour. For example, on a nursing programme, does successful completion of an essay on the principles of care management predict whether the graduating nurse will have achieved the outcome of becoming a safe and effective practitioner in that sphere? In reality, we need an assessment process which more closely judges the students' capacity to act as well as to express their factual and conceptual knowledge of the topic.

The discussion in Chapter 2 highlighted the problems associated with valid assessment in higher education, with difficulty increasing as the learning to be assessed moves towards higher levels of both dimensions of

Table 3.1 Analysis of case studies in assessment

Principle	Link to purpose of assessment	Case study 1	Case study 2	Case study 3
Validity	Student learning, certification	**Strong:** The cases presented to the students require the ability to apply understanding of the law to legal problems. The exercise also assesses working as a team, solving complex problems and communicating effectively.	**Weak:** Results suggest students are focusing on the content of topics rather than understanding the underlying concepts that the tutor intended them to learn. May be testing examination technique.	**Medium:** Tests assess knowledge outcomes but are less successful at assessing higher-order outcomes concerned with application.
Reliability	Certification, quality assurance	**Weak:** One marker, without second marking or moderation. Marking open-ended problems has low levels of reliability.	**Medium:** Second marking and moderation take place to sector standards. Marking open-ended essay questions has low levels of reliability.	**Strong:** Testing instruments and marking independent of assessors.
Effectiveness	Student learning, lifelong learning	**Strong:** The task promotes learning through encouraging student activity and interaction, providing a motivational context by offering an authentic task and affording a means to help students structure their knowledge through working	**Weak:** Encourages students to memorise material rather than develop understanding. Summative examination limits opportunity to learn from feedback	**Medium:** Regular testing is likely to capture students' time. Immediate feedback is likely to support learning. The method may encourage rote memorisation of material.

Principle	Link to purpose of assessment	Case study 1	Case study 2	Case study 3
		on an encompassing case study.		
Comparability and consistency	Quality assurance	**Weak:** The task generates little evidence for comparison across other courses. The open-ended nature means it is difficult to judge how the task should be weighted in comparison with other assignments or examinations	**Strong:** The course generates evidence of the quantity of assessment and the level of student achievement. It is possible to judge if assessment load is comparable with other cognate disciplines in the institution.	**Strong:** The course generates evidence of the quantity of assessment and the level of student achievement. It is possible to judge if assessment load is comparable with other cognate disciplines in the institution.
Transparency	Student learning, quality assurance, lifelong learning	**Strong:** The formative feedback from the tutor, participation in judging other students' work and giving and receiving feedback on contribution to the group all promote skills of evaluation and self-assessment.	**Medium:** Clear information is available on examination rubric and contribution to module mark. Students have access to previous papers but assessment criteria are implicit.	**Strong:** Clear information is available on test process, content and contribution to module mark. Repeat tests enable students to develop clarity regarding assessment method. Assessment criteria are explicit.
Practicability	Student learning	**Strong:** Student workload is managed by class time devoted to team meetings and use of a virtual learning environment to facilitate	**Medium:** Student workload is acceptable although the examination contributes to end-of-semester bunching of assessment. Staff marking	**Strong:** Assessment method distributes student workload across module. Test design is staff-intensive but automated marking

Principle	Link to purpose of assessment	Case study 1	Case study 2	Case study 3
		communication. Marking group presentations is swift	workload concentrated although faster than coursework because detailed feedback is not required.	significantly reduces staff workload, of great benefit for large student cohorts.
Equity	All purposes of assessment	**Weak:** Students with disability or English as an additional language may have more difficulty contributing to a group learning situation and/or communicating their learning in a presentation format.	**Weak:** Time-constrained examinations may pose difficulties for students with certain specific learning difficulties. Additional time may be given but this does not necessarily help (Robson 2005)	**Medium:** The test format can be altered to assist students with some disabilities. No time limit on test supports students with specific learning difficulties and those using an additional language.
Attribution	Certification	**Weak:** The tutor relies on the group members to peer-assess contributions to the team. Students could collude in misrepresenting individual contributions	**Strong:** Controlled conditions enable robust evidence that scripts are students' own work.	**Strong:** Controlled conditions enable robust evidence that tests represent student's own achievement. Procedure must ensure students can only log on in their own name.
Conclusion		**Strong** on student learning and lifelong learning. **Weak** on certification and quality assurance	**Strong** on quality assurance, **medium** on certification and student learning, **weak** on lifelong learning	**Strong** on quality assurance and certification, **medium** on student learning and lifelong learning

Anderson and Krathwohl's (2001) taxonomy (see Table 2.1). Case study 2 (Box 3.2) about the philosophy examination is a good illustration. Students may successfully compose answers to examinations because they have learned the relevant knowledge as organised for them by the tutor, rather than because they have grasped the meaning of key concepts in such a way that they can apply them to new situations. In general, examinations are valid for assessing recall and understanding of factual and conceptual knowledge.

Overall, the biggest threat to validity arises from attempts to ensure 'reliability' and 'practicability' (see the relevant sections below).

Reliability

Assessment tasks should be generating comparable marks across time, across markers and across methods. For example, reliability is demonstrated when different markers make the same judgements about an assignment or when one marker makes consistent judgements about a piece of work at different times. Overall, despite the QAA (2006c) urging higher education institutions to implement principles and procedures for reliable assessment, the evidence on this matter is depressing (Elton and Johnston 2002; Falchikov 2005), with little evidence of reliability in the marking of written work in higher education. Murphy (2006) argues that reliability (dependability) of assessment in UK higher education has traditionally been of little concern, with assessment decisions largely confined to those who have taught the students. Knight (2001) describes reliability in higher education as 'ramshackle' in comparison with secondary/high school education.

In addition, reliability requires that assessment of the same learning by different modes should render similar outcomes. Research on the latter hardly exists, although there have been studies comparing student achievement on two examination papers (Elton and Johnston 2002) which suggested the papers did not produce reliable measures of the same learning outcomes. Yorke *et al.* (2000) show a similar discrepancy in relation to the difference between examination and coursework and argue that the two methods must be assessing different things if the results are so consistently different.

The causes of unreliability are related to the nature of what is being measured by assessment in higher education. Knight (2006) argues that complex learning cannot be reduced to something simple enough to measure reliably; the more complex the learning, the more we draw on 'connoisseurship' (Eisner 1985) rather than measurement to make our judgements. However, he does accept that achievements in some disciplines may be more determinate, and therefore more open to reliable judgement. On the other hand, Maclellan (2004a: 312) would reject many assignments, for example essays, as contradicting the fundamental belief 'that there can be universality of meaning as to what any grade or score represents'. An inter-pretivist view (see Box 3.4) would argue that there is a level of professional judgement in some elements of undergraduate assessment whatever the dis-cipline, particularly if we take Knight's (2006) view that all graduates should be learning complex capabilities such as initiative, adaptability and critical thinking. According to Broad (2000), conferring grades in complex written work is impossible and misleading. It is interesting to note that the Quality Assurance Agency in the UK, in its recent code of practice for assessment (2006c), is advocating broader grades or mark bands, perhaps recognising the difficulty of precise percentage grading.

Box 3.4 Leads into literature: assessment policy and practice

Elton and Johnson (2002) provide an excellent discussion and review of the litera-ture in relation to the key dilemma in higher education between assessment for certification and assessment for learning, setting out the different positions of the positivist and the interpretivist approaches. Essentially, a positivist approach believes in the importance of validity and reliability, assuming that objective standards can be set. The alternative, interpretivist, approach rejects objective truth and conceives of assessment as based on a local context, carried out through the judgement of experts in the field. In their view, it is a social practice whose credibility emerges from a community of practice which shares a consensus about what constitutes accepted knowledge, rules and procedures. It is a 'good enough' (2002: 39) approach in which 'dependability is parallel to reliability in positivist assessment' (2002:46)

On a more general front, Knight and Yorke (2003) provide a well-argued challenge to much current assessment practice, and Falchikov (2005) presents a useful critique of traditional assessment practices and the paradigm of assessment as quality control. Heywood (2000) offers a wide-ranging review of the literature on principles and practice in higher education assessment.

Academics, as 'connoisseurs', are considered able to make expert and reliable judgements because of their education and socialisation into the standards of the discipline and of their local context (Ecclestone 2001). Knight (2006) argues that this situated and socially constructed nature of standards means that measurement of complex learning can only take place effectively within its context, a local judgement made within that social environment, be it a teaching team, department or subject discipline. This local nature of standards means it is unsurprising that many studies have found considerable marking discrepancies between tutors. This is discussed in depth in Chapter 6.

While reliability is particularly important for the purposes of 'certification' and 'quality assurance', it may well work against validity. For example, an overriding concern for demonstrably reliable marking may prevent the use of group assignments or may encourage use of assessments that usually foster low-level learning such as multiple choice question tests (Scouller and Prosser 1994). However, quite reasonably, positivist approaches to assessment would argue that without reliability, there is no validity (Elton and Johnston 2002).

Overall, there has to be a 'trade-off' between reliability and validity, and, whereas American universities have erred towards reliability, validity has taken precedence in the UK (Hornby 2003). Perhaps the best we can do is attempt to achieve a reasonable balance across a student's programme. The concern with moderation and reliability as a key element of quality assurance and certification is discussed further in Chapter 8.

Effectiveness

Assessment tasks should be designed to encourage good quality, 'deep' approaches to learning in the students. Various researchers list different purposes for assessment (Gibbs 1999; Elton and Johnston 2002; Dunn *et al.* 2004), several of which are directly related to assessment as an effective tool for promoting learning. They include 'capturing student time and attention, generating appropriate student learning activity, providing timely feedback which students pay attention to, helping students to internalise the discipline's standards and notions of quality' (Gibbs 1999: 47) as well as motivation and preparation for life (Elton and Johnston 2002). Dunn *et al.* (2004) add the purpose of diagnosing student difficulties. Chapter 2 has set out the research on the relationship between assessment and student approaches to learning and achievement, and there is considerable consistency within the literature on what is required for assessment design to support effective learning.

Overall, Elton and Johnston (2002: 39) link effectiveness to validity: 'Newer notions of validity stress that a "valid" procedure for assessment must have a positive impact on and consequences for the teaching and learning'. Black and Wiliam (1998a) argue that in general the grading function of assessment is overemphasised in comparison with the learning function.

Comparability and consistency

There should be consistent and comparable approaches to the summative assessment requirements of awards of the same level across programmes and institutions. Interpretations of this differ, but normally it involves consistency to be shown in the level of learning demonstrated and in the learning hours required to complete the assessment for a particular number of **credits**. 'The primary concern should be whether standards compare favourably with those in similar institutions or against appropriate benchmarks' (Dunn *et al.* 2004: 69). Within programmes, consistency implies that modules offering similar credit must have comparable assessment requirements. This need not, necessarily be interpreted as exactly similar word lengths and should not mean similar types of assessment. It is the level of learning to be demonstrated and the notional hours required to complete the assessed tasks that are important.

Comparability and consistency also apply to multiple campus and collaborative provision, ensuring that students studying for the same awards have a comparable experience with similar outcomes, workload and standards applying across the different sites. Another element contributing to this principle is consistency in determining how individual assignment and module marks combine to generate an overall classification of award such as a upper second class degree, merit or grade point average, but there is clear evidence in the UK that practices vary significantly between and within universities (Yorke *et al.* 2004; QAA 2006a), leaving degree classification unreliable and inconsistent (Elton, 2004). Above all, comparability and consistency are related to ensuring quality standards and fairness rather than a direct link to assessment for learning.

Comparability and consistency apply specifically to summative assessment and are regulated through course approval, second marking and external monitoring, with all the costs and bureaucracy involved. As Gibbs (2006b) points out, the difficulty of engaging those students with a strategic approach to their learning has led staff to make all assignments summative, which means the full panoply of expensive procedures comes into force with precious resources diverted away from teaching.

Equity

Students enjoy equal opportunity to effectively demonstrate their learning. There is an overriding need to improve the performance of higher education in promoting equity, and assessment has its part to play in that drive. This principle may be considered from a compliance point of view, for example ensuring that practice complies with legislation. Alternatively, programmes and institutions can take a proactive approach which encourages students to celebrate and express diversity and difference within their assessed work.

Chapter 10 on supporting widening participation and student diversity tackles this principle in a practical way. It recommends that, in general, good assessment practice is also inclusive assessment practice. Implementing equity includes making reasonable adjustments for students' special educational needs and/or disabilities and ensuring cross-institutional consistency in assessment procedures such as **extenuating circumstances** claims, providing for specific learning needs (see precept 5 in QAA 2006c), blind **second marking** and anonymous marking.

The principle of equity is important for all the four purposes of assessment – certification, student learning, quality assurance and lifelong learning capacity.

Practicability

Assessment tasks must be practicable for both staff and students in terms of the time needed for completion and marking. There is always likely to be a trade-off between other principles and practicability. Knight (2006), for example, in discussing students' performance as professionals, points out that reliable judgements can only be made when there have been several observations by multiple observers in a range of contexts, which is not very practicable in terms of resources. Practicability also relates to the amount and timing of assessment, and the need to avoid bunching of assessment deadlines. Availability of staff, venue, equipment and technical support for examinations and assignments is also an important issue of practicability. Imaginative and valid assessments have come unstuck at the point of finding sufficient space, staff or equipment to operate.

Modular degrees have brought concerns about over-assessment. Ross (2005) argues that streamlining assessment is necessary to enable staff and students to cope with the changing environment in higher education, particularly growth in student numbers. He also proposes 'stripping-back' of assessment to 'its fundamental relationship with learning outcomes' as a means of making it practicable in the contemporary context. Chapters 12 and 13 discuss methods of managing the student assessment workload.

Transparency

Information, guidance, rules and regulations on assessment should be clear, accurate, consistent and accessible to all staff, students, practice teachers and external examiners. This principle has been of growing importance over the last decade in the UK as institutional processes have become more clearly subject to external audit and review. Transparency is seen as a key element of institutional accountability (Orr 2005), where clear procedures and rules facilitate external scrutiny. These include identifying learning outcomes and marking criteria, extension and extenuating circumstances rules, and second marking and moderation procedures. While much of this may not necessarily improve learning from assessment, it does allow the system to be 'judged in relation to its overall coherence and transparency' (Crook *et al.* 2006: 96), suggesting that reliability in assessment has been substituted by a concern for reliability of assessment procedures (Brown and Knight 1994).

On a more positive note, many academics associate transparency with fairness, better communication and avoiding confusion between staff and students as the rules and structures are made less opaque (Gosling and Moon 2002; Orr 2005). Sadler (2005) supports the drive towards transparency, noting that mysterious criteria and standards lead to a relationship of dependency between student and tutor. Students rely on tutor judgement because they have no concept of how their work is being judged, leaving them unable to regulate their own learning.

The drive towards transparency is seen in various forms. UK institutions are required to write and publish programme specifications. In relation to assessment, it is the view of the QAA (2006c) that clear, public marking criteria and **marking schemes** are important in ensuring that marking is carried out fairly and consistently across all disciplines. However, evidence discussed under 'reliability' would suggest that transparency in relation to 'complex' assignments is an enormous challenge. Orr (2005: 178) argues that tutors develop ideas and beliefs about assessing students which determine how they judge work and 'this implicit approach may contradict the explicit require-ments' given to students. Price (2005) cites a range of studies where variation between staff continued despite the use of assessment criteria.

Furthermore, information such as assessment criteria provides limited help to students as they require interpretation within the context of the given situation (Crook *et al.* 2006). As a consequence, O'Donovan *et al.* (2004) argue that, rather than dispense with 'transparent' information, teachers in higher education need to use participative methods in order to help students learn the tacit knowledge associated with assessment, to begin to make the hidden more visible (see Chapter 5).

A further feature of transparency is demonstration of fair and transparent mechanisms for marking and moderating marks (QAA 2006c) so that all stakeholders are able to judge their appropriateness. Case study 1 is an example of a response to this pressure. The moderator's concern for evidence that the students have individually met the learning outcomes entails time spent by students (writing) and staff (marking) which may add little in terms of student learning.

Overall, transparency is important for 'student learning' but also for 'quality assurance' because of the links to institutional accountability. In the UK, quality assurance is based on the academic infrastructure which is con-trolled by the QAA (2006d).

Attribution

Tasks should generate clear evidence that the work (of whatever nature) has been produced by the candidate. This relates to a range of malpractice including plagiarism but also collusion – for example, where a student team is prepared to represent one or more of their members' contributions inaccurately. This principle has come to the fore in recent years as the internet and electronic communication have significantly increased concerns about plagiarism and cheating.

This is important for 'certification' as institutions and external stakeholders, quite reasonably, want to be assured that students have achieved the learning for the award they have gained. Stringent efforts are gradually developing across the higher education sector to tackle malpractice, with a holistic approach recommended which includes both prevention and detection (MacDonald and Carroll 2006). The emphasis in this book will be on incorporating malpractice prevention into the teaching of modules (Chapter 4) and the design of assessment strategies which help to prevent it (Chapters 11 and 12).

Conclusion and possible ways forward

The foregoing discussion has illustrated the conflicting nature of established principles underlying assessment practice. If we link these principles back to our initial discussion of the purposes of assessment, we can see that each purpose emphasises different principles and is hindered by others:

1. **Certification** emphasises validity, reliability, equity and attribution.
2. **Student learning** emphasises validity, effectiveness, practicability, equity and some aspects of transparency.
3. **Quality assurance** needs validity, reliability, transparency, equity, comparability and consistency.
4. **Lifelong learning** emphasises validity, effectiveness, equity and elements of transparency.

Therefore, in designing our assessment strategies, we need to be aware of the different purposes and principles of assessment and the need to achieve balance. Traditionally assessment has focused on measurement, the summative assessment *of* learning (Boud 2000), and most institutions still stress the measurement aspects of assessment with little concern for other purposes (Gibbs and Simpson 2004–5; Hounsell 2006). In addition, in the current era of accountability, universities are now placing considerable emphasis on the quality assurance aspects of assessment with comparable, consistent and transparent procedures which may also have little to do with supporting learning.

However, researchers are now stressing the importance of balancing concerns about assessment *of* learning (certification and quality assurance) with assessment *for* and *as* learning (student learning, lifelong learning), as discussed in Chapter 2. 'We are not arguing for unreliable assessment but we are arguing that we should design assessment, first, to support worthwhile learning, and worry about reliability later' (Hounsell *et al.* 2006: 1). Of course, this idea of abandoning the quest for reliable and transparent university assessment in an age of accountability would be institutional suicide, and it does not take great powers of imagination to predict the newspaper headlines. Consequently, a pragmatic approach has to be one of balance across a student's programme. It has to be one where care is taken in assignment design to reconcile the potential contradictory effects of different assessment purposes and underlying principles. This is a key proposition underpinning the content of this book as the different principles discussed earlier are developed in relation to all aspects of the assessment cycle.

That process is commenced here by returning to our case studies in order to consider ways to tackle the shortcomings that they illustrate (see Tables 3.2–3.4).

Table 3.2 Case study 1: group presentation

Principle	Potential enhancements
Reliability	Use two markers for the student presentations. Markers (and students) agree marking criteria in advance and share understanding by marking a formative presentation or video of a presentation.
Comparability and consistency	Staff estimate learning hours required by students to complete the assessment and compare these with learning hours for alternative assessments in order to judge weighting.
Equity	Consider putting international students in common language groups to ease communication. Discuss requirements with disabled students and identify any reasonable adjustments.
Attribution	Students are required to keep 'minutes' of their group meetings identifying attendance, decisions made and action taken. These allow the tutor to gain some indication of individual contributions. Alternatively, group pages are set up on virtual learning environment and the tutor can check individual contributions to the discussion.

Table 3.3 Case study 2: unseen examination

Principle	Potential enhancements
Validity	Change examination paper to part B type questions only. Give no choice but provide exemplar questions early in the programme so that students direct their efforts towards the intended learning.
Reliability	Develop assessment criteria and marking scheme in discussion with module tutors. Staff team pre-mark sample scripts to discuss and agree interpretation of marking scheme.
Effectiveness	Change examination as above but include mock examination part-way using self- and peer assessment to help students explore their achievement against standards.
Transparency	Publish assessment criteria and marking scheme. Peer and self-assessment of mock paper to help students better understand the scheme.
Practicality	Consider shorter examination with focus on key concepts to assess whole course but reduce marking.
Equity	Consider second mode of assessment for module which offers students an alternative way to demonstrate their learning.

Table 3.4 Case study 3: online multiple choice quiz

Principle	Potential enhancements
Validity	Ensure that the second mode of assessment for the module focuses on application of knowledge, perhaps through an investigation or project.
Effectiveness	Generate each test uniquely from question banks and allow students to sit a test as many times as they like in each week with only the last attempt counting – to encourage students to engage with feedback. Use second assessment as above to encourage deep approach to subject matter.
Equity	Discuss test format with disabled students and disability officer or learning technologist to identify appropriate adjustments.
Attribution	Procedure must ensure students can only log on in their own name.

PART 2
DEALING WITH ASSESSMENT

4 Teaching a module: maximising the potential of assessment

Many university tutors find themselves teaching a module that they have had no part in designing. The module has been approved and the assessment methods are fixed, at least for the moment. Indeed, where you are part of a module team, the teaching programme, assignment titles, examination questions and submission dates may well be out of your control too. However, this does not mean that you cannot have a significant influence on the assessment strategy of the course and how students perceive and engage in assessed tasks.

While Chapter 12 is concerned with designing module assessment, this chapter aims to help staff working with previously approved courses to ensure that the assessment practice facilitates student learning while meeting the demands of institutional quality assurance. A key element of improving students' achievement is the guidance they receive in relation to assessment, particularly with unfamiliar assignments. Given the importance of this matter, it is dealt with in depth in Chapter 5.

Assessment basics

Assessment information

Students' perceptions of what assessment tasks require can vary significantly and are influenced by their prior experience and preferences. Efforts to make the requirements more transparent through written guidance are insufficient on their own because of the unfamiliar language and the tacit knowledge inherent in assessment (O'Donovan *et al.* 2004). Consequently, other processes are needed to effectively communicate assessment expectations to students (see Chapter 5). Nonetheless, basic written information about each module is an important feature of good practice and welcomed by students (Crook *et al.* 2006). It provides baseline guidance and is especially important for students with disabilities, significant personal responsibilities, or those trying to cope with a demanding workload, because it enables students to organise their time and plan in advance where necessary. As in most aspects, good assessment practice is inclusive assessment practice. Accuracy is important with assessment information. The high stakes involved mean that apparently minor errors can cause considerable trouble and anxiety.

Module guides should provide students with:

- an outline of the assessment task(s) and examinations for the module, including the learning outcomes addressed by the different components of assessment;
- the relative weighting of the assessment components and whether students need to achieve a pass mark in each component or only the overall module mark;
- how the module grade contributes to overall degree classification or progression requirements;
- the assessment criteria and/or marking scheme (see Chapter 6);
- the required format, for example, word-processed, double-spaced and stapled (no plastic?) – unsuitable bindings and inappropriate formats may waste the marker's time and even create bias through the irritation that they cause;
- any arrangements for peer or self-assessment;
- deadlines and procedures for submission of assignments;
- when and how examination dates will be notified;
- requirements for referencing and penalties for failure to reference accurately;
- penalties for excessive length in assignments, poor grammar, spelling and expression;
- procedures to follow if the student is having difficulty or thinks they will not be able to complete the assessment on time;
- when and how the marked work will be returned to students, if applicable;
- a reminder to students with disabilities or specific learning needs about how and when to request alternative assessment arrangements

In some cases the module guide will refer to further detail provided in the programme handbook.

Scheduling of assignments

There are a number of factors to take into account in scheduling coursework:

- The spread of assessment deadlines is often dealt with on a programme basis, so it is worth checking with the relevant person whether there is a submission dates' timetable and if your module has been allocated certain fixed submission dates. Assessment submission dates should come well after the relevant topics have been addressed in the module.

- Where possible, the student workload should be spread across the module to reduce bunching of deadlines. Many students will put off work until just before it is due to be submitted, and if all the assessment comes at the end of a semester or term, they will do very little work in the intervening weeks.
- It is good practice to provide at least four weeks' notice of summative assignments, although small tasks may have shorter notice. Check if your department has guidelines for the notice required for assessment.
- Assessment deadlines need to allow you sufficient time for marking prior to examination boards.
- Scheduling work also needs to take in the desirability of providing formative feedback to students early in modules. If a module has two assignments, it is not helpful for student learning if they have to submit the second one before they have received feedback on the first.

Returning work to students

Students benefit from a prompt return of marked assignments with the accompanying feedback. There are situations where this is not always possible because the work is needed for moderation. In this case, various strategies should be employed. For example, global feedback comments can be published identifying the main strengths and weaknesses in the assignment and action needed to improve future assignments. Alternatively, the students could be given an opportunity to see their marked work in class or by another means so that they can read feedback and annotations. A copy of the comments and the unconfirmed internal mark should be given to the student as soon as possible.

When work cannot be returned to students in person, it should be available for collection from an office, posted or emailed. It should not be left in public places for collection, as this risks other students taking work for their own use.

You might consider arranging for a sample of assignments to be photocopied for retention in the department. These are useful for later use in audit exercises, inducting new members of staff into local standards and (with the permission of the students concerned and anonymised) for use as exemplars with future student groups.

Assessment and learning

Chapter 2 summarised the relationship between assessment and learning. The following paragraphs outline practical ideas for implementing assessment which encourages learning.

Capturing student time

It is important to think carefully about how much your particular module engages students from week to week. Assessment is key to capturing student time and effort and there is a range of effective ways to increase student activity through assessment without incurring extra marking workload:

- online tests which provide automated, immediate feedback;
- peer marking of assignments in class;
- submission of weekly short assignments of which the tutor randomly selects a small proportion for summative marking and feedback;
- submission of a log book indicating work undertaken during the module.

Preparing students for assessment

Chapter 5 is devoted to the important matter of preparing students for assessment. Practical activities can include marking exercises, creating and working with assessment criteria, using **exemplar** assignments and model answers, practising assessment tasks and mock examinations, and peer and self-assessment.

Formative assessment

Feedback on assessment activities can provide information to learners on their progress. Unfortunately, many modules leave assessment until the end so it is difficult for students to judge how well they are doing until the module has finished. Therefore, it is argued (Juwah *et al.* 2004: 3) that formative assessment 'should be an integral part of teaching and learning' in higher education. There is considerable confusion about definitions of formative assessment. For our purposes, we use the term to describe any activity during a module which provides information to students and tutors on their progress.

Staff often say that students will not do assessed tasks unless they count towards final grades, and this is a good reason to include one or more elements of your summative assessment part-way through the module.

However, students can also take part in formative assessment in many informal ways both in and out of the classroom. For example:

- you can introduce true–false or multiple choice questions during lectures to test how well students have grasped the ideas you have been explaining, providing the answers immediately. The results will help them know if they are on the right track and help you know if you need to adjust your teaching. The increasing provision of personal response systems (electronic) speeds this process and enables you to collect their answers quickly and efficiently for electronic display. In-class formative assessment of this nature gives students an active role in class and helps them gain instant feedback on progress.
- ask students to bring drafts of assignments to class where you devote some of the session to peer marking. A small proportion of the final mark can be allocated to submitting a draft if an incentive is needed.

Juwah *et al.* (2004) provide practical information and case studies on a range of tested approaches to formative assessment across several disciplines. Chapter 7 provides information on feedback in relation to formative assessment.

Changing your teaching

Formative assessment during a course is valuable for students to monitor their progress and diagnose difficulties, but it can have considerably more power if it is also used to inform your teaching *as you go along.* It is important to modify teaching plans in response to information about students' learning. This information may come from a range of different sources: questions students ask; in-class exercises; online quizzes; and formal mid-course assignments. The more information you have about the progress of your students, the more likely you are to be able to help them. Angelo and Cross (1993: 148) detail an extensive range of classroom assessment techniques specifically designed to help teachers discover how well students have learnt something. The 'minute paper' involves the tutor asking students to conclude a session by writing the answer to a simple question such as 'What was the most important thing you learned during this class?' or 'What important question remains unanswered?' on a scrap of paper. As students are asked to limit their reply to a sentence or two, tutors can quickly read the responses (or a sample). The 'muddiest point' activity involves a similar technique, but the question is 'What is the muddiest point in the topic, lecture, reading, etc.?' (Angelo and Cross 1993: 154). Both these techniques take very little staff or student time but can provide rich information on which to base decisions about adjusting your teaching. Angelo and Cross argue that the 'muddiest point' is most appropriate in modules where students are having to cope with large amounts of new information. A further suggestion (Nicol and Macfarlane-Dick 2004: 8) is to ask students to note what they found difficult when they hand in an assignment or to ask 'students in groups to identify "a question worth asking", based on prior study, that they would like to explore' during a session.

You can then use the information you gain about student progress to tackle the areas where students are having difficulty. Black *et al.* (2003) found that opportunities which allowed students to reveal their problems were seen as worthwhile, leading to help. This 'help' will depend on context, but may mean going over something in more detail, explaining a point in a different way, discussion of problems or suggesting additional reading.

Writing assessment tasks

While the modes of assessment may be prescribed for you, you may be able to control, or at least influence, the quality of that assessment tool through careful design of examinations and assessment tasks. Chapter 2 discussed the importance of students' 'cue-seeking' behaviour, and the selection of questions and tasks is an opportunity for you to give your students clear cues regarding the nature and level of work that you expect.

Writing examination papers

Examinations are a time-honoured means of assessment in higher education and continue to be taken for granted as an effective means of assessing student learning. Chapter 11 discusses the advantages and disadvantages of using examinations, whereas this section is designed to provide practical help in making your examinations effective.

- Consider alternative examination formats which reduce emphasis on memory and make higher-level academic demands (see Chapter 13 for examples).
- Avoid 'narrowly technical questions, or those closely aligned to the taught course, [which] allow weaknesses in understanding to be disguised' (Entwistle and Entwistle 1997: 155), as students may just reproduce material from your lectures.
- Do not have a choice of questions. Either set a number of short-answer questions which survey the syllabus or set fewer long-answer questions which encourage students to draw on material across the module. An alternative is Elton and Johnston's (2002: 30) suggestion

that lower-order knowledge and comprehension should be comprehensively tested and involve no choice, whereas higher-order skills 'can be exhibited with any basic knowledge' and therefore students can be given a choice. Thus an examination paper might include a range of compulsory short-answer or multiple choice questions followed by a choice of essay-type questions, the latter focusing on key concepts or application of knowledge.

- If students are allowed to bring notes to the examination (for example, for a seen paper or where they have had materials in advance), limit the amount by number of words, not number of pages. Otherwise, students will cram thousands of words onto a page. Ask for the notes to be handed in the day before so that they can be checked for word length.

- If disabled students or those with specific learning difficulties have been recommended extra time in an examination, it may also be a reasonable adjustment to provide them with the same proportion of extra time for preparing a seen paper or advance materials.

Preparation of students for examinations is essential. Elton and Johnston (2002) discuss how 'operational' words used in examinations, such as discuss, analyse, and explain, can have different tacit meanings for assessors and students if their definition in that context is not clarified. Examination techniques are also vital to success, and student preparation will be discussed in the next chapter. In addition, it is important to consider ways to give students feedback on their examination performance.

Writing effective questions

Many forms of assessment require the tutor to write questions. The nature of the questions can have an impact on several of the different principles of assessment. Among the issues to consider are the following:

- Do your questions allow the students to demonstrate that they have achieved the relevant learning outcomes?
- Offering a choice of questions reduces the reliability of the grades because it is very difficult to write equally challenging questions. In relation to essays, it may be more appropriate to set one core question but ask students to answer it in relation to one of a choice of topics, cases, or problems.
- Avoid the word 'discuss'. Provide a more precise instruction (Elton and Johnston 2002).
- Avoid 'closed' essay questions.
- Are your questions clear? This is particularly important for students

who have English as an additional language. Are you testing their learning or their ability to understand your question? Questions will need to present increasingly complex problems to students as they move up the levels. However, test your questions out with colleagues to check that they are challenging rather than unnecessarily complicated.

- Do your questions allow a range of responses (see taxonomies of educational objectives in Chapter 2)? Do they allow students to go well beyond the threshold requirements if they are able to?
- For higher-level learning outcomes, do your questions require students to discern the critical aspects of problems and issues for themselves or are they identified in the wording of the question (Bowden and Marton 1998; Boud and Falchikov 2006)?

An effective way to ensure that questions are well written is to subject them to internal scrutiny. Discussion of questions among colleagues can highlight ambiguous and overcomplicated questions and is generally considered good practice (see Chapter 8 on internal moderation). Banks of essay questions with marking guidelines are becoming available. For example, the economics subject centre of the Higher Education Academy in the UK has a range of examples (www.economicsnetwork.ac.uk/qnbank/).

Multiple choice questions

There is considerable debate regarding multiple choice questions (MCQs) which is developed in Chapter 14. If an MCQ test is already specified in your module assessment plan, then you will need to invest some time in designing or obtaining suitable questions because reliable and valid MCQs take considerable time to construct. Less concern with reliability is necessary if they are being used for solely formative or diagnostic purposes. Chapter 14 provides advice on finding, creating and using MCQs.

Designing and setting up group assignments

Group tasks

Tasks for group-based assessments can be enormously varied, from completing a production or project, and analysis of a problem or case study, to development of teaching materials, posters and presentations on a topic. In general, tasks should be designed which involve high levels of collaboration and negotiation between the members, otherwise the benefits of working in a group may be lost. This might happen, for example, if the task can be done by merely sharing the work out at the beginning and then combining each person's contribution together at the end.

Establishing groups

The ideal size for a group will depend on the scale of the team task but three to five is an ideal size for a group. Larger groups may be appropriate where there is some level of facilitation or direction such as in problem-based learning or a performance. Normally, when the group size extends beyond five, it is much harder for everyone to be involved in the discussion (encouraging freeloaders) and co-ordinating meetings and work can be very difficult. There are conflicting views on whether groups should be self-selecting, with evidence that mixing students of all abilities with high-ability students raises their achievement (Falchikov 2005). In general, tutors should allocate students to groups to reflect the reality of most work teams and encourage students to work with a wider range of people.

Preparing student for group assignments

It should not be assumed that students will automatically be able to work effectively in assessment teams. Research suggests that students are not always positive about group assignments (Falchikov 2005) and they can fail to work well for a variety of reasons (Helms and Haynes 1990). For example, students with high performance goals are more likely to be negative about group assignments, taking on too great a proportion of the work rather than collaborating with others in order to achieve a high mark (Volet and Mansfield 2006). Therefore, you are storing up potential problems for yourself and your students if you do not prepare them for group assignments.

The first stage is to ensure that students know the rationale for using a team approach and what the purpose of it is. Volet and Mansfield's (2006) research recommends helping students to see the wider benefits of group assignments. They found that students who value social forms of learning behave in ways that help the functioning of the group, creating positive outcomes for both individuals and the group. There is a discussion of the benefits of group assessment in Chapter 13, Box 13.8.

There are many skills involved in effective team working, and it is important that students are helped to develop these skills at an early stage through activities in class and, for example, discussion in personal tutor groups. Gibbs (1994) suggests that groups need assistance with:

- establishing the group (bonding);
- setting ground rules/contracts;
- clarifying the task;
- running effective meetings;
- recording decisions and who is doing what;
- dividing and sharing out work;

- reviewing how the group is going;
- giving each other feedback.

These matters should be discussed in class, and further guidance can be found in Gibbs (1994).

A useful way to help students relate these general skills in running a group to their own group is to ask them to draw up a contract or charter including agreements about the group will manage itself. You can suggest including details regarding conduct of meetings, how the work will be divided up and how they will tackle any problems that arise such as non-attendance at meetings. Groups can be asked to submit a copy of their contracts to you as a first task. Care needs to be taken that contracts are used by groups to evict students who are perceived to be performing badly, rather than attempting to address the problem in a constructive fashion (Volet and Mansfield 2006). Instead, provide students with information on what to do if one or more of the group are unable or unwilling to fulfil their role.

Further support can be given by devoting a short period of a contact session to a discussion of how the group is going. A simple questionnaire can be used to start the discussion (are meetings productive, is everyone turning up, are people completing tasks agreed at meetings, does everyone get a fair opportunity to contribute to discussion, is the team making good progress?). Completed individually and then shared in the group, this can be a powerful tool to help groups identify the causes of any problems at an early stage and agree ways to deal with such problems. Preparation should also include information on how group marks will be awarded and whether students will receive a team or an individual mark. Techniques for awarding group marks and differentiating between group members are discussed in Chapter 6.

Group meetings

Students often complain that they cannot meet easily to work on group assignments. It is the case that many students do not come to campus except for programmed sessions, particularly if they are part-time or mature students (and hardly at all in the case of distance learning students). Tutors need to be creative in tackling this problem so that students can gain the benefits of group assessment. Here are some ideas:

- Provide time in class for groups to meet. For example, the first half hour of weekly sessions could be devoted to group meetings allowing groups to raise any questions or queries with you during the main session.
- Set up a discussion board on your virtual learning environment for each group or show them how to establish a **wiki** (a collaborative

website whose content can be amended by anyone who is allowed access to it). In this way, students can communicate with each other, compose work together and share documents in progress.

- Encourage students to consider other forms of communication as well as face-to-face meetings. It has never been easier for students to communicate using telephone and e-mail.
- Suggest that the programme identifies an extra 'timetabled' session each week which can be used for group meetings as well as other important activities such as personal tutorials, course consultative committees and programme information sessions.

Monitoring groups

Pickford (2006) recommends using assessed 'deliverables' as milestones during a group assignment to enable formative feedback on progress and to help groups develop strategies for working under pressure. These deliverables may be a group contract, draft plan or summary of work to date. Some form of monitoring may also be important to reduce the chance of freeloaders in the group. You could ask groups to submit a record of their meetings, including details of attendance, follow-up on action from last meeting and agreed action. If group meetings are to be held online through asynchronous discussion, you can request a transcript of the discussion (Carroll 2002) or monitor it online.

Writing assessment criteria and standards

Although the term 'assessment criteria' is sometimes used broadly (Gosling and Moon 2002), Sadler (2005) argues that it is important to distinguish assessment criteria from assessment standards (see also Box 4.1). Criteria are the aspects of an assessment task which the assessor will take into account when making their judgement. These are likely to be specific to individual tasks and might include such things as quality of argument, use of evidence and presentation (see the example in Box 4.2). Standards, on the other hand, refer to a level of attainment 'established by authority, custom or consensus' (Sadler 2005: 189). Institutions or departments often provide 'grade descriptors' which attempt to set out the standards for achieving different grades (see Table 6.1 for an example). Marking schemes combine criteria with standards by providing the detail about how performance in each of the criteria will be graded. In this chapter, we are concentrating on writing assessment criteria, whereas writing marking schemes will be tackled in Chapter 6.

Assessment criteria may focus solely on the learning outcomes to be demonstrated, but they are likely also to include relevant generic attributes

---

Box 4.1 Leads into literature: the debate about assessment criteria and standards

Criterion-based assessment is strongly supported in educational literature (Sadler 2005). Criteria clarify the link between the stated learning outcomes and the specific assessment task; they can help focus students' efforts in the right direction and provide the basis for them to judge their own progress, and they present a starting point for staff discussion about marking standards. Finally, they provide evidence of the basis for assessment decisions and enable you to justify your judgements. Overall, they are considered essential in the drive towards consistency and transparency, and therefore, in the UK, the Quality Assurance Agency (2006c: 16) state that 'Publicising and using clear assessment criteria and, where appropriate, marking schemes, are key factors in assuring that marking is carried out fairly and consistently across all subjects'.

Despite this advice, there is plenty of evidence (discussed in Chapters 3 and 6) of the difficulty of explicitly specifying, communicating and using assessment criteria and standards at university level. Whereas criteria may be explicitly stated, standards nearly always require an element of professional judgement and thus their interpretation can vary across markers. In addition, they often provide limited help to students as the specific language and discourse mean that they can only be easily understood by someone familiar with the context. The latter problem has led to a number of strategies to help students understand assessment criteria and marking standards, and these are discussed in Chapter 5. Detailed criteria can also encourage a mechanistic, mark-oriented approach in students where they become over-dependent on tutors, wanting them to define the criteria more and more closely, and this can work against students seriously engaging with the learning process (Norton 2004; O'Donovan *et al.* 2004; Bloxham and West 2007). Generic criteria or standards may struggle to reflect disciplinary differences.

In addition, experienced staff have usually developed their own criteria and standards for marking which are both difficult to articulate and resistant to change. Ecclestone (2001) suggests such staff may oppose explicit guidance as a threat to their professional judgement. Indeed, they may ignore formal criteria in favour of their own approach (Wolf 1995). Nonetheless, such guidance is useful for the induction of new staff (Ecclestone 2001) and considered essential for modules with multiple markers (Price 2005).

Consequently, all parties should recognise that the issue of creating and using assessment criteria and standards is not straightforward (Woolf 2004), but we would argue that the processes involved in creating criteria, revising and sharing (and possibly creating) them with students, and using them in marking can only act to improve the quality of judgements. As Woolf argues, just the process of making criteria explicit can encourage tutors to think about the examinations and coursework they are setting and how well they test the desired learning. This is particularly important when we are thinking of inclusive assessment in relation to disabled students. Clarifying exactly what is being assessed makes decisions regarding 'reasonable adjustments' and alternative assignments simpler, and this is discussed further in Chapter 10.

Box 4.2 An example of assessment criteria for a first-year undergraduate essay

The following are generic criteria. In order to reflect module outcomes, tutors will need to amend the first two to identify the topic area and framework for analysis.

Your essay will be marked using the following assessment criteria:

1. You demonstrate evidence of a sound knowledge of the topic and use the appropriate terminology accurately.
2. You show an ability to analyse the subject using the principles/ideas introduced during the module. You show some evidence of critical thinking about the topic.
3. You make use of relevant reading and reference it accurately using the Harvard system.
4. Your essay structure helps make the argument and discussion clear and coherent.
5. Use of language: you display a good standard of English with few grammatical errors or spelling mistakes and it is written in an academic style.

---

such as structure, presentation or use of source material. The following is a list of points to consider when you are devising assessment criteria:

- Ensure your criteria follow directly from the learning outcomes being assessed.
- Ensure the criteria reflect the level of the students' course (see the discussion of taxonomies in Chapter 2 and of levels in Chapter 12).
- Revise the criteria in discussion with other tutors to help ensure that they reflect the real basis on which staff make their judgements. If the range of sources and quality of English are important, make this explicit to students. This process may help you realise that undue weighting is being placed on lower-level skills such as presentation or accurate referencing.
- Remember that clarifying assessment criteria is just as important for examinations as for coursework. For example, in an examination quality of grammar, spelling and presentation may not be as important as quality of content.
- Provide clear, concise criteria which help in writing feedback to students.
- Avoid too many overly specific (checklist-type) assessment criteria which make marking very time-consuming and may take away students' freedom to show learning beyond those areas, limiting the spread of performance.

- Remember that specifying too much detail may appear to 'give the answers away' and encourage students to take a mechanistic approach to meeting the criteria.

Peer and self-assessment

Peer and self-assessment are methods of marking and creating feedback. Chapter 2 outlined our growing understanding of the vital contribution that they can make to assessment for learning, but tutors often have concerns about using these approaches for fear of inaccurate grading, collusion between students and negative student responses. Furthermore, students think that they are not competent to assess themselves or each other and worry about having to criticise each other including fear of reprisals if they mark a fellow student down. The research on peer and self-assessment is summarised in Box 2.2. Here, we draw on the lessons from research to help you use peer and self-assessment successfully.

Provide a rationale

Take time to explain the reasons for using self- and peer assessment to your students – for example, helping them to understand the academic standards of the module, developing the skills of judgement and giving feedback, learning from each other, and preparation for lifelong learning as they learn to monitor their own progress rather than rely on a tutor to do it.

Guidance

Provide good guidance and training for the students for peer and self-assessment. This includes clear instructions and the use of practice activities. For example, if your module assessment involves a peer assessed presentation, get the students to do a practice run on another topic and assess each other in groups. A brave colleague began by asking first-year students to decide what they thought the criteria should be for judging a lecture, something which they all have strong views about. When the group had identified several key criteria, she delivered her lecture and then asked the students to assess it against the criteria, giving her marks and feedback. It provided interesting feedback for the tutor and allowed the students to practise being in the assessor role in a low-stakes way. Falchikov (2005) suggests that non-western students may need more practice and preparation, but it is likely that all students will benefit from this.

Unreliable marking

Tutors are frequently worried about students colluding with each other to avoid making fair judgements, giving themselves or each other high marks or unfairly penalising unpopular students. Suggestions for avoiding this include the following:

- Use **double anonymous** marking (students do not know whose work they are marking or who has marked them).
- Use multiple markers of work, or pair/group marking.
- Use assessment criteria and require students to justify their mark or feedback against them.
- Involve students in drawing up criteria.
- Tutors moderate peer or self-assessed grades.
- Take an average of several peer or self-assessments.
- Only use peer and self-assessment for formative assignments.

Overall, Falchikov (2005) urges tutors to have patience and persistence in developing peer and self-assessment. There are huge gains to be had from involving students in their own assessment, so try to analyse and remedy problems in your local context rather than assume 'it won't work here'.

Designing tasks to reduce plagiarism

Tutors should be aware of the various ways in which students may be involved in malpractice in their assessment including fabrication of material, collusion with other students and cheating in examinations. This section looks particularly at the issue of plagiarism because there is good evidence that tutors can reduce this form of malpractice through care at the planning stage.

The potential for plagiarism is increased where assessments:

- are repeated year on year;
- are bunched at the end of courses (students become overburdened and resort to cheating);
- require only the use of information and ideas which are easily available in the public domain (for example, on the internet or in a journal article);
- are not systematically checked, for example using plagiarism detection software.

You can reduce the use of plagiarism by:

- regularly changing assessment questions;
- spreading assessment across the module, for example through small tasks that build up to the final assessment, through formative peer-assessed activities and asking to see early drafts of work;
- using your own (regularly changed) case study material as a basis for assignments;
- referring to contemporary events (for example news items, court cases, policy developments);
- making assessments relevant and stimulating;
- setting more specific titles for assignments;
- building in elements of personal reflection or reflection on personal experiences;
- using group assignments;
- asking for photocopies of the front page of four or five key articles, books and internet sources used in an assignment to be appended to the coursework.

Plagiarism detection is discussed in Chapter 9 and use of detection software is included in Chapter 14. A few leads into the literature are given in Box 4.3.

Box 4.3   Leads into literature: plagiarism

The ideas for designing assessment to reduce plagiarism are drawn from professional experience and various texts. Carroll (2002) provides a comprehensive sourcebook including many practical suggestions and resources. Falchikov (2005) summarises research on cheating in higher education and reviews the advice for tutors emerging from studies of plagiarism and cheating. Finally, Park (2003) reviews the literature on plagiarism. Further information can be obtained from the JISC Plagiarism Advisory Service (www.jiscpas.ac.uk/).

When problems crop up

Extensions

There will always be students who are unable to complete assignments in time for good reason. Unfortunately, determining good reasons is often difficult for tutors to do in the absence of independent evidence and will require a level of professional judgement. You can open yourself up to accusations of favouritism or discrimination in granting extensions, so it is important to ensure that you are following your department or institution's policy and procedures. This may require students to arrange extensions in advance of the due date and will normally involve completing a form which they submit with their late assignment

Where you do decide that extra time is appropriate, offer students short extensions (one or two days) wherever possible to prevent their workload building up. Alert personal tutors or the programme leader to the fact that you have granted an extension to ensure that students are receiving advice and support if they are not managing their workload.

Extenuating or mitigating circumstances

Institutions use different terms for this procedure. **Extenuating** or **mitigating circumstances** refers to cases where students have serious difficulties and an extension is unlikely to suffice. For example, where prolonged personal difficulties or illness necessitates students missing an examination or means they are unlikely to complete outstanding work in time for the examination board, they will need to present a claim for extenuating circumstances and present evidence to support their case. This is also the case where students complete assessment or sit examinations but consider their performance was affected by factors beyond their control. Students need to be advised that making a claim does not always mean they will succeed. Claims usually have a range of possible outcomes, including voiding the assessment or allowing the student a second chance to submit. They do not normally allow students to gain extra marks that the work does not justify. Advise the student to submit any claim with supporting evidence to the relevant office as soon as possible, and definitely well before the board of examiners is due to meet. Tutors are well advised to appraise themselves of their institution's practice in relation to extenuating circumstances because you can cause problems for yourself and your students if you misadvise them.

Conclusion

This chapter has summarised ways in which tutors can take control of the assessment in their modules, using it to improve the student experience and their own satisfaction with the task. It has considered basic assessment information, and writing assignments, examinations and assessment criteria. It has also provided advice on using group assignments, peer and self-assessment and designing assessment to avoid plagiarism. In general, we are advocating an approach which puts assessment at the heart of your teaching, planning it carefully from the outset and using it to drive student learning.

5 Preparing students for assessment

Introduction

Students may have a very weak understanding of assessment and fail to exploit it to improve their learning (Maclellan 2001). Indeed, Hyland's (2000: 244) research with history students showed that while students wanted to do better, they seldom knew how to improve because they did not understand the language in assignment briefs and lacked 'clear, precise and practical advice'. Helping students adjust to the demands of writing at university is a key factor in driving up standards of achievement (Davies *et al.* 2006), but Swann and Ecclestone (1999a) suggest that the literature on improving assessment has neglected the complex issue of how we induct and socialise students into an assessment community. This is despite the fact that early difficulties with assessment are associated with **attrition** (Krause 2001). Much good work in improving assessment practice will be undermined if we do not put similar effort into preparing students for assessment and help them perceive the meaning of assignments and the standards expected of them.

What is involved in becoming academically literate?

Communities of practice and tacit knowledge

Within the concept of communities of practice (Lave & Wenger 1991, 1999; Fuller *et al.* 2005), learning is considered to be a social practice where novices in that community become full members through participation rather than formal instruction. Subject disciplines can be perceived as communities of practice, each with a distinct discourse, but they differ from other communities in that the primary form of discourse is through the written rather than the spoken word (Northedge 2003a).

For students to become part of an academic community, they need to become skilled at writing in the discourse of the subject discipline (Northedge 2003a) – to become academically literate. Implicit in this process is the notion of acquiring 'tacit' knowledge (Polanyi 1998), something which is learnt through practice and is difficult to express in words. Defining and differentiating between 'critically analyse', 'systematically appraise' and 'carefully review' in assignment titles is likely to be different for each of us, depending on subject discipline and prior experience. As tutors, we have achieved a form of connoisseurship regarding the standards and protocols of our subject disciplines (Knight 2006), but that has usually been achieved over many years and is not easily understood by novices. Assignment feedback is arguably the chief way in which we communicate with students regarding our standards (Price 2005).

Academic literacy or literacies

An additional difficulty facing academically inexperienced students is the complexity of the community or communities they are joining. Boud and Falchikov (2006: 406) argue that it is not always obvious to students 'what the community of practice is that they should be identifying with, its activities are not necessarily clear'. This problem is heightened for students on interdisciplinary courses faced with different disciplinary conventions, methods of argument, and referencing, and is not helped by tutors not always recognising the differences between subjects (Cowan and Creme 2005). Students have to contend with diverse understandings of academic literacy within and between subject discipline communities because tutors develop their own implicit view of what good writing is. The tutor's view may contradict published criteria and they may be unaware of this (Orr 2005). Staff lay emphasis on different qualities – for example, number of sources used, presentation, and particular perspectives – and students feel they have to decode 'the whims of individual teachers' (Crook *et al.* 2006: 104). Overall, the tacit nature of higher education practice means that elements of the assessment process are not transparent to students, and this is borne out in research (Hounsell *et al.* 2006).

This issue applies particularly to the interpretation of assessment criteria and marking standards. Woolf (2004) argues that criteria only make sense in context. They often include words such as 'appropriate', 'systematic' or 'sound' which are relatively meaningless unless you have a framework in which to understand them. We can try to write criteria and standards more explicitly, but there will always be a degree of professional judgement which comes from being a connoisseur in the discipline. 'Even the most carefully drafted criteria have to be translated into concrete and situation-specific terms' (Knight and Yorke 2003: 23). Just as communities of practice 'induct' their members largely through participation, understanding disciplinary ways of writing can only be learnt through participative methods. Box 5.1 introduces the development of student writing through a focus on 'academic literacies' which offers an alternative to socialisation and study skills approaches.

The difficulty of transferring such tacit knowledge has generated a

---

Box 5.1   Leads into literature: an academic literacies approach

The 'academic literacies' approach (Lea and Street 2000) problematises the notion of student writing. It sees the academic community as heterogeneous where writing is a 'contextualised social practice' always dependent on the situation in which the writing takes place and is assessed. Lea and Street have identified a range of models to explain the development of student writing: 'study skills', 'academic socialisation' and 'academic literacies'. The 'study skills' model sees academic writing as a set of technical skills to be learnt, whereas 'academic socialisation' more closely reflects the idea of 'community of practice' where the task of academic staff is to induct students into the writing conventions of the discipline. However, 'academic socialisation' assumes that the culture, of which students need to become a part, is established, fixed and homogenous. The tacit knowledge which students need to acquire is taken as a given and not contested. In contrast, the 'academic literacies' approach sees academic writing as shifting and dependent on the specific context such as the discipline, the course and the tutor, thus 'literacies' rather than literacy. It emphasises the ideological assumptions, power relationships and sense of identity underpinning academic writing. Creme and Lea's (2003: 26) advice to students is to recognise that academic writing is not just subject-specific but module-specific and dependent on the 'orientation of the course and the academic staff who designed it'.

---

growing range of interventions designed to help students understand what is expected of them. Perhaps the best-known intervention is to involve students in marking exemplar assignments. Rust *et al.* (2003) found that this activity resulted in marks on average half a grade higher (approximately 5%) compared with those who did not take part. The positive impact was sustained over three cohorts and lasted into students' second year. They contend that teachers should make 'use of transfer processes such as dialogue, observation, practice and imitation to share tacit understanding of assessment requirements' (O'Donovan *et al.* 2004: 332).

Student diversity

While 'cue-conscious' students (Miller and Parlett 1974) can quickly learn what is needed to satisfy the markers, other students do not find this easy. Haggis and Pouget's (2002) research suggests that the greater heterogeneity of students in contemporary higher education means that we need to be more explicit with students about assessment, particularly as a discouraging first assignment is associated with student attrition (Krause 2001). In addition, Dunn *et al.* (2004) discuss the reduced opportunity for 'cue seeking' faced by distance learning students whose main form of interaction with academic staff may be limited to assignment feedback. They argue that it is the responsibility of tutors to provide those 'cues' in ways that are accessible to all. Whereas Dunn *et al.* concentrate on implementing this imperative through the written description of each task, we suggest that more participative, dialogical methods are necessary because tacit knowledge cannot be easily communicated through the written word.

Furthermore, students' background and prior language experience will impact on this process, and some groups of students may be particularly disadvantaged, because they do not bring with them the same tacit knowledge of the system as their privileged peers (Yorke and Longden 2004). In addition, they are likely to find the language of assessment less accessible as a result of previous educational experience (Orr 2005). For example, a study (Morias, 1996) showed that middle-class students were more likely to benefit from extra guidance regarding assessment criteria.

Perceptions of the task

A key finding is that students' approach to their assignments and revision is strongly influenced by their perceptions of the task (Snyder 1971; Miller and Parlett 1974). As we discussed in Chapter 2, student learning is a result of an interaction between a student and the learning situation, and this is unique for every student in every different learning context. It is influenced by various factors, including their perception of the learning context. Therefore, in relation to assessment, the students' perception of what the assessment requires affects the approach they take (Prosser and Trigwell 1999). Students will not necessarily tackle the assessment task in ways you expect because they may have a different perception of the meaning of the task (Laurillard 2002). Your report on a 'practical' may have been designed to demonstrate an understanding of the topic area and the scientific methods involved, but the students may believe the purpose is to describe the experiment and its results without thinking about the underlying science. If we want students to take a deep approach to their assessment, then we need to ensure that their *intention* is to make meaning, as opposed to an intention to reproduce material on the topic. Thus changing the assessment alone will not necessarily change the students' approach to assessment unless we can help them perceive correctly the requirements of the task, and discern its important components, its meaning and relationship with their learning.

While the activities suggested in the second half of this chapter are designed to help students understand the requirements of an assessment task, they cannot compensate for poorly constructed assignments, confusing instructions or vague criteria. Chapter 4 provides advice on getting these prerequisites right.

Difficulties with innovative assessment

Gibbs (2006b) argues that students do not relish innovative types of assessment if they are not familiar with them or think they will take more time. Hounsell *et al.* (2006) have also identified students' unease with unfamiliar assignments leading them to question the relevance of the skills involved. Gibbs (2006b) suggests litigious students may challenge assessments where criteria are not explicit or they have not been adequately prepared. Helping students understand the purpose and rubric of innovative methods (including self-, peer and group assessment) may be crucial to their success.

Time management and learner autonomy

A further reason for preparing students for assessment is the struggle that many have in organising and managing their time well. Problems occur when students do not plan their work and leave it all to the last minute. While Chapters 4 and 12 discuss this issue in relation to designing and scheduling assessment, tutors should also consider how students are helped to develop the skills of autonomous learning, including time management. Sambell *et al.* (2006) argue that we need to help students develop 'procedural autonomy' before they can develop 'critical autonomy'. Procedural automony refers to students taking some control over the organisation of their workload, learning to use criteria and working within the rules of their subject (Ecclestone, 2002). Critical autonomy 'enables people to develop their understanding beyond conventional insights and wisdom ... the capacity to see the world another way' (Ecclestone 2002: 38) and is associated with developing subject expertise, the ability to make judgements, and the skills of evaluation and synthesis (Ecclestone 2002).

Summary

Taken as a whole, preparing students for assessment means assisting them to:

- learn to write in the discourse of their discipline(s), through acquiring tacit knowledge of its form and conventions;
- explore assessment criteria within context;
- develop accurate perceptions of tasks, their rationale and purpose;
- recognise the varying emphases of different tutors and modules;
- focus on an intention to gain meaning from completing their assignments;
- recognise the specific requirements, format and purpose of unfamiliar assessment tasks;

- pay attention to instructions, guidance and criteria and manage their study time effectively.

Overall, there is a need to actively support students' entry into the subject discipline community. Institutions have attempted to induct students through the provision of learning support, voluntary study skills workshops and online advice. However, these practices assume that academic literacy is independent of the context, a fact which is not supported by the evidence (Wingate 2006). There is no one way to write an essay or a lab report, and students can only learn how in the context of their modules and assignments.

Price and O'Donovan (2006) point out that this process of knowledge transfer has traditionally taken place using considerable staff–student contact such as seminars and tutorials. In today's mass higher education sector, that luxury may not be available to the majority of tutors and their students. More cost-effective opportunities must be found for inducting students into requirements and standards (O'Donovan *et al.* 2004). This imperative underpins the practical suggestions and advice in the second part of this chapter.

A framework for preparing students for assessment: integrating guidance and feedback

A number of researchers are now concluding that preparing students for assessment is not a distinct stage in a module but should be part of an integrated cycle of guidance and feedback, involving students in active ways at all stages. Price and O'Donovan (2006) describe a cycle commencing with providing 'explicit criteria' followed by 'active engagement with criteria', 'self-assessment with submission of work' and 'active engagement with feedback'. The cycle is seen as iterative, with students' engagement with feedback from one assignment feeding forward to their engagement with the assessment criteria for the next assessment task.

In a similar, but more complex model, Hounsell *et al.* (2006) advocate a guidance and feeback loop with a number of steps. They suggest that reflecting on the steps can help tutors diagnose strengths and weaknesses in the provision of guidance and feedback. We have reproduced the steps in Table 5.1, accompanied by potential questions and practical activities from this chapter that you may find useful for the different steps.

Hounsell *et al.* suggest that staff should be proactive in providing supplementary support because evidence suggests students may lack confidence or opportunity to seek it themselves. A planned approach is likely to provide a more equitable and systematic response to student needs.

The following sections of this chapter will focus on practical suggestions

Table 5.1 Activities to support guidance and feedback

Steps in Hounsell et al.'s Guidance and Feedback loop	Potential supporting questions and activities
1. Students' prior experiences of assessment in the subject and module	Have they done this type of assessment before? Do they understand the terms, know the conventions of the subject, know the referencing protocol?
2. Preliminary guidance about expectations and requirements	Working with assessment criteria
	Working with exemplars
	Referencing and citation advice
(commence assignment)	
3. Ongoing clarification	Monitoring progress through peer marking of draft assignments
	Practice assignments (for example, mock examination, practice presentations)
	Online self-tests
(submit assignment)	
4. Feedback on performance	Summarising feedback in own words
	Drafting action plan for next assignment
(review feedback)	Comparing tutor feedback with self-assessment
5. Supplementary support	One-to-one dialogue with individual weak students to discuss feedback
(feed forward into next assessment)	
6. Deployment of enhanced understanding and/or skills in subsequent assignments	

Source: adapted from Hounsell et al. (2006: 18).

to implement this framework. Following O'Donovan *et al.* (2004), the practical advice is divided into two sections, 'explicit knowledge transfer' and' tacit knowledge transfer' while recognising that there will always be an overlap between the two.

Giving explicit information to students

Students consider that clarity and openness are fundamental elements of a fair and valid assessment system (Sambell *et al.* 1997). In Chapter 4, we set out the basic information requirements that should be included in a module handbook. In this chapter, we will elaborate on assessment information which you can provide for students in order to develop their understanding of the assessment task.

Sharing assessment criteria

Assessment criteria identify what aspects of an assignment or examination will be assessed and, thus, what students should focus their attention on. These provide important cues for students particularly if you use active methods to help them more fully understand the criteria and standards.

Marking schemes and grade descriptors

Marking schemes complement assessment criteria by outlining what standards students need to meet in each of the criteria, both at threshold level and at higher grades. They provide the basis for students to improve their grades particularly if feedback comments link directly to the scheme. If you are using department or institution-wide **grade descriptors** as your marking scheme, it may be worth reproducing them in every module handbook rather than assuming students will refer to a programme handbook or student guide (Bloxham and West 2007).

Assignment guidance

As Dunn *et al.* (2004) argue, careful wording of assignment instructions and guidance can provide appropriate and timely cues for students. They suggest you should:

- provide a rationale for the type of assessment you are using;
- explain the terms you use – for example, if you ask students to 'analyse', 'evaluate' or 'identify', define what you mean as it is likely to differ in other learning contexts;
- explain the form required – for example if you are asking for a lab report, a portfolio, an essay or a reflective journal, you should set out the purpose of the assessment mode, how it should be presented, appropriate genre, 'voice' (should they use 'I'?) and register;
- suggest methods for approaching the task, such as essay-writing advice.

They also suggest that too much information is counterproductive and, to a certain extent, this is supported by the evidence discussed in Chapter 4 (Box 4.1) that over-specification of detail can encourage a mechanistic approach in students. Undoubtedly, there is a fine balance here. Dunn *et al.*'s (2004) solution is to decide what is important for the students' stage in the programme and focus on providing information in one or two developmental areas with any given assignment.

Referencing and citation advice

Incorrect referencing and citation can weaken student writing and may lose marks for what are often only technical errors. Academics differ considerably in how much they value accurate referencing in comparison with other factors and a consistent approach is needed by markers. You can provide additional confidence for your students by ensuring they have access to good-quality advice. The advent of referencing and citation software such as EndNote™ and Refworks™ can make this task much easier for students once they have mastered the software basics. This might be included in an induction to a programme.

Library exercises

Students should be actively encouraged to engage with library resources. While for first-year students this may involve a library exercise to build a reading list for a first assignment, for students in later years a librarian may be invited to run a workshop on advanced searching of academic databases. In either case, it will have more impact if it is directly linked to a current assignment.

Information on regulations and misconduct

As with most areas of assessment information, details about regulations and misconduct are unlikely to be useful unless students are encouraged to actively engage with and understand them in the context of their course (discussed later). However, providing relevant extracts from the regulations in the module handbook is a good starting point, and it will also act to protect you from students who claim that they 'were never told'.

Telling what cannot be told: tacit information transfer

The problem with written guidance on matters such as assessment criteria is that it has been shown to make little difference to students' work (Price and Rust 1999) and students consider it of little benefit. The imprecision of the language means that the criteria are interpreted differently by each person, with a greater level of shared understanding only emerging through further explanation, working with exemplars, and discussion (Price and O'Donovan 2006).

Earlier discussion in this chapter has set out the importance of preparing students for assessment *in context*, and we need to recognise that context does differ not only by discipline but also by module and tutor. There is an obligation on all modules to provide some level of preparation for assessment. This will also differ depending on students' level in a programme, and preparation is particularly important if they are facing an unfamiliar method of assessment. Low attendance at supplementary workshops and students' perception of them as 'remedial' (Harrington *et al.* 2006) supports the view that they need to be delivered as a central part of their programme.

The following section sets out a range of practical methods to help students gain a shared understanding of assignment requirements and criteria. It is supplemented in Chapter 7 with ideas to help students engage with tutor feedback because this may present equivalent problems.

Providing exemplar assignments and model answers

Exemplar assignments provide students with in-context information regarding how the criteria are applied. Sadler (1989) argues that exemplars demonstrating high standards in the assignment help students develop a conception of the task similar to the tutor, a 'pre-requisite for success'. It is important to gain the permission of students before their (anonymised) work is used. Exemplars provide information on suitable (and unsuitable) ways to structure an assignment, types of evidence and appropriate academic conventions. However, Price and O'Donovan (2006) make the point that seeing exemplars alone is insufficient; it is the dialogue surrounding them that assists students' understanding. Tutors need to take care to present exemplars as examples rather than formulas for fear of suppressing creativity.

Engineering, computing and other science-based subjects may be able to provide model answers to similar types of assignments to help students grasp what is expected. Use of model answers needs to be considered in the light of concerns that it encourages students to 'produce formulaic responses' (Hounsell *et al.* 2006), focusing on producing the assignment in a specific way rather than understanding the learning task as a whole. They may be of more developmental use when students are asked to benchmark their completed assignment against a model answer as a form of self-assessment, creating their own formative feedback.

Grading and writing comments on exemplars

Students are asked to read and mark an exemplar using the assessment criteria and marking scheme (or grade descriptors) for the module. Student groups are then invited to discuss their views and agree suggested marks and reasons for their judgement. They should also note where they found it difficult to interpret the criteria or make decisions. These can be shared with a larger group and tutors can comment on confusions, misapprehensions and correct judgements, sharing the final mark that the piece of work was originally awarded. For a detailed description of this approach, including evidence of long-term impact on student achievement, see Rust *et al.* (2003).

A similar process can also take place outside the classroom setting, with student groups debating their views and posing questions using an online discussion forum. The tutor can intervene as necessary to answer questions and post information regarding the judgement on the original assignment. As before, it is important to stress that exemplars are examples, not formulas.

Practising unfamiliar tasks

Modules which introduce unfamiliar tasks should build in **low stakes** opportunities for students to practise the new method, for example a poster, presentation, press release, or critique of a journal article. This is likely to reduce student unease and also help clarify the expectations of the task. Where appropriate, this type of practice activity can follow from initial work with exemplars, as described earlier, or be used as the basis for peer feedback, as described later.

Grading and writing comments on their own work

Students are requested to submit a self-assessment with their finished assignment. The self-assessment questions should focus on getting the student to consider how well they think their work meets the assessment criteria – for example, 'Which of the assessment criteria do you think you met most successfully?', 'Which of the assessment criteria did you find most difficult to fulfil?'. Questions could also include 'What do you think are the strongest points in your assignment?' and 'What aspect of the assignment did you struggle with most?'. The act of completing this self-assessment, of itself, is likely to encourage students to use and think about assessment criteria. In addition, after marking, students can be asked to compare the tutor feedback on their work with their self-assessment (Price and O'Donovan 2006). This can help them to see whether they are focusing on the right areas and assists the process of self-regulation by improving their understanding of what they are aiming for. It is particularly useful if students who self-assessed very inaccurately are provided with advice from the tutor on their misapprehension of either the demands of the task or their own performance. This latter process can be concluded by students completing a brief action plan for future assignments, drawing on the tutor feedback and their own self-assessment.

Students may be concerned that their self-assessment will negatively influence the marker and prefer to submit their self-assessment at a later stage. Self-assessment may also be used to engage students with tutor feedback (see Chapter 7).

Grading and writing comments on their peers' work

As peer assessment can provoke some anxiety (see Box 2.2), it should only take place once students have had some training in working with criteria, either through explanation or working with exemplars. Students should also be made aware well in advance that their work is going to be reviewed by other students. Student anxiety can be reduced by asking students to focus on providing feedback against the criteria rather than trying to allocate a mark or grade to an assessment. Box 5.2 provides examples.

Box 5.2 Using peer feedback

Peer feedback has been successfully used in the Childhood Studies Course where first-year students undertake a short writing task and post their 'answers' to the Blackboard VLE discussion board through which they give and receive peer feedback. Students also bring their writing to a class session where they further compare their writing with tutor-prepared model answers in discussion with peers. Students find this very helpful and tutors have noted marked improvements in early attempts at writing on the course. (Kay Sambell, reported in McDowell *et al.* 2005: 9)

Box 7.4 in Chapter 7 provides a further example of the use of peer feedback to gain formative feedback on draft assignments.

Discussing the meaning of particular assessment terms

Academic terms have specific connotations in different disciplinary contexts and they frequently have similar, if not overlapping, meanings, for example verbs such as 'evaluate', 'appraise', 'review'. Our experience of working with tutors suggests that they can use words interchangeably depending on their own prior experience. You can try to explain what you mean by the terms students will meet in assessment tasks and examinations. However, tacit knowledge such as this is not easily explained, so it may be worth providing students with a short summary of each term followed by a concrete example. You could ask students to study a relevant journal article or extract and attempt to identify the words in action. Of course, you are unlikely to find clear-cut usage of different verbs. Authors will, for example, integrate description with evaluation and synthesis, but the emerging discussion is likely to enhance students' understanding.

Practising correct citation and referencing

Anecdotal evidence suggests that you can provide students with extensive written advice on referencing and citation, only to see it ignored. A useful activity, particularly with students at the beginning of a programme, is to bring to a session a wide range of different types of reading matter: books, edited books, journals, professional magazines, material from the web, reference books, newspaper cuttings and DVDs. You should include examples of discipline-specific resources such as law reports, maps and works of art. Provide the students with a referencing guide in the required style of your department or discipline (Harvard or numerical). Ask the students to construct a bibliography involving one reference from each type of source, written down in the correct style. When complete, get them to pair up with each other and check for accuracy. You need only be available to answer questions and resolve disputes where they cannot agree on the correct format.

Another approach involves students working in pairs or threes. Ask them to choose one academic resource and construct a paragraph using that source for argument or evidence. They write their paragraph followed by an accurate bibliographic entry on a poster. These can be displayed around the room for discussion in relation to the assessment criteria. In general, these exercises will be more effective if clearly tied to a specific assignment.

Helping students avoid plagiarism and malpractice

Institutions should 'encourage students to adopt good academic conduct in respect of assessment and ensure they are aware of their responsibilities' (Quality Assurance Agency 2006c: 27), particularly in the current climate, with growing concerns about malpractice, particularly plagiarism. However, it is not that simple as the following examples illustrate:

- Is it collusion if two students tackle a difficult German translation together?
- Does using material from the internet amount to plagiarism?
- Is it cheating if a student lets a friend in the year below see an old essay?

The answer to all these questions is 'it depends'. These are complex issues and, while there should be institutional guidelines, there will also be differences depending on the specific context.

One of the major reasons for plagiarism is student confusion and ignorance about what it is (Carroll 2002). Plagiarism is often not intentional cheating but misuse of paraphrasing and quoting. Previous educational settings may have had much more lenient rules regarding what can be 'copied' and the automatic referencing of sources is often absent from pre-university education.

At the programme level, explaining malpractice, including practical exercises and examples, should be included in induction. Carroll (2002) argues that it is important to reinforce understanding for specific groups (for example, international students) and to use active methods. Considerable advice is available online from the JISC Plagiarism Advisory Service (http://www.jiscpas.ac.uk), and Carroll (2002) provides a useful range of educational activities. They include giving students a sample of different ways of using a text and asking them to 'draw the line' between plagiarism and legitimate practice.

Some unintentional plagiarism is caused by poor disciplinary skills and lack of understanding of academic conventions and appropriate referencing protocols. Tutors need to make clear that they value explanations in the students' own words rather than lengthy quotations which do not always demonstrate understanding. In addition, and for those who are intentional rather than unintentional plagiarists, consider using plagiarism detection tools. Google™ is very effective but time-consuming to use on an individual basis, and universities are increasingly using plagiarism detection software.

Preparing for examinations

Make sure examination and revision techniques are included in students' programmes. Consider giving students the opportunity to do a mock examination so that they know what the examination will look like and can practise without the stress of the real thing. Students can peer mark against criteria or model answers. Consider providing global feedback on previous attempts at the examination (Hounsell *et al.* 2006), alerting students to common errors so they can take action to avoid them.

Preparing students for self-, peer and group assessment

This element of student preparation is dealt with in Chapter 4 on teaching a module.

Conclusion

This chapter has examined what is involved for students in becoming academically literate. It has stressed the need to go beyond provision of clear written assessment guidance. Students, together with their peers and tutors, need to engage in discussion and practical exercises involving the assessment requirements in order to allow sharing of tacit knowledge. This preparation for assessment is seen as one part of a guidance and feedback loop which programmes need to construct for students. In general, the chapter argues that time spent in preparing students for assessment is time well invested both in terms of their sense of control over their work and their ultimate achievement.

6   Marking

Introduction

'Markers are the gatekeepers for university quality' (Smith and Coombe 2006: 45), with assessment providing the basis for ensuring academic standards (Price 2005). However, assessments in higher education are internally set and marked and, while this offers a level of autonomy not enjoyed in other sectors of education, it means that the responsibility for grading is largely down to the subjective judgement of tutors and other markers. There are increasing levels of accountability including external review together with contemporary concerns regarding student litigation over inaccurate marking (Swann and Ecclestone 1999a; Hand and Clewes 2000) and plagiarism (Smith and Coombe 2006). Altogether one can argue that marking, despite its apparently routine nature, makes significant demands upon tutors and other markers.

The assessment literature has not examined the process of marking in depth (Yorke *et al.* 2000; Smith and Coombe 2006) and offers very little advice on the subject except at the technical level such as urging staff to use criteria (Swann and Ecclestone 1999a). Nonetheless, research has considered marking consistency and, despite the massive increase in quality procedures designed to ensure robust practices, the results are consistently depressing. Marking lacks attention in universities (Swann and Ecclestone 1999a; Smith and Coombe 2006), with staff often feeling unprepared for the role, particularly part-time staff (Smith and Coombe 2006). A lack of discussion on the subject allows assumptions of reliable standards to continue largely unchallenged perhaps because, as Price (2005) suggests, it is too uncomfortable to discuss these matters which are at the foundation of our awards. Sadly, commonly held tutor views regarding marking, such as its onerous, low-status nature, do not encourage time or energy to be put into its improvement (Smith and Coombe 2006).

This chapter is designed to remedy some of the omissions in the assessment literature by recognising the frailty of much marking practice, identifying the limitations to what is possible and providing practical strategies to improve your marking as far as is feasible. The parallel issues of feedback and moderation are developed in Chapters 7 and 8.

Marking and marking practices

Different approaches to marking

Differences in approaches to standards and criteria are central to marking. These fall into two main categories: **norm-referenced** and **criterion-referenced** approaches. Criterion-referenced assessment is firmly linked to outcome-based learning in that student achievement is tested against a set of criteria such as those linked to the learning outcomes for the assignment.

Norm-referenced assessment 'aims to discriminate between students and is designed so that student performance in the assessment is distributed across a range, so that those who do better on the assessment task receive higher grades than those who do less well' (Bowden and Marton 1998: 162). For example, it might be decided that the top 10% of a cohort are awarded an A, the next 30% a B, and so on. Whereas with criterion-referenced assessment all students have an opportunity to do equally well, a norm-referenced approach will almost always create a distribution of grades.

Criterion-referenced assessment is now generally considered desirable (Price 2005) on the basis that it is fairer to students to know how they will be judged and to have that judgement based on the quality of their work rather than the performance of other members of their particular cohort. In addition, it gives protection to markers as it enables them to justify their judgements (Sadler 2005). Sadler has identified four different models of criterion-based marking models used in universities.

In model 1 the criteria are designed to judge how well the student has demonstrated progress towards the desired learning outcomes. This model most directly links to the concept of constructive alignment (see Chapter 2).

In model 2 'percentage grading' is used where tutors use numerical scores to represent how well students have done and these are added together to give overall scores or grades. The nature of individual tutors' criteria for, for example, determining whether a student's work has reached the threshold, is generally hidden or only communicated through feedback. There is 'an underlying softness in the data that typically goes unrecognised' (Sadler 2005: 182), and varying application of the percentage model across subjects results in very different patterns of degree classification. For example, in a recent five-year period 21% of mathematics graduates were awarded first-class honours, compared with only 1.8% studying veterinary science (Hornby 2003). Nevertheless, this approach is a criterion-based method in that students are judged against some implicit criteria (what constitutes a mark of 65%?) and their marks are not determined by reference to how well other students have done as is the case in norm-referenced marking. Marks for individual components are added together (averaged) to determine students' final grades.

Model 3 is similar to model 2 but allows for staff to combine scores in varying ways in order to recognise students' global achievement. For example, in order to gain an upper second-class degree (2i), students might have to gain a B grade in at least half of their modules, with no less than an average grade of C. Criteria for judgement are inherent in these 'combination' rules, with the example given illustrating an emphasis on sufficient consistency of achievement at the higher level even if the average mark falls short.

Model 4 involves specifying qualitative criteria or attributes. The typical department or university grade descriptors which specify what students must do in relation to generic criteria in order to achieve a particular grade (for example, in relation to knowledge, application, use of literature and organisation) fall into this category.

Sadler's analysis is useful because it helps us to see that while models 1 and 4 represent the trend in universities (albeit still represented by numerical scores), they are different approaches to criterion referencing and the difference leaves some room for confusion. For example, if your criteria are focused on generic qualities (model 4) such as quality of argument or presentation, grading and feedback are likely to focus on those qualities, possibly at the expense of feedback on achievement in relation to specific learning outcomes. If the approach taken is model 1, then a focus on learning outcomes may make it difficult to give marks for generic qualities (such as quality of English) unless they are specifically listed in the learning outcomes. Some grade descriptors attempt to combine both criteria based on outcomes and criteria based on generic qualities (see Table 6.1).

The trend towards criterion-referenced marking disguises a residual reliance on norm referencing (Maclellan 2004a). In other words, our interpretation of criteria is influenced by our shared understanding of the 'norms' for a particular assessment at a particular level. It is argued that norm referencing continues to be used in practice because it is easier, it acknowledges that the terms used in marking schemes can be applied at different academic levels and that they can only be communicated and understood with reference to student work (Price and Rust 1999; Baird et al. 2004; Price 2005).

Thus higher education marking relies on a combination of judgement against criteria and the application of standards which are heavily influenced by academic norms. While we can share assessment criteria, certainly at the level of listing what qualities will be taken into account, applying standards is much harder to accomplish and relies on interpretation in context, and therein lies one of the key components of unreliability.

The shortcomings of marking in higher education

Despite the assumption that academics share common views of academic standards, marking in higher education is inherently unreliable (Price 2005). Research shows that staff vary considerably both in the marks they give and

Table 6.1 Grade descriptors for final-year honours undergraduates

80–100 AA	Students meet all the requirements for an A grade. There is evidence of exceptional scholarship, including critical evaluation and synthesis of issues and information that generates originality and challenges existing approaches. Accurate and detailed use of a range of evidence. Comprehensive knowledge and understanding of theories, principles and concepts.
70–79 A	Student has met the learning outcomes (LOs) of the assessment with evidence of comprehensive and up-to-date knowledge and understanding of concepts and theories and their interrelationship. The work shows a detailed appreciation of how aspects of the subject are uncertain, contradictory or limited. The work adopts a well-sustained critical approach using a breadth of evidence, reasoning and reflection. Works shows evidence of a mature and independent approach to problem solving. The student can create appropriate hypotheses and select, justify and use imaginative and innovative approaches in their investigations.
60–69 B	Student has met the LOs of the assessment with evidence of comprehensive and up-to-date knowledge and understanding of concepts and theories and their interrelationship with an awareness of how aspects of the subject are uncertain, contradictory or limited. The work adopts a critical approach using a breadth of evidence, reasoning and reflection. Works shows evidence that the student can act confidently and autonomously in the identification and definition of complex problems and select, justify and use approaches aimed at their resolution.
50–59 C	Student has met the LOs of the assessment with evidence of detailed knowledge and understanding of key concepts and theories, including an awareness of the *provisional nature* of knowledge. The work shows evidence of a general critical approach using individual judgement and reflection, although there is some limitation in the ability to conceptualise and/or apply theory. Works shows evidence that the student can act without guidance in the identification of complex problems and can apply knowledge and skills to their resolution.
40–49 D	Student has met the LOs of the assessment, with evidence of knowledge and understanding of key concepts and theories including basic recognition of the complexity of the subject. The work is for the most part descriptive rather than based on argument and logical reasoning.

Work shows evidence that the student can apply appropriate learning accurately to complex problems and/or practical contexts.

35–39 F	Student has not met all the LOs of the assessment, with only basic knowledge of key concepts and theories and weaknesses in understanding. There is little or no recognition of the complexity of the subject. Work is largely descriptive with some unsubstantiated assertion. Analysis is minimal or contradictory. Unable to always apply learning accurately to complex problems and/or practical contexts. For professional courses any work which contains evidence of, or reference to, unsafe or dangerous practice should be deemed a fail.
30–34 F	Student has not met LOs, with inadequate knowledge or understanding of key concepts and theories. There is no recognition of the complexity of the subject. The work is descriptive and uncritical, with unsubstantiated assertion and a lack of analysis. Insufficient understanding of given tools/methods to apply learning accurately or safely to complex problems and /or practical contexts.
0–29 F	Student has failed the majority of the LOs.

Source: extract from grade descriptors for levels 0–5, University of Cumbria.

in the shape of their mark distributions (Heywood, 2000) – see Price (2005) and Read *et al.* (2005) for recent overviews of variability in tutor marking. Elton and Johnston (2002) describe marker reliability as low for essays and problem-style examinations, except where mere knowledge recall is required, and Knight (2006) suggests that the ability to measure students' achievements reliably may be greater in subjects such as the natural sciences. He contends that 'non-determinate' subjects that deal with the 'human world' such as the arts, humanities and social sciences rely more on the subjective judgement of assessors. Overall, the reasons for marking unreliability were discussed in Chapter 3 and relate to the subject matter, the complex nature of what is being assessed in higher education (Knight and Yorke 2003), individual markers' approaches and standards (Ecclestone 2001) and the difficulty of taking into account a wide range of criteria (Price 2005). See Box 6.1 on how tutors learn to mark.

As pointed out by Partington (1994), the extent of these marker effects should not be underestimated; mark differences of 8 or 9 marks out of 25 in essay marking are common. When this happens cumulatively, then a student's final degree classification may depend as much on having certain examiners as on demonstrating academic competence. It is hardly surprising

Box 6.1 Leads into literature: how tutors learn to mark

Chapter 5 discussed the concept of communities of practice as a way of understanding learning in academic teams as an informal, participative process reflected in staff learning to mark by 'just picking it up' or 'learning on the job' (Hornby 2003: 449). Implicit in this learning process is the notion of acquiring 'tacit' knowledge by which we achieve a form of connoisseurship regarding the standards and protocols of our subject disciplines (Knight 2006). This connoisseurship applies particularly to the process of marking, and, even with explicit criteria and standards, tutors will need to use a degree of professional judgement in order to interpret essentially subjective terms such as 'good' or 'systematic'. Thus, tutors rely on 'their professional knowledge and experience to "know the standard" of work to be set' (Price 2005: 220).

Setting standards in higher education is largely an individual practice (Price 2005), with evidence suggesting that little use is made of past assignments to communicate (albeit informally) standards to new markers (Hornby 2003). In addition, varying professional knowledge, experience and values leads to staff attaching importance to different qualities in work (Read *et al.* 2005; Smith and Coombe 2006). Efforts to increase the reliability of marking, such as assessment criteria and marking schemes, are somewhat undermined by the difficulty of communicating their meaning (Ecclestone 2001) and by tutors' customary approaches to marking. Wolf (1995) contends that markers acquire fixed habits in their marking which they may not be aware of but which can influence their grading. In effect, staff use implicit standards which may contradict the official standards (Baume *et al.* 2004; Price 2005; Read *et al.* 2005).

Despite this unreliability, experienced assessors come to see themselves as expert markers (Ecclestone 2001). Their judgements become more intuitive than conscious, as they develop 'mental models' of marking which they apply regardless of marking guidance (Ecclestone 2001). Indeed, they may deliberately choose to ignore guidance, such as a marking scheme, as a threat to their professional expertise (Ecclestone 2001). In reality, studies have found that experienced markers are no better than novice markers at applying standards consistently, partly because new markers pay greater attention to the task and guidance (Ecclestone 2001; Price 2005). However, casual staff, in particular, may feel under pressure to mark generously, for example when they face evaluation by their students and fear poor appraisal following low marks (Smith and Coombe 2006). Overall, the intuitive and essentially private nature of marking (Ecclestone 2001; Smith and Coombe 2006) and a lack of assessment scholarship and discourse among academics (Price 2005) are not helpful in addressing these issues.

On a more positive note, other researchers (Klenowski and Elwood 2002) believe that common standards do become established among cohesive staff teams, and this is certainly the view frequently declared by tutors. Knight's (2006) view that assessment judgments can only be considered to be local because of their context-bound nature tends to support the view that standards can be established at the local level. Furthermore, where the emphasis of marking is on feedback and learning, anxieties about reliability and consistency may be minimised. However, it is worth noting that staff identify different strengths and weaknesses in the same work (Read *et al.* 2005) and students are aware that feedback from one member of staff may be of limited use because future tutors will value different attributes (Norton 2004).

that we often suspect students of selecting modules because the tutor is known to be an 'easy' marker.

In summary, the research suggests that providing fairness, consistency and reliability in marking is a significant challenge caused by the inherent difficulty of reliably marking complex and subjective material combined with our own marking predispositions. It is not surprising that new staff and postgraduates involved in marking, anecdotally, devote considerable time to marking yet still lack confidence in their decisions.

This depressing picture suggests that it would be foolish to propose simple solutions to some of the problems of marking. Indeed Knight (2006: 450) considers that 'solutions are not to be had'. Advice may be experienced as a series of platitudes, good in theory, but largely impractical to implement. Thus, in the forthcoming sections, we have used the research cautiously to identify potential areas for action, recognising that, above all, we do need to give the key stakeholders confidence in the robust nature of marking while accepting that attempting to create totally reliable, measurable assessment will damage higher education as it stands.

Assessment criteria, grade descriptors and marking schemes

Assessment criteria

Assessment criteria are the aspects of an assignment or examination which the assessor will take into account when making their judgement. These are likely to be specific to individual tasks and might include such things as quality of argument, accuracy, use of evidence and presentation (see the example in Box 4.2). Chapter 4 includes advice on writing assessment criteria.

Grade descriptors

Grade descriptors are statements of standards to be reached across a range of generic criteria in order to achieve different grades. A full set of grade descriptors for a university or department will involve statements of standards across the different levels of award (see Table 6.1 for an example at honours level). Although they are a fairly recent innovation, they are increasingly being developed on an institutional basis to attempt to provide greater consistency in marking across different disciplines in a way that is not provided for by the percentage scale alone (Hornby 2003). Evidence suggests they are valued by staff and students.

Marking schemes

A marking scheme (alternatively known as a rubric) for an assignment or examination combines the assessment criteria for the task with the appropriate standards (for example, from a set of grade descriptors) and provides the detail about how performance in each of the criteria will be graded (see Figures 6.1 and Table 6.2).

Using criteria, grade descriptors and marking schemes

It is the view of the QAA (2006c) that clear, public marking criteria and marking schemes are important in ensuring that marking is carried out fairly and consistently across all disciplines. Although they are not the universal panacea to accurate marking, they do have a number of important benefits:

- They give confidence and guidance to novice markers and help them become part of an assessment community more quickly (Ecclestone 2001).
- They provide guidance for experienced markers who may have developed inaccurate marking practices (Ecclestone 2001).
- They provide the starting point for staff discussion about marking.
- Staff consider them more reliable and valid than the percentage scale approach (Hornby 2003).
- They help individual markers feel that they are being more consistent in their marking (Price and Rust 1999).
- They have some standardising effect on marking across multiple markers (Newstead and Dennis 1994; Baird et al. 2004), and at lower levels of education this was found to be particularly true with the use of model answers and trained assessors (Heywood 2000).
- They provide a public language and terminology for assessment requirements.
- They provide an infrastructure to defend and support marking decisions (Swann and Ecclestone 1999a).
- They make outcomes more transparent to students (Swann and Ecclestone 1999a; Gosling and Moon 2002; Hornby 2003), and students value them (Granleese 1996; Price and Rust 1999).

- They have a diagnostic value for students (Sadler 2005), providing a guide to learning (Baume *et al.* 2004) and improving achievement (Price and Rust 1999).
- They can speed up marking and make it easier to write feedback (Price and Rust 1999).

On the other hand, problems regarding marking schemes, grade descriptors and criteria include the following:

- It is difficult to change marking habits (Ecclestone 2001) and there-fore judgements will be made possibly in contradiction of explicit marking guidance.
- Staff ignore them or choose not to adopt them (Price and Rust 1999; Ecclestone 2001; Smith and Coombe 2006).
- Staff struggle to understand the terms used (Price and Rust 1999).
- Assessors may not understand or agree with the outcomes they are judging (Baume *et al.* 2004).
- Generic standards are not seen as robust by staff, creating difficulty in applying them to a specific module (Price 2005).
- There is a risk that explicitly stating standards has the effect of raising them (Price and Rust 1999; Baume *et al.* 2004).

The aforementioned evidence suggests that these devices have some value and, perhaps more importantly, are seen to have value by staff and students. And although our ability to describe and communicate criteria and standards in such a way that they are amenable to standardisation between markers remains doubtful (Ecclestone 2001), training staff with marking schemes can reduce marking differences even if it cannot eliminate them (Baird *et al.* 2004). Overall, it is difficult to see how any argument for consistency and fairness can be put forward if at least minimum criteria and standards are not in place. Ecclestone (2001: 312) makes the important point that they 'encourage staff to take moderation activities seriously since they provide an explicit reminder of the agreed public standards about fairness and rigour'.

Writing marking schemes

Marking schemes should be devised at the same time as the assignment or examination is written (Partington 1994). A scheme should clearly identify the criteria by which the task will be judged as one dimension, with the grading scheme as the other dimension. The individual 'descriptors' in each cell are indicators of how the criteria are demonstrated at different levels to achieve higher or lower grades. See Figure 6.1.

Research suggests that assessors are able to state the reasons for the

GRADING (institution-specific)	CRITERIA			
	Criterion 1	Criterion 2	Criterion 3	Criterion 4
80–100% AA				
70–79% A				
60–69% B				
50–59% C				
40–49% D				
35–39% fail				
Under 35% fail				

Figure 6.1   Template for a marking scheme

judgements they make in marking (Baume *et al.* 2004), and therefore the easiest way to create a marking scheme is inductively, using work that has been marked or from a model answer you have written yourself (Race 2003), and then teasing out the substantive reasons for deciding on different marks – in other words, abstracting the standards from real judgements, then clarifying and codifying them into a marking scheme (Sadler 2005).

Caution is advised in relation to over-specification in marking schemes because detailed criteria can encourage a mechanistic, mark-oriented approach in students which can work against students seriously engaging with the learning process (Norton 2004). It may also prevent students being rewarded for difference and originality.

Woolf (2004) suggests that schemes should be written on a 'sufficiency plus' basis, describing what is needed to achieve threshold grades and then what additional qualities are required for each higher grade. This contrasts with some marking schemes in which the descriptors are couched in negative terms, listing what is missing rather than what is present. See Table 6.2. for a generic marking scheme for an essay.

Writing a scheme in theory (perhaps determined by your institutional or departmental grade descriptors) is one thing, but using it in practice can be very different. You will find that elements which you had not predicted emerge as important when you start applying the scheme to scripts. Race (2003) suggests that you should revise your marking scheme once you have seen how a few candidates are tackling the question in order to write an 'even better' scheme. However, in the interests of fairness to current students, it is better not to change the scheme for current work but to make notes so that the scheme can be adjusted for future assignments of a similar nature.

Table 6.2 Year-1 essay: marking scheme
The statement in each column describes what the tutor will be looking for in order decide what grade your essay should be given.

	Knowledge and understanding	Analysis	Reading and referencing	Essay structure	Use of language
80–100% AA	As for A, plus demonstrates exceptional comprehension of topic	As for A, plus sophisticated analysis using ideas and principles beyond those introduced in the module	Essay fully supported by reference to relevant up-to-date material. Accurate use of Harvard referencing technique	Clear structure which enriches the discussion and argument	Essay displays an excellent use of standard written English
70–79% A	Shows thorough knowledge and understanding of the topic, with evidence of reading beyond the key texts	Essay shows a resourceful and imaginative analysis using ideas and principles beyond those introduced in the module	Clear evidence of wide and relevant reading. Accurate use of Harvard referencing technique	Clear structure which enhances the argument and discussion	Essay displays an excellent use of standard written English
60–69% B	Shows evidence of relevant and sound knowledge and understanding of the topic	Shows evidence of analysis using ideas and principles introduced in the module	Essay well informed by reading which goes beyond key texts. Accurate use of Harvard referencing technique	Structure is clear and supports coherent discussion and argument	Essay displays a very good standard of written English with all statements clearly expressed
50–59% C	Shows relevant knowledge of the topic	The essay is largely descriptive with some discussion using ideas and principles introduced in the module	Effective use of key reading. Accurate use of Harvard system	Structure supports the discussion and argument	Essay displays a good use of standard written English with few, if any, grammatical or spelling errors. Written in an appropriately academic style

	Knowledge and understanding	Analysis	Reading and referencing	Essay structure	Use of language
40–49% D	Shows basic knowledge of the topic	The essay is limited to description and includes frequent unsupported facts and opinions	Appropriate use made of a limited range of reading. Largely accurate use of Harvard system	Evidence of structure relevant to the title	The work is written to an acceptable standard of English. There may be some grammatical errors and the work may need more careful editing
35–39% fail	Signs of emerging knowledge of the topic but insufficient for progression to level 2	Essay is generally descriptive and uncritical. Some inaccuracy in the material	Some use of very limited reading, although fairly superficial. Inaccurate use of Harvard system	Some structure although key issues may be omitted. Some repetition	More care needs to be taken with elements of grammar, spelling and sentence construction
Under 35% fail	Shows inadequate knowledge of the topic to meet learning outcomes	Descriptive and uncritical. Some discussion irrelevant to the title	Poor use of reading. Poor or incorrect use of Harvard system	Little evidence of planning the essay	Poor standard of written English. Inappropriate register

Using marking schemes

Tutors should not be unduly worried if they make different judgements from their colleagues, because this is to be expected, given all the potential for subjectivity in marking discussed at the beginning of this chapter. However, the capacity to use a scheme to improve consistency is enhanced where markers have had an opportunity to discuss it and establish common meanings, particularly of the terminology (Price and Rust 1999). Therefore all schemes should be discussed with the marking team where possible (Gosling and Moon 2002), both in advance of marking and as part of the moderation process.

A student's work does not typically fit one grade descriptor and judgement is needed (Sadler 2005). Baird *et al.* (2004), albeit discussing GCSE marking, suggests that a 'best fit' approach is adopted for each criteria. This involves identifying which of the statements is nearest to the student's performance for any criterion. Once the best fit has been identified for each individual criterion, it will be easier to identify the overall band for the work by examining where the majority of criteria lie or by compensating strong performance in one area with weak performance elsewhere. It then remains to decide whether the work should be placed in the upper or lower level within that overall grade.

This approach avoids the overly precise marking that is often associated with a percentage scale, something which the evidence of marking accuracy cannot support. Using all points on a percentage scale, while appropriate for quantitative assessments such as multiple choice tests, may not be appropriate for most higher education assessment, and some universities have deliberately adopted a grade-based approach. Some of the problems of a percentage scale can be mitigated by marking by band. This involves limiting the range of marks that staff can use to broad bands – for example, five marks in each band as shown in Table 6.3. Grades are limited to 52%, 57%, and so on, and other marks are not permitted. It avoids the problem of borderline marks for individual work and forces staff to make decisive judgements.

Table 6.3   Grading by band on a percentage scale

AA/1st	77% and above
A/1st	72%
B/upper 2.i	67%
B/lower 2.i	62%
C/upper 2.ii	57%
C/lower 2.ii	52%
D/upper 3rd	47%
D/lower 3rd	42%
E/bare fail	37%
E/clear fail	32%
F/fail	27% and below

The banding of grades will need to take into account the norms and regulations within your institution. For example, if considerable use is made of marks above 80%, the grades available will need to reflect that. The intention of grading bands is to simplify marking decisions and avoid the problem of borderline marks, therefore staff should not be discouraged from awarding marks above 77% or below 27% if the work deserves it.

Other approaches to improving accuracy of marking

Using exemplar answers

It is argued that marking schemes on their own are of little use unless they are given meaning by contextualising them with reference to exemplar assignments. However, there is very little research on the use of exemplars to establish standards (Baird *et al.* 2004).

Using pre-moderation

This refers to markers pre-marking a selected number of scripts and discussing the marks before marking the main batch. For example, Price (2005) reports an approach where staff all mark the same sample work and meet to agree the mark as an approach to improving consistency. On the face of it, this would appear to be more useful than post-marking moderation, but it may increase workload if post-moderation is required.

Maintaining your own consistency in marking

The research discussed in Box 6.1 suggests that it is important for each of us to be aware of the influences on our approach to marking. For example, Wolf (1995) reports that tutors can 'compensate' in their marking under various circumstances, and these include where a person has performed uncharacteristically badly or they are known to the tutor. Ecclestone (2001) reports other ways in which assessors' subconscious judgements may affect their marking such as using criteria other than those listed or weighting them differently. She notes that research has found evidence of subconscious bias in relation to factors such as cultural origin, gender and confidence.

Other factors which may affect the scores tutors award include varying the amount of time spent marking individual items (Baume *et al.* 2004) and the order in which work is marked, with good work which is marked after poor work receiving better appraisal (Baird *et al.* 2004). Tutors should also be alert to their academic prejudices which may unfairly sway marking too far up or down, giving weighting to a factor you particularly care about (Brown *et al.* 1997). Some lecturers will 'punish' poor grammar or inconsistent referencing particularly harshly and beyond the agreed criteria. Hartley *et al.* (2006) found that tutors gave significantly higher marks on average to essays typed in 12 point font rather than 10 point font!

Brown *et al.* (1997) also recommend marking examination scripts by individual questions rather than whole scripts, as this is faster, more reliable and avoids the potential of the halo effect which might occur when you have marked one excellent question in a script and thus tend to see only the good points in the next question by the same candidate.

Finally, Hornby (2003) discusses the concept of 'defensive marking', where staff choose to mark in a fairly narrow band, avoiding too many high or low marks, in anticipation of challenges to their marking from students and internal or external moderators. Where an assignment is blind **double marked**, a tutor may feel at greatest risk from this challenge and may practise 'risk-averse' marking, erring towards giving average grades.

Managing your marking

There are several issues to consider in terms of planning for marking:

- Plan your marking time in your diary immediately following submission dates. Protect the time vigorously; the task will take no less time by being delayed, but its usefulness to students will be severely reduced. A long gap means that you are producing most of the feedback for the benefit of external examiners and quality assessors, which is not its primary purpose at all. You should also be alert to your levels of tiredness.
- Identify blocks of time, and in order to avoid distractions you will almost certainly be best at home or hidden in a quiet corner rather than in your office where distractions will tempt or force you away from the task in hand.
- Use support staff for the administration of submission, handling and sorting of assignments. As a tutor you need to spend your time reading, making judgements and writing feedback. Ensure that the submission process is formally arranged and that the appropriate scripts will be sorted, prepared and presented 'ready to mark' to each lecturer.
- The first few scripts of an assignment or new examination may take slightly longer until you get into the swing of a particular assignment, but it is critical that you have a target time in mind for each one and work to it. It is too easy to allow the marking of each script to expand and then run out of your allocated marking time. The marking of remaining scripts in *ad hoc* time slots is likely to be more inconsistent.
- New tutors may suffer considerable angst because of the considerable effort students may have invested and the importance of the grade to students. These factors must, however, be balanced against the benefits of prompt feedback and the maintenance of a reasonable work–life balance by tutors.

Issues in marking

Data protection

See Chapter 9 for important information on data protection legislation as it pertains to information you hold regarding marking, including comments on examination scripts.

Anonymous marking

There is a growing trend towards systems of anonymous marking in universities – and even where it is not policy, the increase in student numbers and use of casual markers in many programmes is having the same effect by default. The earlier discussion of tutor bias provides the central rationale for anonymous marking. It is impossible for tutors not to be affected, at least subconsciously, by their prior knowledge of students, and therefore there is strong support for the policy.

On the other hand, tutors may argue that knowledge of the reader allows them to provide more effective feedback. If the work is a significant improvement on previous attempts, the tutor can be very encouraging even if the final mark remains low. The same feedback for a student who has performed poorly in comparison with their previous assignments would be inappropriate. Crook *et al.* (2006) refer to the dislocation of author and reader in higher education assessment, with impersonal feedback appearing irrelevant or inaccessible and lacking dialogic quality. In practice, tutors usually have to work within the guidelines of their institution, but the topic is certainly worth further debate.

Holistic versus analytic grading

Criterion-based marking raises the question of holistic or analytic grading, and teaching teams will need to determine whether the final mark for an assignment will be obtained holistically by considering the overall impression of the assignment or whether it will be arrived at by adding the scores obtained for each criterion.

Biggs (2003) makes a firm plea for a holistic approach as a better representation of judgement in real life, where you do not judge a building by assessing the quality of individual bricks. While the individual parts are important to the quality of the whole, it is the way they are used to create the overall task, whether that be an essay, dissertation, painting or performance, which is important. Such a holistic approach allows markers to discount limited achievement against some criteria if the overall product is sufficiently good.

On the other hand, Gosling and Moon (2002) argue that analytic marking will tend to produce greater consistency because otherwise individual markers will weight component parts differently in coming to their overall judgement. They recommend that the relative weighting of different criteria should be specified. Clearly, this is a matter for teaching teams and may be influenced by the requirements of a professional body for some programmes.

Borderline marking

Institutions have different policies regarding whether tutors are permitted to award grade borderline marks for assignments (for example, 59%). In addition, the aggregation of marks for different assignments or parts of assignments can create a grade borderline mark for a module.

However, borderline marks can frustrate students who may wonder where the missing percentage point could be found. They are also likely to request (quite reasonably) remarking. Our advice would be to use your grade descriptors or marking scheme and your assessment criteria to clearly identify what grade band a student's work is in. If this is difficult, request that the item is second-marked by another tutor. If you really cannot decide whether an assignment is in one grade or another and thus you want to award a borderline mark, it may be better to give the student the benefit of the doubt.

Over-length work

Guidelines on length of assignment (for example, number of words or pages, or timing of presentation) are important as they are part of the strategy to provide consistency and reliability. It may be easier for a student to meet the assessment criteria if they use considerably more words. Consequently, where a specific length is stated in the assignment description, staff should apply penalties to students who exceed the length. The nature of the penalty should be decided in advance and publicised to students. In practice, institutions use a range of penalties such as refusing to take into account anything over the maximum length or reducing marks on a sliding scale. Assessed presentations may be terminated by the tutor when the time is reached.

Peer marking

Peer marking is dealt with in depth in Chapter 4.

Marking group assignments

Group-based assessment tasks are becoming increasingly common across higher education, and their benefits are discussed in Chapter 13. However, they do pose some difficulties if not handled well, foremost amongst which is the allocation of individual marks to a piece of work completed by a group of students. This section will discuss approaches to the issue with particular emphasis on the use of peer assessment.

Assessing group products and processes

We can think about a group assignments in two ways:

- the product created by the group such as a report, presentation or performance;
- the group process, including all the skills and effort put in by members of the group in creating the product.

The group product can be assessed using the normal procedures for marking, including use of assessment criteria, as outlined in this chapter. In this respect, these products are no different than any other item of coursework. The greater challenge is in assessing the group process.

It might be tempting to avoid marking the group process and award each student the same 'product' mark or ask them to submit the 'product' as a set of individual sections which are given separate grades. We would counsel strongly against this approach. Separate submissions are likely to disrupt the spirit of collaboration (Raeside and Goldfinch 1990), and an important reason for group assessments is their role in the development of students' skills in working with others. Good team-work skills are highly valued by employers (Lejk and Wyvill 1996) and form an important element in most QAA benchmark statements and professional body requirements in the UK. Consequently, effective team working is likely to contribute to one of your programme learning outcomes (see Chapter 11) and thus it will be important to assess whether students have met this outcome. In addition, Webb (1995) argues that active participation by all members of an assessment team benefits everyone's learning, and an emphasis on process is important in helping sustain a group over several weeks (Falchikov 2005).

How can you assess the group process? Tutors, fearful of peer assessment, have typically tried to assess the group process by asking students to write an individual reflection on the team work, their own contribution and the skills they have developed. This creates extra work for markers and does not necessarily achieve the aim of assessing the group process. Indeed, while it is tempting for staff to retain control over how the marks are distributed, the only people who can really judge what happened in the group are the members themselves; the tutor is not able to assess it (Kilic and Cakan 2006). Therefore, we would advise asking students to peer assess each other in relation to their contribution to the group process and product.

Using peer and self-assessment

This approach brings with it the general benefits of peer assessment discussed in Chapter 2 and has several additional benefits. Students are more likely to contribute to the group process if they know the effort will be rewarded (Helms and Haynes 1990), it can provide them with feedback on their team-work skills and contribution to the group and, finally, it can also help to divide the 'product' mark more fairly in relation to individual students' contribution to the group (see Figure 6.2). This gives students a reward for meeting the 'process criteria' which we will discuss later. This is very impor-tant because students are usually resentful if all the members of the group gain the same mark regardless of their contribution to the task (Falchikov 2005). Research suggests peer assessment in this context is effective in dis-criminating between different students' contributions (Warren and Cheng 2000) and thus, despite the fact that it is 'a complicated and problematic task' (Lejk and Wyvill 1996: 268) it is worth taking time to solve the problems (Falchikov 2005).

Assessment criteria for group 'process'

Assessment criteria will be needed for assessing the process, and various cri-teria have been used in practice (Goldfinch 1994; Lejk and Wyvill 2001; Kilic and Cakan 2006). Heathfield's (1999) criteria include both contribution to the group process (for example, attendance at meetings, being co-operative, and supporting and encouraging others) as well as contribution to the group task. Heathfield's general criteria were translated by a student working party into a meaningful description of effective and ineffective group contributions (see Figure 6.3). Whatever the criteria, it may be helpful to develop them with students, as evidence suggests that this increases their confidence in using them (Heathfield 1999).

Once the assessment criteria are devised, there are a number of strategies for carrying out the self- and peer assessment (Lejk and Wyvill 1996). Fal-chikov (2005) provides a useful review of published studies using different methods, and there appears to be no conclusive right way to do this. Many of the approaches use some form of peer assessment of 'process' criteria to create an individual weighting factor (Kilic and Cakan 2006) either by open dis-cussion or rating in private. Software is now available for this, as discussed in Chapter 14. The resulting weighting is used to determine what proportion of the 'product' mark each student is given. In other words, there is only one final mark per student for the group assignment. See Figure 6.3 for a worked example. Current experience in our institution suggests this is an effective and acceptable method for describing student contributions to group process in terms of a mark (inasmuch as you can do such a thing). Its main short-coming is dealing with students who have made very limited contributions (for example, through illness) having the effect of unduly lifting the grades of the remaining group members. In this case, students are requested to exclude

This sheet is designed to divide a group mark between the members of a group, based on their contribution to the task.

Students are asked to complete Figure 6.3 (self-assessment). They are asked to award themselves a mark out of 20 for each of the six categories. The criteria are there to help them decide what they deserve with an empty box to note the reasons why they feel their contribution was worth that mark. When all group members have completed a self-assessment sheet, the group should have a meeting to discuss the self-assessments and agree each person's mark for each category. Groups are instructed that, as it is very difficult for all group members to make exactly the same level of contribution, the totals (*) for each student should not be the same unless they attach a short statement explaining why. The group then submits the final group grid accompanied by each individual's self-assessment at the same time as they submit the assignment/do the presentation/complete the performance.

Names of group members

Categories							
Regular attendance at group meetings							
Contribution of ideas for the task							
Researching, analysing and preparing material for the task							
Contribution to co-operative group process							
Supporting and encouraging group members							
Practical contribution to end-product (e.g. writing, presenting, making materials)							
Total for each student(*)							Total for group ——

Signatures of participating group members:_____

Each student's final mark is calculated by dividing their total mark (*) by N, and multiplying the answer by the group mark.

N is found by dividing the total for the group by the number of students in the group. Therefore when the group total is 360 and there are four students in the group, $N = 360/4 = 90$.

Example: a group of four is awarded a joint mark of 60%. Jane gets a peer assessed score on the grid above of 94. Her final percentage mark is $94/90 \times 60 = 63\%$

Figure 6.2   Group assessment sheet

Please award yourself a mark out of 20 for each category. Note the justification for your mark in the empty box. The criteria are designed to help you with your self-assessment.

Worth 20	Worth 0	Justification for mark	Mark
Regular attendance at group meetings Attended all meetings, stayed to agreed end, worked within timescale, active and attentive, prepared to be flexible about meeting times	Missed several/most meetings, always or often late, left early, digressed, giggled, day-dreamed or gossiped most of the time		
Contribution of ideas for the task Thought about the topic in advance of the meeting, provided workable ideas which were taken up by the group, built on others' suggestions, and were prepared to test out your ideas on the group rather than keep quiet	Didn't come prepared, didn't contribute any ideas, tended to reject others' ideas rather than build on them		
Researching, analysing and preparing material for the task You did what you said you would do, you brought materials, did an equal share of the research and helped to analyse and evaluate the material	You did no research, you didn't do what you promised to do, you didn't manage your workload, you didn't get involved with the task and allowed others to provide all the material		
Contribution to co-operative group process Left personal differences outside the group, willing to review group progress and tackle conflict in the group, took on different roles as needed, kept group on track, willing and flexible but focused on the task	Did not take initiative, waited to be told what to do, always took the same role (leader, joker, etc.) regardless of circumstances, created conflict, and were not prepared to review group progress		
Supporting and encouraging group members Keen to listen to others, encouraged participation, enabled a collaborative learning environment, sensitive to issues affecting group members, supported group members with special needs	Sought only to complete the task, spoke over others and ignored their opinions, kept ideas and resources to yourself, insensitive to individuals' needs, and did not contribute to the learning process		
Practical contribution to end-product Willing to try new things, not hogging the tasks, made a high level of contribution, took own initiative, were reliable and produced high standard work/presentation	Not willing to take on any task, did not take any responsibilities, were unreliable so others felt the need to keep checking up, and made a limited, poor-quality contribution		

Figure 6.3 Team assessment: marking criteria

such students from their deliberations, leaving the tutor to identify an appropriate resolution.

What is important is that you decide what approach you are going to use at the programme level and use this across all group assignments. Each tutor devising their own method is likely to confuse students (Gibbs 2006b) and make them more resistant to the process.

Anonymous rating?

Students may prefer to give anonymous assessments of their peers in the team, and this may reduce the anxiety about assessing each other which is discussed in the peer assessment literature (Falchikov 2005). Open assessment has the advantage of helping students develop feedback skills, whereas anonymous marking leaves students unable to put their point of view or defend themselves. You will need to decide whether anonymous feedback is appropriate to your groups, depending on their experience of group assessment, but either way it is important to help students develop the skills of marking and reporting judgements (see Chapter 5).

Conclusion

This chapter has summarised a range of issues which impact on the accuracy of marking in higher education and has attempted to provide some practical suggestions for enhancement. Marking is difficult where assessment tasks reflect complex learning. There is no simple route to reliability and consistency which protects the validity of our assessment methods. Yet sadly, perhaps because of concerns regarding bad press or potentially litigious students, there is little debate among the higher education community on the inherent frailty of marking practices. Read *et al.* (2005) call for more open discussion on the variability of standards, and a greater level of openness might give greater confidence to new tutors who mistakenly think that it is possible to be a faultless marker.

There is much that individuals and teams can do in reflecting on their own practice as markers. Improving consistency of marking through creating assessment criteria and marking schemes, training markers and developing shared understanding of such documents through discussion is resource intensive. However, we should regard these activities as valuable use of our time because of the crucial role that marking plays in maintaining confidence in higher education's standards.

7 Providing effective feedback

Introduction

The significance of feedback for learning and the potential of formative assessment to enhance pedagogy (Yorke 2003) provide a strong argument that all assessment activity in universities should aim to produce effective feedback for students. Indeed, feedback is arguably the most important aspect of the assessment process in raising achievement (Black and Wiliam 1998a; Gibbs and Simpson 2004–5), yet there are many difficulties with current practice.

Chapter 2 outlined recent research indicating that feedback should be viewed as an essential element integrated into the learning process. Some structural problems affecting feedback, such as assessment in modular programmes tending to become entirely summative, may need to be tackled at institutional level (Taras 2006). However, working within existing structures, it is possible to develop a more integrated guidance and feedback loop (Hounsell *et al.* 2006) – or perhaps it would be more appropriate to call this a 'spiral', to include the dimension of progression through a programme. This means integrating guidance, feedback and target setting into the programme structure and student entitlement. Chapter 5 provides general strategies on how a guidance and feedback spiral might be achieved, while this chapter focuses on the feedback element in particular.

The 'academic literacies' approach (see Box. 5.1) problematises student writing, and within this approach Lillis (2001, 2003) argues for the central importance of developing feedback as a dialogue. Despite this plea, the formalisation of assessment procedures may 'decouple' student from tutor, distancing the reader from the author of their assignment (Crook *et al.* 2006). Feedback may be generally limited to one-way, 'monologic' communication (Lillis 2001). While peer dialogue may compensate for this to some extent, Northedge (2003b) warns that students working together may continue to employ an 'everyday' discourse rather than practise using academic language. Therefore, he stresses the importance of tutor–student dialogue. Lillis (2001) draws on the notion of 'addressivity' to explain how a tutor's response to writing in progress can help the student develop and clarify the meaning in their work: 'are you trying to say . . . ?' or 'what is the point you are trying to make in this paragraph?'. In other words, the dialogue taking place with reference to an assignment can help the student develop the emergent meaning in their writing and provides the opportunity for the teacher to respond to and reorient the student's thinking. Dialogue may also be seen as a way to mitigate some of the lack of trust and misunderstandings that form unintentional outcomes of the feedback process (Carless *et al.* 2006).

These two challenges – of integrating guidance and feedback throughout programmes and of encouraging feedback as dialogue – form underpinning principles for this chapter. It will draw on both research and developing practice to provide general advice on providing and using feedback and to offer a basis for tutors and teams to review and enhance their approach.

Timely feedback

Students benefit from a very prompt return of marked assignments with accompanying feedback. This may not always be easy to achieve, and Chapter 4 offers strategies for providing feedback to students before the fully marked and moderated assignments are available. Where there are two or more elements of assessment in a module, students should receive feedback on the first assignment in time to apply it to subsequent assessed work. While online tests may have some limitations, their great advantage is being able to provide prompt feedback to students. Ways to speed up provision of feedback are discussed later in this chapter.

Written feedback

The nature of written comments can vary enormously, and there is evidence of student dissatisfaction at the amount, timing, frequency, helpfulness and consistency of the feedback they receive (Hounsell 2006). The following paragraphs outline elements of good practice in written feedback which tackle these concerns.

Feed forward

Feedback needs to provide specific and sufficient comment and suggestions on strengths, areas for development and strategies for improvement. Student perception and mediation of written feedback is an under-researched area, but Weaver (2006) found that students identified negative and over-general feedback as unhelpful. A key principle of feedback is that it will usefully inform the student of ways to improve their performance, or 'feed forward' (Torrance 1993; Hounsell 2006). General praise is not useful, whereas comment on a specific strength acts as advice for the future because it is telling the student to use that particular strategy in future assessments. Likewise, general or obscure criticisms will not be useful. Give specific examples from the script of positive or weak sections. On the other hand, if comments are too grounded in the specific assignment, then students may find it difficult to generalise from them (Carless *et al.* 2006).

It is important to build from specific comments towards providing more generalised strategies for improvement in future assessments. For example, you could complement this specific praise comment:

> In your discussion of [key concept] on page 'X' you very effectively highlighted the contrasting views of two different authors as part of building your own argument.

with this more forward-looking *addition*:

> You should consider how this kind of critical engagement with the literature might become a more widespread feature of your writing.

It should be possible to prompt the transfer by students of strategies suggested in written feedback to future assessments (albeit requiring adaptation to a new context). For example, a module booklet may signal the links to other modules:

> The feedback for this assessment in module X101 will help you to set targets by considering both what you did well (keep on doing it) and what you need to do to improve. Comments on this essay should particularly help you to successfully tackle the essay assignment in module X201. The feedback will also assist you in completing the assessed report in module X104 which builds on the key concepts introduced in this module to investigate topic X in more depth.

This approach does require a coherent programme design and a carefully thought out assessment strategy (see Chapter 11).

Limit the amount of feedback

It is important not to overload the student with too much detailed information and certainly not to over-correct written work. These issues are also important from a tutor workload perspective. The tutor should perhaps consider writing just three or four comments that would be most helpful to the student in understanding the grade awarded and in improving their future work. In order to achieve an encouraging overall impact, at least part of the feedback should build on a positive aspect of the assessed work. Detailed corrections such as those for spelling and grammar could be limited to the first paragraphs with a note directing the writer to the problem and potential sources of help.

Encourage positive motivation

Tutors need to consider their purpose(s) in providing written feedback and reflect on how this compares with what they actually write, how their students perceive it (Orrell 2006; Weaver 2006) and the impact of feedback on students' approaches to learning. They should focus on positive achievements and on suggesting strategies for improvement that are within the control of the student. Written feedback will impact on the self-efficacy beliefs of the student, and this may be a major influence on how they approach their studies; students will be more likely to perform better if they believe they are capable of improvement. Box 7.1 provides an introduction to some of the underpinning theory. In general, feedback needs to be encouraging despite the fact that it should also present the areas for improvement required to gain a higher grade in the future.

Speeding up feedback

Handwritten comments can be quick and allow tutors to keep away from a computer screen, but a basic and genuine problem is that students may be unable to decipher handwritten feedback. The widespread use of e-mail and the development of electronic submission systems are also creating considerable pressure for the word-processing of feedback. There are advantages to this because feedback can be e-mailed individually to students, it helps to speed up feedback and also means that students are not relied upon to physically collect their marked assignments. Although there are dangers of cut-and-paste editing, it seems likely that thoughtful use of word-processing will be able to, at least, match the quality of handwritten feedback.

Word-processing of feedback also allows the use of comment banks (for an example, see Falchikov 2005) which may speed up the writing of feedback. They can create the core of effective feedback quickly and thus allow more time for individualised comment. Word-processing of feedback also allows easy editing; if the work is double marked then this can be particularly useful. Although use of comment banks may seem a rather mechanical process, it is important that when new procedures are being scrutinised the traditional process they are replacing should be subjected to the same level of analysis.

Feedback grids can also speed up the provision of feedback, especially when they are tailored to the assignment. See Figure 7.1 for an example used to give prompt feedback to community work students on their management supervision skills. Where a marking scheme exists (see Figure 6.1 for an example), this can be also be used as a marking grid, with tutors highlighting

---

Box 7.1   Leads into literature: impact of feedback on student motivation and self-efficacy

The conceptions of learning and, in particular, of intelligence held by tutors as well as those held by students are important influences on the writing and reception of feedback. Building on the work of Dweck (1999), Yorke and Knight (2004: 27) use the terms 'fixed' and 'malleable' to describe a spectrum of beliefs about intelligence held by tutors and students. A fixed belief means that intelligence is viewed as an ability level that is resistant to change. A malleable position is that 'with effort one simply can achieve more and, in doing so, ascend a virtuous spiral'. Yorke and Knight (2004: 33) argue that a malleable view of intelligence 'is more conducive to learning'. They promote the concept of 'practical intelligence' which may help tutors to move towards a malleable position because it relates to learning gained through experience and offers considerable developmental potential. Tutors should hold a malleable position on intelligence combined with an ambition to advance the practical intelligence of the student as a prerequisite for writing effective, encouraging feedback.

Pertinent to this challenge is the work of Bandura (1997) on social cognitive theory and, in particular, on self-efficacy. Self-efficacy is seen as a major influence on approaches to learning and will affect the response of students to feedback. Self-efficacy in this context is considered as the level of belief held by a student that they can influence their performance in future assessments. As Pintrich (2003: 671) asserts, 'Students who believe that they are able and that they can and will do well are much more likely to be motivated in terms of effort, persistence, and behaviour than students who believe they are less able and do not expect to succeed'. From the perspective of social cognitive theory, written feedback can be viewed as an opportunity for the tutor to influence the student's self-efficacy beliefs through 'social persuasion'. However as Pajares (2002: 7) points out, 'Effective persuaders must cultivate people's beliefs in their capabilities' and not be confused with 'knee-jerk praise or empty inspirational homilies'. He further warns that 'it is usually easier to weaken self-efficacy beliefs through negative appraisals than to strengthen such beliefs through positive encouragement'.

---

the cells to reflect student achievement. There is some evidence that students find it difficult to interpret checkbox feedback (McDowell *et al.* 2005), and it may be wise to practice using peer assessment in order to help students understand the meaning of different statements.

A useful way to provide prompt feedback when handwriting feedback comments or marking exam scripts is to keep a note of general strengths and weaknesses. This group feedback is then typed up and e-mailed to the students typically as one page of very prompt generalised feedback which avoids the delay caused by second marking and moderation. This summary

Having listened to your supervision tape, I have ticked the points that I think you need to pay attention to:

Agenda setting: • Checking out whether your supervisee has things to add to the agenda • Explaining the purpose of talking about x – why you have put it on the agenda • Agreeing the timing of the session • Agreeing how the session will be recorded	
Structure of the session: • Focusing on all the details of the incident rather than moving quickly to the wider issues raised by situation/incident • You are moving straight from description to what could be done differently another time without asking 'why'. This means that the supervisee has no analysis of the situation to help them think what they should do another time. It is just guess work • Accepting the first reason/explanation for the situation that is offered by the supervisee and not challenging them to think about other possible explanations • Not dealing with the underlying issues in sufficient depth • Not dealing with the different issues raised by the situation separately – lumping them together so that the learning is rather vague	
Questioning: • Asking closed questions • Asking 'Do you feel/think . . . ?' type questions which tend to be suggestive • Asking follow-on questions when the supervisee doesn't reply immediately. For example, an open question, followed immediately by a suggestive question: 'Why do you think it happened? Was it because . . .?' Ask the first question and cope with the silence. It will get their brain ticking • Asking several questions at once • Asking questions in a long, complicated way	
Supervision skills: • Allowing a chatty supervisee to control the session • Accepting the supervisee's moans and blaming of others without challenging them to consider their contribution to the situation • Not focusing the discussion	
Action planning and ending supervision: • Not summarising the discussion • Not identifying the key learning/action points • Not agreeing what will be recorded	

Figure 7.1 Using a grid to provide speedy feedback

document can also be used as guidance for future cohorts (Hounsell *et al.* 2006), will provide useful evidence to tutors for module evaluation, and may even inform the future development of a comment bank. The grid in Figure 7.1 was assembled in this way.

Feedback style

The overall strategy suggested here is for tutors to position themselves as far as possible as 'co-learners' within the subject discipline community (Northedge 2003a). This requires attention to the nature of the written feedback provided and a willingness on the part of tutors to acknowledge that marking student work may contribute to their own professional learning. In written feedback consider to what extent you may be able to use a more questioning approach, for example replacing apparently confident statements such as:

> The report had no clear structure and the argument was weak.

with more questioning comments such as:

> I found it difficult to follow your argument. Consider how a more explicit structure may have helped the reader and also helped you as writer in forming your argument.

Even when commenting more directly on understanding of concepts within the subject discipline, it may be possible to be more tentative by encouraging the student to self-assess their knowledge, for example replacing:

> The argument is undermined by poor understanding of [key concept].

with more of a prompt for self-assessment such as:

> I found it difficult to follow your argument. You might consider how you need to further develop your understanding of [key concept].

Evidence suggests that students do pay some attention to feedback (Carless *et al.* 2006; Hartley *et al.* 2002), and using a style that attempts to at least approach a dialogue appears to be a reasonable and achievable strategy.

Feedback language

Care should be taken to align the language of feedback to the mark, avoiding mismatches such as '65%, excellent'. In this regard, it is important that teaching teams work towards ensuring that there is consistency in the use of assessment language. This needs to extend from the published assessment guidance and the information provided orally by tutors to the written feedback. However, as Mutch (2003: 37) argues, 'feedback, even of the most carefully crafted type, could be fated to be misunderstood and ignored'. A potential conflict is that tutors try to ground the feedback very much in the specifics of the individual student's assignment and in terms they will understand, which may mean that they do not use the same language as the assessment guidance.

Northedge (2003a) argues convincingly that tutors and teaching teams need to take care to ensure that the subject discipline language used in assessment documents and in feedback is realistic about the level of participation that students will have gained within the subject discipline community and to allow for the use of 'intermediate levels of discourse' at different stages of the programme. Helping students to understand terminology and feedback is therefore important (see below and Chapter 5). In relation to this matter, there is evidence that students find feedback produced by their peers easier to understand (see Box 7.2), and they will accept criticism more readily from other students as it is not as 'emotionally loaded' (Black *et al.* 2003: 77).

Box 7.2   Students generating feedback

First-year students used assessment criteria to anonymously mark their peers' posters. In order to help students engage with the process, they were also given marks for the quality of their feedback, particularly for how well it reflected the assessment criteria. Research with the students discovered that they were able to describe the main points of the feedback they received and they were able to articulate these points in very concrete ways: 'the bridge they were making for themselves in interpreting what they were marking in terms of "academic" criteria was helping them to generate feedback for others that also bridged that divide' (Bloxham and West 2004: 729)

An additional factor, which adds to the complexity, is that the language of institutionally produced assessment documents (for example, institutional grade descriptors) may be at odds with that of the assessment criteria which are written by the teaching team at a local level and within a subject discipline.

Structure of feedback

The design of feedback forms (cover sheets) is worthy of some thought because it can shape the feedback provided in terms of focus and detail. Students should be able to see the links between comments in the feedback and the assessment guidance provided for the assignment. There are various choices in the structure of written feedback and, ideally, the choice should be agreed at the programme level in order to provide consistency to students. The feedback can be organised to link principally to one or more of the following:

- the module learning outcomes;
- the marking scheme or grade descriptors;
- the assessment criteria.

Chapter 6 provides a fuller discussion of the approaches to marking that underpin these different choices and the implications of marking analytically or holistically.

In considering and adapting these possible choices for written feedback, tutors should perhaps include the key elements of the feedback 'sandwich'. This means that the overall structure should start with a layer of specific praise for strengths within the assignment. This is followed by the filling, which consists of key areas of weakness and strategies for improvement. The final layer is again a statement that is as positive as possible providing an overview of the assignment.

Above all, then, the structure of feedback needs to be thought through, justified and reviewed by teaching teams so that it provides feedback in a format which aids student understanding, is linked clearly to the assignment guidance and hopefully does not create unintended effects on the marking process.

Formative feedback

Assessment *for* learning conceives of the role of assessment as predominantly formative and diagnostic – an opportunity for students to judge how well they are doing against the requirements of the course. It is widespread practice across the academic world to receive formative peer feedback on draft research publications before completing the final version. This approach is also common in some postgraduate programmes where students receive provisional feedback and then have an opportunity to improve their paper – in Sadler's (1998) terms, to 'close the gap' – before final submission. Taras (2006) argues for equity for undergraduates in the provision of formative feedback on their writing, with no penalties other than the need to do some editing. However, it is relatively uncommon except for major tasks such as dissertations and is sometimes dismissed as 'writing it for them'. Disciplinary traditions vary radically on this matter. Weaver (2006) found significant differences between the feedback experience and perceptions of business studies compared to art and design undergraduates. This was partly because the art and design modules provided more built-in opportunities for formative feedback. Overall, students will pay attention to feedback at the draft stage because attending to it is likely to influence their grades (Gibbs and Simpson 2004–5). In providing such feedback, you need to ensure that you are working within institutional regulations and that the process is fair to all students.

Peer and self-assessment can help to reduce the workload on staff associated with generating formative feedback (see Box. 7.3). Using peers to provide formative assessment has the added benefit that it reduces the technical and affective problems considerably compared to its use in summative marking. Chapters 4 and 5 provide advice on using peer and self-assessment.

Box 7.3 Gaining formative feedback on draft assignments

Students were asked to bring a draft assignment to class. The class of 30 was divided into two halves, groups A and B, and the tutor collected the assignments from each half. The group A assignments were distributed randomly to group B students and vice versa. The students were asked to read the assignment with reference to the criteria, and write comments. After the students had completed this, group A were asked to find the owner of the assignment they had marked and spend 10 minutes discussing their comments. After 10 minutes, group B students did the same. The session concluded with a discussion about points or queries that arose from the reading and the use of criteria. Students valued it for helping focus their attention on the criteria, seeing alternative ways of going about the task, getting feedback at a stage when they could use it to improve their work and reassurance that they were 'on the right track'.

Alternatively, the workload for staff of writing feedback can be transferred to the formative stage, limiting the feedback provided at the final submission to a grade, alone or with very brief comment. This approach, while beneficial to student learning, will probably challenge quality-assurance procedures so you need to negotiate it with both students and relevant colleagues. In practice this will create a small amount of additional assessment workload for tutors, and it may only be possible to resource it for one or two modules within a programme, one of which would ideally be early in the course.

Other similar solutions involve breaking up the assignment so that students gain formative feedback but also a small proportion of their module grade from a provisional submission – for example, an essay plan and introduction explaining the approach they plan to take. See Cooper (2000) for a further example. This approach may, however, increase tutor workload considerably.

Building dialogue

While we recognise that the resources required for meaningful dialogue between student and tutor are not available for most modules and programmes, we would urge tutors to consider how opportunities for meaningful conversation with students can be built into their teaching. This is particularly important for students in the early stages of a programme. For example, let students know that you are happy to take questions on the assessment tasks by e-mail, but all replies (disguising the identity of the questioner) will be answered on the module's website or virtual learning environment for everyone to read. Students should be encouraged to visit the website before posting a question or just to see what others have asked. Our experience shows that sometimes the questions are of a technical nature – 'How do I reference a handout used in class?' – but they can also raise more significant issues regarding the assessment requirements. Box 7.4 provides a practical example of creating tutor–student dialogue in a seminar group.

Box 7.4   Feedback dialogue

First assignments were returned to a group of business studies students and they were asked to bring the assignment to the following session with any questions or issues they wanted to raise about the feedback. At the next two-hour session, the tutor asked the class of 20 students to work in groups on a structured task using a resource book, while she held a five-minute tutorial with each student. This provided an opportunity for the tutor to check students understood the feedback and to provide further explanation. It ensured students read the feedback with some care and there was demonstrable increase in overall grades compared with the previous year. Student evaluations picked out that session as one of the aspects that helped them to meet the learning outcomes (N. Metcalfe-Meer, personal communication).

In visualizing and developing the feedback process as a dialogue, it is necessary to at least attempt to address the power imbalance between tutor and student. Moving the marking effort by tutors forward from end of module to formative feedback on a provisional submission is one way to shift the role and power position of the tutor away from 'assessor' and towards 'critical friend'. Even if this only occurs within one or two early modules, it could contribute positively to building a different relationship between tutors and students.

The central challenge is that it will be difficult to establish written feedback as a dialogue when it is written rather than spoken, it is linked closely to grading, the student may not have access to the tutor, and it involves a significant power imbalance between the tutor as assessor and the student as writer.

Engaging students with feedback

Preparing students for feedback

Evidence discussed in Chapter 2 suggests a vicious 'downward spiral' created by students choosing not to or being unable to use feedback that may be combined with staff cynicism that their efforts are wasted (Hounsell 2003). While efforts can be made to improve the quality of feedback, it is equally important to help students use it effectively, and this section will provide advice on promoting active engagement with feedback.

First, students should be briefed on feedback (Freeman and Lewis 1998), its nature and purposes, so that they recognise the different forms feedback takes (written comments, tutorials, mentor feedback on placement, feedback from peers, question-and-answer sessions) and they are ready to be challenged and spurred into action by feedback comments. They should also be made aware of their right to ask for clarification of feedback from a tutor and have an opportunity to comment on the usefulness of tutor feedback through the evaluation process. See Chapter 5 for general information on preparing students for assessment.

Self-assessment

Within the assessment process it may be difficult to identify or construct places for peer and self-assessment in which students feel safe. The modular structure of many programmes does create one possible advantage which may be exploited, in that once a student has been credited with an agreed mark then it cannot be taken away. Self-assessment after tutor marking of the assignment for a module is therefore relatively unthreatening and is useful in terms of students identifying the possible relevance of the feedback to future assignments and modules. Rust *et al.* (2005) advocate several approaches, such as providing students with generic feedback for the cohort and asking them to identify which of the comments apply to their work. They can then compare this self-assessment with the tutor comments. Alternatively, they can be asked to complete a self-assessment informed by tutor comments on their work. In this case Taras (2001, 2003) suggests that the grade should only be revealed after the completion of self-assessment. Comments without a grade are associated with more learning (Rust *et al.* 2005), although students may be resistant to this unless the rationale is carefully explained.

An important part of self-assessment in this context is setting targets for future assignments, and students can be asked to do this as part of their self-assessment. Alternatively, paired discussion of feedback during a class session or online discussion can be used to help students turn feedback into feedforward. Ideally they will be able to critically consider their self-assessment and response to tutor feedback and question their underlying assumptions about their approaches to study and to their writing.

Personal development planning activities

The design of personal development planning (PDP) within the structure of personal or group tutorials is a possible way to build in dialogue about written feedback from tutors. Students might be required to bring their PDP progress files and the written feedback on two or three of their most recent assessed assignments to a session. Students can then be asked to work individually on identifying the transfer of targets from feedback towards their next assignments. During the individual work the tutor circulates and enables individuals to raise questions arising from feedback which are relevant to their next assignments. Such a session encourages student engagement with feedback but may need confident handling of some questions regarding the marking and feedback if other tutors have marked the work. The focus needs to be on students interpreting feedback rather then the session tutor 'translating' it because of the different meanings that tutors ascribe to academic terms (see Chapter 6 for a discussion of this issue).

Contrasting feedback

An opportunity for promoting feedback as a dialogue may arise wherever there are two tutors involved in providing feedback. The two voices of perhaps a tutor and a work-based mentor may risk at times frustrating and possibly even confusing the student. However, it does present the feedback as contested and may help to entice the student to critically engage with the comments. This approach already occurs in some double-marking situations, is common in some arts subjects and sometimes arises in work-based learning within professional programmes. This proposal appears to conflict with the need to carefully control tutor workload, and teaching teams might only consider it as a possibility where two tutors are already involved in the assessment. The student might be allowed to hear both tutors' voices rather than a single feedback script which has involved the extra work of merging the second marker's comments.

Evaluating the student perspective

As a tutor or as a member of a teaching team, you need to evaluate your students' experiences, perceptions and responses to feedback. Feedback is a complex and contested form of communication and, despite the general messages arising from the literature, the impact of feedback practice on learning in universities will be strongly influenced by particular subject disciplines, departments, teaching teams and groups of students. Attempts to enhance the feedback process will need to address the student perspective and the issues of discourse, identity and power that this raises (Higgins *et al.* 2001). The need to establish this student perspective is signalled very strongly by the work of Crook *et al.* (2006), who argue that the accountability agenda in higher education, together perhaps with pressure on resources, creates forces which work towards 'an enforced distancing of the principal participants, tutor and student' (2006: 111).

Informal gathering of evaluation data by tutors takes place during marking and through analysis of result profiles during moderation. However, the systematic qualitative analysis of assignments (see, for example, Hatton and Smith 1995; Maclellan 2004b) and of the associated tutor feedback sheets (Randall and Mirador 2003) is an approach with considerable potential for enhancement of learning.

Conclusion

Many of the suggestions in this chapter involve making the provision of feedback a messier and more contested process, and they require confidence and good levels of trust across the teaching team. They may appear to conflict with the apparent need for a tightly organised system that is able to robustly defend itself against threats from individual students or external audit. However, as Crook *et al.* (2006: 113) found, an 'audit-inspired, well ordered process may disturb rather than enhance the students' participation in educational practice' – for example, a robust moderation procedure may prevent prompt return of work or deliver feedback when it is too late to have much impact.

This chapter has summarised key aspects of research and practice in feedback in order to provide advice and suggestions. However, this still leaves the responsibility on tutors and teaching teams to evaluate their own practice, including the perspectives of their students, in order to critically evaluate and develop effective feedback processes within their local context.

8 Moderation: towards greater consistency in marking

Marion Nuttall

Setting the context

Chapter 6 focused on the skills and challenges of marking student work accurately and acknowledged that much of higher education assessment, by its very nature, is hard to assess reliably. There are pressures for accountability, transparency and consistency from government and from potentially litigious students as consumers which make reliable marking more important now than ever before (Holroyd 2000). In the UK, for as long as 20 years there has been a growing national concern over higher education standards (O'Donovan *et al.* 2004) and as a result, the Quality Assurance Agency has developed a number of strategies and policies designed to create greater confidence in the sector. These include, for example, subject benchmark statements, the Framework for Higher Education Qualifications (see Chapter 11, Box 11.3) and a Code of Practice including sections on assessment (QAA 2006c) and external examining (QAA 2004). The section on assessment specifies that 'Institutions have transparent and fair mechanisms for marking and for moderating marks' (QAA 2006c: 16). Despite this entreaty to institutions, a number of problems are evident in the management of assessment, including variability of standards and poor moderation (QAA 2006a).

Therefore institutions and academics need to pay attention to good practices for marking and moderation, if only to inspire confidence in standards among all concerned. Key procedures designed to achieve this are second/double marking and moderation, which in a number of countries can involve working with external examiners. This chapter builds on Chapter 6 on marking and Chapter 7 on feedback by clarifying the role of moderation practices. This will include discussion of some of the issues as well as practical advice on implementation.

Moderation

Moderation is a process for ensuring that grades awarded are fair and reliable and that marking criteria have been applied consistently. Interestingly, while reliability is discussed in depth, 'moderation' as a term hardly surfaces in assessment texts for higher education tutors. This is probably a reflection of how mechanistic and taken for granted the activity is seen to be, failing to raise the passions associated with other aspects of assessment. Despite this, the effort to demonstrate fairness, reliability and consistency through moderation is expensive and diverts resources from more learning-related aspects of assessment (Gibbs 2006b). In fact, it may harm student learning, for example where it creates an undue delay in students receiving feedback.

Nonetheless, there are a number of benefits accruing from effective moderation which make it necessary even when each marker in a teaching team has been provided with clearly stated assessment criteria and a marking scheme. These include improved reliability resulting from the opportunity to surface major differences in the interpretation of criteria and marking schemes, prevention of undue influence by 'the predilections of the marker' (Partington 1994: 57) and mitigation against the influence of 'hard' or 'soft' markers. In addition, transparent moderation procedures are likely to increase students' confidence in marking and they provide 'safety in numbers' (Partington 1994), giving staff confidence in dealing with students (Swann and Ecclestone 1999a). Finally, as discussed in Chapter 6, the process of seeing others' marking and discussing marking decisions can have an important role in staff development and the creation of an assessment community among the marking team (Swann and Ecclestone 1999a).

A number of circumstances make the process of moderation particularly important, including when:

- courses are delivered collaboratively and/or over a number of campuses;
- members of a marking team are newly appointed and inexperienced in assessment practices (Ecclestone 2001);
- there are multiple markers for a module (Price 2005);
- part-time markers are employed specifically for marking, for example postgraduate teaching assistants (Fransson 1977);
- practitioners contribute to or are involved in marking because of their professional expertise but are not experienced in higher education marking practices or standards (for example managers, nurses, teachers);
- workload pressures mean that markers are fitting marking into a hectic, fragmented schedule.

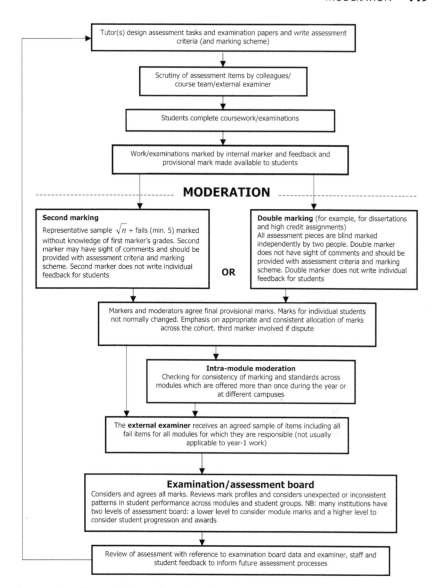

Figure 8.1 The marking and moderation process for tutors

The flow diagram in Figure 8.1 is provided as a model of good practice and shows that moderation usually includes both internal and external processes, the latter in the UK and elsewhere possibly involving external examiners. Figure 8.1 demonstrates that a good deal of the work of moderation takes place *before* the marking period, and Chapter 6 emphasises the importance of preparatory tasks such as clarifying assessment criteria and marking schemes. Dunn *et al.* (2004) recommend that decisions are made in advance about how to tackle unexpected but appropriate student answers that are outside the marking scheme; for example, such work might be passed to module leaders for their decision (Price 2005).

Internal moderation

There are various component parts to internal moderation:

- Programme approval (validation) procedures test whether the module learning outcomes reflect the level of study and whether the assessment tasks will enable students to demonstrate appropriate learning. This process moderates the validity of the programme design in terms of the appropriateness of its aims and learning outcomes and its assessment strategy.
- Internal and/or external scrutiny of assessment tasks to support staff in the effective design of coursework tasks and examination papers. This may take place informally, through a 'scrutiny committee' or via an external examiner.
- Second or double marking of the work, usually by sampling. The policies vary from one university to another and it is imperative to follow your own institution's guidance.
- Intra-module moderation is essential where a module is offered to several different groups in the same academic session with different module leaders (for example, on several campuses). The programme leader should ensure that moderation takes place to check that assessment standards have been applied consistently across the groups.

The remainder of this section will focus on the latter two components listed above, particularly second and double marking (see also Box 8.1). These should be common practice for all summative assessment, and evidence suggests that staff see them as essential for providing fairness to students and ensuring the quality of work (Hand and Clewes 2000). Nevertheless, research indicates that second and double marking may be patchy (Maclellan 2001).

Box 8.1   Leads into literature: second and double marking

There is relatively little written about the processes of second and double marking as currently practised in our universities, although many researchers have investigated tutor differences in marking (see Chapters 3 and 6). The exception is an interesting, if rather polemical article by Partington (1994).

According to Partington (1994), time-consuming double marking ceases to be necessary if there are published mark schemes moderated by external examiners. However, as discussed at length in Chapter 6, mark schemes can be interpreted differently and it is hard to disagree with Dunn *et al.* (2004) when they emphasise that they are a necessary part of the preparation for moderation but do not render double/second marking unnecessary.

Second marking

Second marking is not actually marking, but a process of moderation by a second person. It involves a sample of the assignments or examination scripts being read by a second marker. It does not mean remarking the work or writing additional feedback but involves the verification of standards by checking the marking of the sample. The main purpose of second marking is to ensure that markers have graded the assessment tasks appropriately in accordance with the defined assessment criteria and the relevant grade descriptors or marking scheme.

Second marking with sight of the first marker's comments and grades is the most light-handed. However, Partington (1994) discusses at length the difficulty in second marking with regard to convergence of the two markers when the second marker knows the mark which has been awarded by the first marker. He suggests this convergence is likely to be aggravated where the second marker is moderating the work of a more experienced colleague, despite evidence discussed in Chapter 6 that experience does not automatically bring with it greater accuracy in marking.

Alternatively, when the mark is not known (blind second marking), the individual markers might be expected to value the characteristics of the students' work differently and ultimately this may lead to students being treated more fairly. On the other hand, in this situation 'defensive marking' (see Chapter 6) may apply, with staff erring on the safe side with average marks for fear of contradiction by double markers if they choose high or low grades.

When writing their moderation policies institutions should think carefully about the effective use of staff time and resources in specifying requirements for sampling and the extent to which double marking (see below) is obligatory. The marking task must be practicable without compromising quality assurance, although there is some argument that, in higher education, a sample can never be 'taken as indicative of the whole' (Partington 1994). A helpful way of deciding on the sample size is to use the square root of n where n is the number of assignments or examination papers in the cohort studying a module. This reduces the pressure of second marking on large cohorts but maintains a reasonable minimum number for small cohorts. In the case of multiple markers, the same principle applies: sufficient scripts should be scrutinised to assemble a reliable picture of each assessor's standard. The sample size should be sufficiently large to be representative of all the major dimensions being assessed (Brown *et al.* 1997) and should normally include any provisional fails and grade borderline items.

Double marking

Double marking means that the work is marked independently by two different people without sight of each other's comments, marks or grades (known as blind double marking). It is usually used instead of second marking for large assignments such as dissertations, projects or exhibitions, and institutions may require double marking of all assignments in modules where an individual assignment contributes 100% of the assessment weighting. The intention here is to provide a greater check on marking standards in acknowledgement of the greater contribution the assessment makes to the student's overall profile. Markers should not write comments on the work as this may prejudice the other marker (Race 2003). Submission of two copies by students helps to avoid this problem.

Resolution of marks

When second or double markers have completed their reading of student work, it may be necessary to resolve differences in grading between the first and second markers. In the case of multiple markers, the module leader may make the final decision. Where the two markers are asked to agree final marks, it is suggested that in order to avoid regression to the mean, resolution of the marks is as follows for second marking:

- Where there is general agreement, the first marker's marks stand for the whole cohort; small differences in grading should be ignored as they are inherent in higher education marking.
- If there is substantive variation in the marks and an adjustment is needed to the first marker's grades, further second marking will be needed to examine the extent of the difference. Whatever adjustment is made must be applied fairly to all relevant candidates. For example, if the first marker appears to have been too generous with work at the lower end of the spectrum, all work that falls into that

category may need to be adjusted and not merely that sampled by the second marker.

- If the two markers cannot agree, a third internal marker is used in the same way as the second marker. The final agreed marks are those that reflect the closest consensus of two of the three markers.

For double marking where every assignment is marked twice, the two markers can negotiate the agreed mark of individual students through discussion, although averaging of marks should be avoided.

Intra-module moderation

The growth of multiple campuses and modes of study, distance learning and partner arrangements, for example with further education colleges, means that modules and programmes may be running in different modes, on different sites, taught by different staff teams. Intra-module moderation is designed to test consistency of standards across different cohorts of the same module. Such moderation will consider both the quality of the work produced and the fairness, reliability and consistency of the marking across the cohorts. Intra-module moderation will involve second marking but will also include a review of the range and spread of marks. Sets of marks which vary significantly across cohorts are not unusual, but moderation will want to test whether this is a result of student differences, marking inconsistency, or aspects of the learning environment.

Recording moderation

Evidence of second/double marking and moderation is required for quality audits and reviews, so it is worth designing administrative procedures that capture this without creating too much additional bureaucracy. An example of how you might record this is shown in Figure 8.2.

External moderation

External moderation involves a range of activities and differs internationally. All undergraduate awards in the UK have external examiner or examiners appointed to them, whereas in Australia it is more restricted to research degrees and some honours degrees. In New Zealand external examiners are appointed to postgraduate degrees and undergraduate degrees at honours level (Muir 1999).

In the UK, external examiners are appointed with a responsibility to consider comparability of standards and quality of the programme and

Module code: _____
Module name: _____

Semester: _____ Academic Year: _____ Location _____

Module Coordinator: _____
1st marker(s): _____
2nd marker(s): _____

| Name | Assignment 1, weighted ...% | | | | | Assignment 2, weighted...% | | | | | Assignment 3/Examination, weighted...% | | | | |
	Date received	Marked by	1st mark	2nd mark	Agreed mark	Date received	Marked by	1st mark	2nd mark	Agreed mark	Date received	Marked by	1st mark	2nd mark	Agreed mark

Figure 8.2 Example of form used for recording moderation of assessment

assessment procedures. The external examiner system is designed to bring a level of external accountability to assessment decisions in higher education, that is, to ensure that all the awards of an institution meet internal standards as well as external standards of the QAA and professional statutory and regulatory bodies, and that the institutions' academic regulations, assessment processes and procedures are effective and fairly applied. The focus has changed over time towards ensuring 'due process', internal consistency and acting as consultant to programme teams: 'The key to real influence [over programmes] ... seemed to be the careful construction over time of a relationship that allowed for both a proper element of distance to enable rigorous scrutiny, backed up by the existence of formal powers, and the growth of a sense of trust and collegial sharing' (Hannan and Silver 2004: 5).

External examiners carry out their role using a range of processes such as meetings with staff and students and reviewing course documents (Higher Education Academy 2004). However, their most important task continues to be the moderation of examination scripts and coursework assignments to test standards and facilitate the comparability of treatment between students. There is very little research on the process of external examining, although recent work is beginning to investigate conceptual understanding of the examining process as a basis for offering greater support for the role (Higher Education Academy 2004). There is some concern that elements of the external examiner system work against quality enhancement (see Box. 8.2).

Working with your external examiner

Here are some suggestions for building a productive relationship with your external examiner(s):

- Regard your examiners as peers, able to provide an external perspective against the 'local' context for assessment. Use them to discuss issues and dilemmas, but remember that knowledge of the local context is very important in making judgements and recommending changes.
- Invite them for an informal induction at the start of their term of office, an opportunity to meet the programme leader and teaching team, to help them understand both the structure and philosophy of the course. Provide them with a copy of the previous examiner's report so they can offer continuity.
- Normally, unless the number of assessment items is sufficiently small for all of them to be scrutinised, reach an agreement with your examiners on the sample of work to be sent to them for moderation. There may be institutional guidelines on this. Samples should include representative examples of each grade or class of degree.

Box 8.2 Leads into literature: external examiners and quality enhancement

Quality assurance arguably diverts attention away from innovations in teaching and assessment. Biggs (2003) suggests that the use of external examiners may discourage innovative assessment practices as institutions restrict themselves to approaches that can easily be understood out of context. Case study 1 in Chapter 3 illustrates this, and Chapter 3 in general explores how aspects of quality assurance may conflict with the use of a range of assessment methods and limit the use of more innovative methods of assessment such as peer assessment or team assignments. Biggs (2003) suggests that external examiners cannot be fully aware of, and in sympathy with, the aims of the teaching and the approach to assessment of a programme, and yet responses to their comments are part of the quality assurance system, hence the pressure to make assessment comprehensible.

In Britain the external examiner system has been regarded as the 'guarantor of quality' (Heywood 2000: 247). Yet, as pointed out in Chapter 2, there is a paucity of research evidence on the effectiveness of external examiners, and what exists does not inspire confidence. Their impact is regarded as 'light touch' (Murphy 2006: 40) and unreliable (Price 2005), particularly as the system has diversified (Heywood 2000) and with modular schemes (McGhee 2003). Brown et al. (1997) comment, in their observations on quality assurance systems in universities, that the duties of external examiners and their impact on the operation of programmes varied considerably, as did mechanisms for ensuring appropriate and timely action on the recommendations in their reports. More recent evidence (QAA 2005) suggests that most UK institutions have now established sound external examining procedures in terms of appointment, induction, powers, communication and reporting of examiners, but, as with other aspects of quality assurance in higher education, these ensure the reliability of the procedure, rather than the reliability of the underlying practice (Brown and Knight 1994; Knight 1994; Brown et al. 1997).

Thus, despite overall confidence in the system, the role of external examiners needs re-evaluating and changing while the positive inputs of their work are retained. Above all, it appears necessary to retain some externality in the moderation process if we are committed to a fair and comparable system of assessment (Partington 1994; Brown et al. 1997; Biggs 2003). Biggs (2003) suggests this can be achieved by calling examiners consultants who advise universities but do not perceive their roles as simply judging students' assessments. Universities should not use external examiners as markers nor as final arbiters, and should not follow their advice slavishly where it is contrary to the philosophy of the programme. Chapter 9 elaborates on this point.

Sometimes examiners will view the work at the institution during the visit, for example where it is not suitable for posting (portfolios, exhibitions and performances).

- If a student is likely to be discussed at an assessment board, then it is helpful if the external examiner has had an opportunity to review his/her work.
- Where possible, encourage your external examiners to meet with students to hear their perspectives on the course and its assessment.
- When samples of work are sent to the external examiner, provide copies of the module outline, marking schemes and assessment criteria. Without assessment criteria, the examiner will need to create their own (if only implicitly), and these are likely to vary from the teaching team's local agreement, perhaps causing unnecessary disagreement.
- A copy of the final unconfirmed marks for all candidates should be included with all samples so that the examiner can review the overall performance of the cohort.
- If at all possible, send work in plenty of time for them to moderate it. It may be helpful to use a 'drip-feed approach' where as soon as the internal assessment of a particular module is complete, the sample should be sent to the external examiner.
- Avoid using external examiners as adjudicators of individual marks. Staff should resolve any differences of opinions, using a third marker, before submission to the examiner.
- Where external examiners are involved in visiting work-based settings used for student placements or practica, ensure that mentors/supervisors receive a briefing on the examiner's role and responsibilities.
- The main concern of the external examiner should be the assessment of the subject or programme in its entirety rather than the correction of the marks given to individual students. If a problem with marking standards is identified this should be raised with the assessment board and if necessary a scaling exercise should be undertaken to adjust the marks of all relevant work. Evidence shows that the practice of changing individual marks is fading but has not yet completely disappeared (Hannan and Silver 2004).
- Consult your external examiners when significant changes are proposed to the assessment or other elements of a module.

External examiners' reports

In the UK, external examiners submit an annual report for each award that they examine to the head of the institution, and in addition an end-of-appointment summary may be required on completion of the term of office. In the report, which should not contain the names of individual staff or students and for which a template is commonly used, comments are invited on the following:

- overall comparability of standards in relation to similar programmes in other higher education institutions;
- the quality of programme;
- the quality of assessment procedures;
- organisation and arrangements for the assessment process;
- lessons from the assessment process;
- specific recommendations;
- the extent to which issues raised previously have been addressed.

There is opportunity to submit comments in a separate confidential report if deemed necessary. The reports are a significant part of the quality assurance procedures of institutions and a formal response to the issues raised by the external examiners is often required as part of programme evaluation and action planning, although universities appear to differ in this regard (Hannan and Silver 2004).

Conclusion

This chapter has considered moderation and its important role, albeit in our collective psyche if not in substance, in safeguarding standards and creating confidence in higher education. In addition, the moderation process has the potential for a positive professional development opportunity for tutors and other markers by facilitating shared understanding of standards and debate about assessment practice. This is developed in Chapter 15. Certain aspects of moderation, particularly those focused on external accountability, have been shown to possibly mitigate against enhancement of teaching, learning and assessment.

9 Managing assessment in different roles

Introduction

Assessment is a complex enterprise involving students, tutors, managers, administrators and employers, each with a role to play in developing an effective assessment system. The diverse, sometimes conflicting, purposes of assessment can create a tension between the different responsibilities staff hold as they try to satisfy the various demands of the system. Despite the fact that assessment procedures have become tightly managed institutional processes (Crook *et al.* 2006), evidence suggests that assessment systems do not always function well, with problems such as lack of information to students on assessment matters, poor moderation, variability of standards and lack of assessment criteria (Quality Assurance Agency 2006a). In addition, although reliable procedures give the appearance of 'good order', they do not necessarily deliver good-quality assessment practice (Crook *et al.* 2006). Institutional energy has focused on equitable and consistent assessment procedures at the expense of enhancing assessment practice. The gap between procedure and practice is reflected in a conspicuous divergence between how well institutions think they do assessment and general student dissatisfaction with it (Crook *et al.* 2006).

This chapter attempts to tackle this challenge of maintaining reliable assessment procedures capable of satisfying independent scrutiny, with an emphasis on defining roles and responsibilities in the assessment system which promote good practice. It will clarify the responsibilities associated with typical roles in an accessible checklist style. Clearly there will be institutional differences in the organisation of assessment, and this chapter aims to provoke thinking about those roles as much as provide a template for management. The chapter will also debate some of the particularly difficult elements of the management of assessment.

Procedures included in an assessment system are (extended from the list in Crook *et al.* 2006: 96):

- deciding aims and outcomes;
- specifying assessments and assessment criteria;
- setting coursework assignments and examinations;
- providing information to students;

- submission of assignments and sitting of examinations;
- timing and receipt of feedback;
- making and deciding claims for mitigating (extenuating) circumstances;
- dealing with suspected malpractice in assessment;
- responsibilities of examination boards and their use of discretion;
- communication of results to students.

Promoting equity

In advance of guidance regarding different roles, it is important to briefly consider the responsibility at every level to promote equity. The QAA (2006c: 14) states that 'Institutions [should] ensure that assessment is conducted with rigour, probity and fairness'. However, promoting equity (fairness) is not a simple process of ensuring the same treatment of individuals because 'unfairness may arise from treating unequals equally as much as from treating equals unequally' (Stowell 2004). Thus it is considered equitable to make alternative assessment arrangements for students with disabilities. In general, equity in assessment is seen as having transparent and consistent assessment procedures such as those listed earlier, with the possibility of suitable reasonable adjustments for students facing unequal circumstances such as a disability, illness or personal difficulties. However, the procedures and discretion in granting adjustment must also be transparent and consistently applied. There are responsibilities at all levels of management, and the issue does not simply fall to individual tutors. This topic will be discussed in more detail in Chapter 10 on supporting diverse students.

Tutor level

Tutor responsibilities normally involve:

- adhering to institutional procedures and regulations for the conduct of assessment;
- providing reasonable help and advice to students concerning assessment;
- following departmental or institutional procedures in respect of coursework extensions and students experiencing mitigating or extenuating circumstances;
- ensuring that assessment practices promote equity in outcomes as far as possible (see Chapter 10);
- marking students' work with reference to standards, and in a timely way;

- maintaining an accurate record of student marks;
- keeping secure all assignments and examination scripts, and protecting all student data from third parties;
- being aware of the potential for academic malpractice and following institutional procedures where malpractice is suspected;
- attending examination and progression boards as required;
- referring students with difficulties to a relevant person or service (for example, student support services).

Module leader level

In addition to the responsibilities in managing assessment listed for tutors, module leader responsibility normally involves:

- drawing on subject-specific and pedagogical research in the design of assessment;
- writing assessment tasks and assessment criteria in good time to ensure that they can be shared and discussed with the teaching team, and included in module guides;
- writing module guides including information on the teaching, learning and assessment strategies used in the module (see Chapter 4 for details);
- writing examination papers in time for them to be scrutinised by the external examiner as necessary and responding to any feedback from the scrutiny;
- maintaining the security of examination papers;
- planning how the module prepares students for assessment particularly with unfamiliar assessment methods, and how it contributes to students' academic skills development;
- establishing a common view on marking standards and feedback among the module team (Price 2005), paying particular attention to training new and casual markers (Smith and Coombe 2006) (see Chapter 6);
- ensuring that assignments are marked and returned to students with feedback as swiftly as possible (within institutional guidelines if they exist) and in time to influence further module assessment;
- ensuring robust second marking/moderation of assignments (to institutional guidelines) and providing feedback on marking to the module team (see Chapter 8);
- maintaining an accurate record of student marks and grades and submitting them to the relevant administrator as directed;
- considering how students can be helped to engage with feedback;

- preparing samples of assessment for external examiners, including full mark lists and course outlines;
- retaining sample copies of student work for future use and reference;
- evaluating module assessment drawing on data from analysis of results, student feedback, the external examiner and the teaching team, and using the information to improve future practice.

Programme leader level

Carefully planned assessment systems can be largely paper exercises which have no serious effect on assessment practices and are invisible to students who experience different 'interpretations' of the system across their different modules (Knight and Yorke 2003). Individual tutors may comply with procedures but deliver their modules in ignorance (or defiance) of broader drives to create a coherent learning environment for students. Therefore the programme leader role is vital in obtaining the co-ordination necessary if we want assessment to appear to students as coherent and supportive of their learning. The following list combines aspects of culture and structure (Knight and Yorke 2003) in identifying the responsibilities of programme leaders:

- co-ordination of a programme assessment strategy, including building a shared understanding between staff regarding the purpose of assessment and planning for future enhancement (see Chapter 11);
- ensuring articulation of programme assessment standards (for example, grade descriptors by level of study – see Chapter 6);
- ensuring student induction to programme assessment *procedures*, including assignment submission, progression and award requirements, referencing and citation and procedures for claiming mitigating circumstances;
- ensuring programme-wide preparation for assessment *practices*, including good academic practice and understanding and avoiding malpractice;
- co-ordination of an assessment scheduling across the programme which spreads student and staff workloads;
- taking responsible steps to ensure that programme assessment strategy promotes equity in outcomes (see Chapter 10);
- co-ordinating the preparation, support and monitoring of placement-based assessors;
- setting programme arrangements for granting and managing extensions on coursework (within department or institutional policy);
- informal recruitment of external examiners (usually to be confirmed through institutional appointment procedures);

- providing external examiners with induction to the programme and ongoing liaison with them, particularly in relation to reviewing samples of student work (see Chapter 8);
- co-ordinating evaluation of programme assessment data, including analysis of results and module evaluations, in order to examine effectiveness of assessment in relation to intended learning outcomes, co-ordinate responses to external examiners, identify and pursue programme-wide issues, and provide information for annual programme evaluation and subject review.

Head of department level

Heads of department (and equivalent middle-management posts) clearly have an important role through their programme leaders, administrators, external examiners and chairs of examination boards in *managing* good assessment procedures. They are key figures in mediating the implementation of institutional policy in ways sympathetic to the subject discipline (Mutch and Brown 2001). Furthermore, variability in assessment arrangements across departments can provide inequitable treatment for students in the same institution, particularly those on joint or combined degree programmes (QAA 2006b). It is worth benchmarking your department's approach against institutional norms and testing whether variance is the result of legitimate disciplinary issues (for example, professional body requirements) or merely traditional custom and practice. It may be wise to appoint a senior department member as assessment officer with responsibility for managing and monitoring departmental procedures as listed earlier.

However, managing good assessment *procedures* is not a substitute for leading good assessment *practice*, as discussed in the introduction to this chapter. Mutch and Brown (2001) recommend developing a department assessment strategy, and this can contribute to ensuring quality enhancement as well as quality assurance at the department level. A department assessment strategy might include:

- setting any institutional assessment strategy within the context of your academic subject, for example identifying which are the priority areas for your discipline;
- ensuring staff are inducted into, and maintain, appropriate standards for setting and marking assessment across the department;
- using department meetings or away-days to discuss assessment issues; consider having a departmental 'assessment forum';
- auditing the range and appropriateness of assessment methods used in the department (Rust 2002);

- ensuring that programme and module evaluation and staff–student liaison groups capture, analyse and respond to student views on assessment;
- providing opportunities for staff to deepen their understanding of assessment and providing visible support for staff who are trying to develop their assessment practice;
- ensuring that assessment strategies in the department promote equity in outcomes as far as possible and monitoring the progress of students by ethnic group (Commission for Racial Equality 2002);
- managing departmental procedures for dealing with suspected malpractice.

Chairs of assessment boards

Stowell (2004) points out that although there is increasing pressure to demonstrate transparency and comparability of standards within and across higher education, there is still potential for considerable discretion and concealment in the confidential proceedings of examination boards. She sets out two ideal-type approaches to academic standards, equity and justice: a 'professional judgement' approach and an 'outcomes' approach.

The professional judgement approach emphasises drawing on the experience and subject expertise of the board of examiners in order to exercise discretion, for example in **condonement** and **compensation** decisions and agreeing the award of borderline cases. It involves staff at examination boards acting as advocates for students whose circumstances they know. Judgement of overall worth (degree classification) is based mainly, but not exclusively, on students' assessment outcomes. Stowell argues that this approach makes it difficult to ensure equitable treatment for all students as some students may be better 'represented' than others, the information used is inherently unreliable, and some tutors can make a student's case more effectively than others.

The outcomes approach is characterised by the examination board focusing on the standard application of regulations and conventions. 'Individual candidates either meet the criteria for progression or for a particular award, or they do not' (Stowell 2004: 505). Applications for mitigating circumstances are usually decided by an independent panel and, where accepted, are only grounds for a second opportunity to complete the assessment. Where discretion is applied, it is regulated by a clear set of rules rather than professional judgement or knowledge of the student. The second approach facilitates equity in the treatment of students.

In the UK, the QAA Code of Practice on assessment (QAA 2006c) clearly favours the 'outcomes' approach, recommending that members of assessment boards should declare any 'personal interest, involvement or relationship with a student being assessed' and noting that, in some institutions, equity of treatment is protected by not disclosing student identities at assessment boards. They also recommend that institutions consider providing guidance on the exercise of discretion in relation to borderline cases and mitigating circumstances.

This is an interesting and complex area for discussion, but, for the purposes of this brief guide, it is important that as chair of an assessment board you are clear on your own institutional policies and practice in this regard, particularly as adopting an outcomes approach is not always popular with academic staff who see it as undermining their professional judgement (Stowell 2004).

Some guidelines for good management of assessment boards include the following:

- Where there are different levels of boards (for example, module assessment boards and programme assessment boards, or departmental boards and faculty boards), you need to ensure that you are aware of the relevant responsibilities of each board: for example, does a module assessment board have any discretion to adjust borderline marks?
- Good communication and planning with relevant programme or module leaders, administrators and academic registry.
- Draft an agenda well in advance and circulate it to ensure all relevant courses and other matters are included.
- Carry out a pre-board scrutiny to check all marks are available or reasons are provided for gaps in mark lists. Discuss any regulatory matters or difficult student issues with your academic registry.
- Check that information is available regarding mitigating circumstances (this may be part of your board's procedure or may have been dealt with by an independent group).
- Ensure you are aware of the relevant regulations and rules for exercising discretion (have copies to hand for reference and for more complicated cases).
- Make sure board members, particularly external examiners, sign relevant documents before they leave the room.
- Ensure the safe return or disposal of all confidential documentation.

Institutional leadership

Many of the shortcomings identified in the QAA (2006a) review related to institutional approaches to assessment arrangements and policies, and senior managers could do worse than test existing approaches against the revised UK QAA (2006c) code of practice for assessment. Yorke (2001a) recommends a series of questions that senior managers should reflect on in order to test the efficacy and robustness of their assessment systems and their responsiveness to national and international developments in the field.

Development of policy and regulations must embrace both assessment *of* learning and assessment *for* learning (see Chapter 2). Senior managers should also be aware of the tension between seamlessly managed assessment procedures and good assessment practice. Policies and procedures may actually work against assessment enhancement (Biggs 2002). Here are examples related to feedback:

- Feedback given at the draft stage of an assignment may have significantly more impact on learning than feedback on summative work. However, if the institution judges quality by significant feedback on the cover sheets of summative coursework, staff will direct their efforts to that end.
- Timely feedback is extremely important, but this aim is thwarted if your regulations do not permit the release of marks and feedback until after the examination board.

Appoint external examiners as consultants, not as final arbiters. Be prepared to listen to their advice but do not require your departments to follow it slavishly if they can provide a reasoned response for not doing so. Your tutors may be better informed about effective assessment than an individual examiner who is basing decisions on tradition rather than research evidence.

Chapter 3 set out a number of the conflicts in managing the different purposes of assessment, balancing 'certification of students' and 'quality assurance' with 'student learning'. Institutional managers will be tempted to privilege the first two at the expense of the last in order to demonstrate robust standards to the wider community. However, perhaps your most important stakeholders in assessment are students themselves, and they are not currently giving a strong vote of approval to university assessment arrangements (Crook *et al.* 2006; National Student Survey 2006). Listen to what they have to say about assessment.

Institutional approaches to plagiarism

The changing context for plagiarism creates a need for a holistic institutional response which balances consistent and fair treatment of suspected students with methods to prevent it in the first place (Park 2003). Such institutional strategies should include ensuring students are helped to acquire academic conventions, skills and integrity; providing staff development in support of deterring plagiarism; creating consistent decision-making procedures for malpractice cases; and collecting evidence on the incidence of plagiarism and its detection in the institution (MacDonald and Carroll 2006). While institutional leadership is required, there is a role in plagiarism prevention and detection for all levels of staff. Chapter 4 provides guidance on designing assessment to avoid plagiarism, and Chapter 5 outlines how students can be helped to avoid it.

A note on data protection

Data protection legislation seeks to provide the individual with a degree of control over the use of their personal data and has a number of implications for assessment practice in universities. In order to alert staff to the issue, some key rules and considerations are briefly set out here, but we strongly recommend that all staff who manage assessment are trained to understand and implement the key principles as set out in the JISC (2001) Data Protection Code of Practice. This includes placement-based assessors. The following are précised from that guide by way of an introduction only:

- With the exception of examination scripts, all personal data related to assessment may be obtained by the student.
- Internal and external examiners' comments, written on scripts or separately, must be made available to students 'in intelligible form' if requested. Comments should be both intelligible and appropriate – so writing 'this is rubbish', while tempting, is not appropriate. We suggest that comments should be directed clearly towards assessment criteria.
- Institutions should consider how the recording of internal examiners' comments could be made more appropriate for students (for example, tear-off comment sheets in examination script booklets).
- Where universities use assessment or classification and grading systems which are based entirely on automated means, they should provide a formal statement that explains the logic behind that assessment or system.
- Students may have access to minutes of examination boards and boards considering applications for 'mitigating circumstances' that contain discussion about them if they are named or other information by which they can be identified (for example, student number) is included. Such documents can be exempt if they cannot be disclosed without disclosing information about a third party. However, this can usually be done by erasing names of third parties.
- Students' results should not be disclosed to third parties, including

fellow students, employers or parents. This may be problematic for some institutions which have an obligation to publish results. JISC suggests that local, limited publishing of results may be acceptable but suggests using personal identifiers rather than names. It states that institutions should explain how results will be published and provide a mechanism so that students can exercise their right not to have their results published. Results should not be displayed outside the local area or on the internet and they should not be passed to third parties without the consent of the student.

- Universities should not withhold results from candidates who are in debt to the institution.
- Personal data should be kept secure at all times. This is of particular concern when personal data are taken offsite, for example, on a laptop. Staff should be aware of the importance of good security in these circumstances.
- Secure transfer of personal information is also important. Normal e-mail communication does not usually offer sufficient security.

Conclusion

Assessment features high in the range of responsibilities resting on academic staff in different roles. This chapter has outlined the scope of those responsibilities which span tasks that support all the purposes of assessment. Information has been provided by job role (tutor, module leader, programme leader, and head of department), which includes responsibilities related to quality assurance, certification of students, enhancing student learning and lifelong learning. Clearly institutional roles and responsibilities will vary considerably, and this chapter aims to provoke thinking about roles and responsibilities in your particular context rather than provide a template for management of assessment.

10 Supporting widening participation through assessment

Introduction

There has been a considerable increase in participation in higher education in recent years, leading to a more diverse student population. While evidence suggests that promoting diversity has benefits for all students' academic and social growth (Gurin *et al.* 2002), this change is also producing powerful challenges to teaching and learning in universities because of students' levels of preparedness and expectations (Northedge 2003a; Murphy 2006).

We are defining diversity and diverse learners broadly to include all those categories of people who are under-represented in higher education. This will, of course, differ by institution and local context, but might include factors such as age, gender, ethnic group, socio-economic background and disability, and includes international and non-English-speaking students and those in rural and isolated areas.

McDowell and Sambell (2005) warn us that experience of assessment does not differ markedly between non-traditional and traditional students and that we should avoid thinking of them as 'problem' cases or groups. Similarly Haggis's (2006) research with access students suggests that there are strong individual differences concealed within these groups and we should resist the temptation to only think about such students in stereotypical ways. An alternative method would be to develop assessment strategies based on individual difference, but this is not feasible. A third approach is to adopt an inclusive approach to assessment practice which provides for all, but reflects the particular needs of specific groups (Robson 2005). That is the approach adopted here. The chapter begins by briefly reviewing evidence about the achievement and retention of under-represented groups, examining particular assessment strategies, followed by more detailed discussion and practical advice in relation to specific groups.

Widening participation, retention and achievement

Widening participation is concerned with both access to, and achievement within, higher education of people from under-represented groups. In general, research on identifying the causes of failure and attrition is inconclusive and we lack detailed evidence of who drops out (Johnson *et al.* 2003), although the majority who leave do so in their first year (Yorke 2001b). Taken as a whole, there is a strong relationship between the characteristics of students on entry and non-completion rates (Yorke and Longden 2004). The results of studies conflict (Johnson *et al.* 2003), which suggests that factors are specific to institutions and might be related to location, courses, student characteristics and other features. Failure to cope with academic demands, lack of familiarity with university life and difficulty adjusting to the middle-class culture of university are among reasons cited for withdrawal (Yorke 1999; Forsyth and Furlong 2000; Davies and Elias 2003; Yorke and Longden 2004).

There is a growing body of evidence regarding successful strategies to improve student outcomes and increase retention (Leach and Zepke 2005). Interventions have generally focused on the academic and social integration of the student (Tinto 1993), with both UK and international studies revealing consistent findings (Higher Education Funding Council for England (HEFCE) 2002). Successful strategies are those that increase students' personal networks, contact with tutors and sense of belonging. Retention is also enhanced by accessible and comprehensive pre-enrolment and academic advice, student satisfaction with the institution, and a student focus in teaching practices. Furthermore, induction activities which develop appropriate expectations and skills for higher education study and assessment are linked to positive outcomes (Abramson and Jones 2003; Rust *et al.* 2003). In relation to assessment, academic difficulty – including problems with the first assignment – is associated with attrition (Krause, 2001). Evidence suggests that formative assessment in the early stages of a programme assists retention (Yorke 2001b; Yorke and Longden 2004). Experience of assignments on pre-university courses may have been very different and may not have prepared students well for higher education assessment.

Most retention strategies focus on:

- sorting (recruitment and admissions);
- connecting (fostering relationships between students and the institution);
- supporting (students' lives outside the university – finance, childcare, counselling) (Johnson 2001)

(see Beatty-Guenter 1994).

These are relatively easy to instigate, usually involving largely admissions and support staff and a short time frame. However, this assimilationist approach is criticised as negating rather than valuing the students' existing identity and culture and not investigating the interaction between student and the institution (Tierney 2000; Johnson 2001; Thomas 2002; Haggis 2004; Leach and Zepke 2005).

Alternative 'transformative' (Beatty-Guenter 1994) or 'adaptive' (Leach and Zepke 2005) interventions involve changing fundamental institutional practices; these are difficult to implement and take time to deliver results (Johnson 2001). They require improvements to all aspects of teaching and learning and the working environment in order to develop a student-focused approach. This approach requires change by academic staff (Blythman and Orr 2002) rather than focusing on student support or personal tutoring (Johnson 2001) and is being addressed by approaches such as 'first-year experience' initiatives.

Minor and manageable improvements to assessment practice do have a valuable part to play in improving equity of outcomes for under-represented groups, and the following sections will identify a number of practicable strategies. Ideally, they should contribute to a more strategic institutional approach to promoting and catering for increased student diversity.

Using assessment to support retention and achievement

Preparation

Diversity of students means that prior assumptions about their readiness for higher education cannot be taken for granted (Gibbs and Simpson 2004–5). Thorough preparation for assessment is important, including helping students to understand expectations of university writing, developing academic skills, and understanding assessment criteria. The evidence for this and practical ways to involve students are set out in Chapter 5.

Scheduling assessment and reassessment

Early assignments are helpful in integrating students into academic life and good study habits (Cook *et al.* 2005). Box 10.1 provides some leads in the significance of early experiences. The freedom of university life in comparison with the structured assessment demands of school or further education can be difficult for some students to cope with (Krause 2001) and they will benefit from a well-designed transitional period. Scheduling assessment to allow formative feedback at a point where students can respond to it before their next assignment is important. In general, it is better to avoid summative assessment at an early point in courses (Yorke 2001b) and therefore some universities are running year-long modules in year 1 with limited summative assessment in the first semester. An alternative approach has been taken in an

---

Box 10.1 Believing that students can succeed

Boud (2000) stresses the importance of communicating positive expectations to students. Tutor belief in students' ability to develop through their efforts rather than innate ability is important (Yorke and Knight 2004; see Box 7.1), and assessment design has a part to play in this. One course used negative marking with first-term modern language students, deducting a mark for every mistake on a short essay. It was very easy for students to obtain fail marks, particularly if they tried to use more complex constructions but did not get them quite right. This assessment method worked against risk taking on the part of the students and quickly made even well-qualified ones feel that they were not up to the demands of the course. Consider how your early assessment opportunities build in a belief that success is possible and in the control of the student.

---

experiment at the University of Wolverhampton (McLaughlin and Sutton 2005). Examinations in the first semester were replaced with slightly earlier 'informal' assessment followed by timetabled feedback sessions. Failing students then took resits two weeks later. This has led to enhanced retention which staff think resulted from a early opportunity to recoup failure supported by feedback and a greater involvement of students in the learning process. Student engagement may also be enhanced by allocating some marks to class participation, as described in Dunn *et al.* (2004). See Chapter 4 for a discussion about scheduling of assessment on your modules.

Formative and peer assessment

Discussion in Chapters 2, 4 and 7 highlight the importance of formative assessment and the use of feedback to improve student achievement. A key guideline from the Student Transition and Retention Project is that 'students should receive regular, formative evaluations of their work early in their course' (Cook *et al.* 2005: 4). Consistent evidence shows formative assessment in programmes will have particular benefits for low attainers and disadvantaged learners (Black and Wiliam 1998a). Peer assessment has specific advantages in helping students understand what they should be aiming for in their assignments. In this way staff can help to provide a supportive learning environment for students where they can 'safely' develop the practices of their discipline (Lawrence 2005). Chapter 4 discusses how to use peer assessment, and Chapter 7 provides information on effective use of feedback and formative assessment.

Group assessments

Social integration and developing a sense of 'belonging' to the course and institution can be assisted by the use of group assessments. These require students to meet (if only virtually) and work collaboratively outside of timetabled sessions, and this can facilitate social relationships and motivation (Volet and Mansfield 2006) as well as discussion of course matters. Group tasks can quickly help to build group cohesion, and provide an informal opportunity for students to teach each other sympathetically. Lejk *et al.* (1999) found that lower-ability students did better in examinations after participating in a mixed-ability group assessment. However, group assessments can go wrong, and Chapter 4 discusses how to prepare students for them.

Intervention in the case of learning difficulties and academic failure

Cooke *et al.* (2005) recommend that student retention is helped by early recognition of students with difficulties and referral to support services as appropriate. This is easier to do if there has been some early diagnostic assessment. It also means that students can receive help before the marks begin to count. Monitoring late and non-submitted work and instituting early, supportive intervention are also important.

Cultivating awareness and use of support services

Research suggests that students are not always aware of the central support services that are available to them (Dhimar and Ashworth 2005), for example to improve their information literacy or enhance their use of English or academic writing skills. Academic staff should build a partnership with such services to support their teaching (Lawrence 2005) and to increase students' awareness of provision. Chapter 5 suggests ways that you can integrate central services into your teaching.

Equal opportunities in assessment practice

There is an overriding concern among policy makers to enhance the record of higher education in promoting equal opportunities (Northedge, 2003b; CRE 2006; HEFCE 2006). Nevertheless, in the UK, black students are heavily over-represented among those who leave early (Connor *et al.* 2003). Legislation exists requiring universities to promote race equality and it is being extended to promoting equality on the grounds of gender and disability (Northedge 2003b). Assessment should encourage students to achieve by celebrating diversity and difference, demonstrating how these differences enrich their academic work. This section provides some practical examples for both ensuring that assessment arrangements do not advantage any one student over another and for actively promoting equality. It is followed by more detailed advice on assessment issues involving disability and race in particular.

Individual differences

Individual differences in students can be the result of many different factors in addition to their cognitive ability on arriving at university. Differences may result from their previous experience of education; their perception of the learning situation; their family and ethnic background; a learning or other disability; having English as an additional language; gender; and age. The purpose of paying attention to equity in assessment is to ensure that students enjoy an equal opportunity to effectively demonstrate their learning; the medium of assessment should aim to reduce as far as possible elements of discrimination.

Range of assessment tasks

There is no doubt that different styles and formats of assessment will advantage some students in relation to others. For example, some students have difficulty expressing themselves in written form, whereas others find the prospect of presentations terrifying. Some students struggle with group tasks, whereas others will thrive (Volet and Mansfield 2006). Some students benefit from the tension and adrenalin of examinations, whereas others become frozen by the anxiety they provoke. 'Unfortunately, there is no known assessment which suits everybody (including the assessor). The simple answer to this problem is to utilise a diversity of assessment techniques wherever possible' (King, n.d.).

Robson (2005: 86) argues that as well as offering variety of assessment across a programme, students could be presented with a choice of ways to complete an individual assignment: 'same assessment, different process'. She suggests that genuine alternatives assess the same learning outcomes but allow students to demonstrate their learning in ways that suit their preferences. This is quite a daunting idea for many tutors because of the logistics involved. In addition, such an approach requires absolute clarity about what learning outcomes should be assessed, and quality assurance demands consistent and comparable assessment across all students on the programme.

On the other hand, concerns about providing reasonable adjustments for disabled students (see later) can be dealt with in this manner without singling out such students for special treatment. There are many different potential methods of assessing (see Chapter 13), particularly if you are prepared to draw from other disciplines (Robson 2005), and Robson suggests piloting alternatives as a first stage. Clarity of learning outcomes is essential – for example, if you normally use an essay, you might consider whether clear, grammatical, written English prose is one of your outcomes or whether your emphasis is on knowledge of the subject, argument and examining different points of view. If the latter is the case, then perhaps a web page, oral presentation or poster could be offered as a different choice.

Access to resources

Staff should reassure themselves that students have equal access to sufficient resources – for example, computers, reading material and equipment – to complete the assessment tasks. If students are expected to participate in an online discussion, can a wheelchair user gain access to the computer centre, is the desk height suitable, can arrangements be made for a visually impaired student to use assistive software to read other participants' comments? If a student is working in an additional language, will support be available to enable them to access the meaning of the text?

Similarly, care needs to be taken to offer equal opportunities to students with specific learning difficulties. Assignment questions, guidance and criteria should be written in clear English. Over-long sentences should be avoided.

If you are prepared to give students tutorials during the preparation stage of an assessment, all students should know that that resource is available to them. You need to consider whether full-time students are advantaged compared to part-time or distance students in, for example, access to learning resources or tutors. If students are speakers of English as an additional language, then it is important that they receive a written record of the tutorial so that they can refer to this later.

See the next section on assessing disabled students for a discussion about the provision of additional or different resources to enable students with disabilities to fairly demonstrate their learning.

Inclusive assessment tasks

In addition to the choice of assessment method and access to resources, staff can contribute to equal assessment opportunities by considering the content and context of their assessments. For example, do your tasks and case studies:

- reflect the multi-cultural nature of our community;
- avoid placing people in stereotypical roles;
- include positive images of different cultures and backgrounds;

- show members of different communities and disabled people carrying out a full range of roles and behaviours;
- reflect the contents of the module that has been followed?

Good, timely assessment information

All students are assisted by the provision of good and timely assessment information. See Chapter 4 for a checklist. Students with disabilities may need more time, or need to make extra arrangements in relation to assessment. Part-time students may need to prepare well in advance to fit their studies around work obligations. International students may wish to examine the assessment criteria very carefully to ensure they understand what is needed of them in the UK context. Therefore, thorough, advance information helps all students in their planning and organisation and reinforces the idea that good assessment practice is also inclusive assessment practice.

Marking

Anonymous marking is an aid to avoiding bias in marking for whatever reason, conscious or unconscious. See Chapter 6 for advice on consistency in marking.

Prejudice in peer and self-assessment

There is a lack of conclusive evidence about whether peer and self-assessment is affected by factors such as race, age or gender (Falchikov 2005). Chapter 4 provides advice on promoting fairness in peer and self-assessment.

Assessing disabled students and those with specific learning difficulties

We are defining disability broadly to include mobility impairments, sensory impairments, medical conditions, mental health conditions and specific learning difficulties such as dyslexia. The term 'disabled students' is used throughout to include all those within the above definition.

The essence of this section is to show how we can ensure that we do not discriminate against disabled students in the assessment process. The UK's Quality Assurance Agency (1999: 17) states that 'Assessment and examination policies, practices and procedures should provide disabled students with the same opportunity as their peers to demonstrate the achievement of learning outcomes'.

Learning outcomes

When determining your learning outcomes for a programme or module, take care to ensure that they do not unnecessarily present barriers to disabled students. The following example is taken from the UK Disability Rights Commission Code of Practice for providers of post-16 education (2002: Section 6.3):

> A student with a speech impairment is on a Hotel and Tourism course. Part of the assessment relates to customer service. The assessment usually considers a number of factors including the verbal fluency of each candidate, and on grounds of academic standards, the department refuses to make any changes to the assessment practice. However, fluency is not an essential element of customer service, it is simply an aspect that the assessment to this course habitually takes into account. It is likely to be reasonable, therefore, to make an adjustment that allows the student to show his customer service and conversational skills without demonstrating verbal fluency.

This is a challenging example at first sight. However, consideration of successful teachers and other professionals with speech impairments indicates that it is probably the quality of service and communication skills which should feature in the learning outcomes rather than verbal fluency. The assessment should attempt to measure those achievements.

Reasonable adjustments and academic standards

In the UK, the Special Educational Needs and Disability Act 2001 (SENDA) makes discrimination against disabled students illegal. The Act places a legal obligation on all higher education institutions (HEIs) to make 'reasonable adjustments' for disabled students. The Act also requires HEIs to anticipate 'reasonable adjustments'. This means that we should consider what adjustments future disabled students may need when developing assessment methods.

Maintenance of academic standards is paramount and protected within UK legislation. Offering reasonable adjustments does not mean changing or lowering academic standards to accommodate disabled students, it means designing assessment so that disabled students have an equal opportunity to demonstrate their learning. Where existing methods do not meet this criterion, it is important to consider how to adjust the assessment process so that disabled students still have an equal opportunity to demonstrate their learning. In some cases creating equality of opportunity may require an alternative assessment, as compensation for a difference in skill. The following example of an alternative assessment is provided by the South West Academic Network for Disability Support (1999–2002):

> An arts and humanities student with cerebral palsy is required to complete an 8000 word dissertation. An alternative assessment method was suggested: the student submitted a collection of audio tapes containing research and interviews on the subject. The assignment was passed. The student reported that they had to spend a significant amount of time on the project.

In practice, as the number of disabled students grows, the practice of making individual examination arrangements is no longer manageable, nor founded in evidence of effectiveness (South West Academic Network for Disability Support 1999–2002). Furthermore, disabled students themselves, while appreciating special arrangements, are also ambivalent about them (Higher Education Academy 2006: 10). A different approach to providing fair opportunities for disabled students is that discussed earlier of providing a choice of alternative assessments (South West Academic Network for Disability Support 1999–2002; Robson 2005). This sort of flexibility may be particularly important in relation to aspects of fieldwork and practical activities which may be inaccessible to students with certain disabilities.

Professional courses

In the case of professional programmes (such as nursing, occupational therapy, social work), there is an overriding requirement that students demonstrate that they meet all the professional standards associated with the award. For example, in teacher education in England and Wales, there is a requirement that all entrants to courses must be able to communicate clearly and grammatically in spoken and written English, and, where appropriate, Welsh:

> It is essential that where a candidate has a specific learning difficulty (such as dyslexia), this should not interfere with the candidate's ability to teach effectively and to secure effective learning in the written work of their pupils or trainees. The onus is on the candidates to prove that their condition does not limit their capacity to teach.
> (Department for Education and Skills 1999: Section C.1.2.)

Reasonable adjustments may be made to assessments to enable students to demonstrate that they have met these professional requirements. However, the professional requirements themselves cannot be changed. Consequently, at the admissions stage, clear information, in general terms, should be provided to all candidates on the professional requirements that they will need to satisfy.

Assessment information

As discussed earlier in this chapter, good and timely assessment information is vital. All students should be aware of the procedures for requesting modifications to assessment (for example, use of a computer in examinations), and this should be included in your module handbook. These arrangements can take time to organise, so tutors have an important role in reminding and supporting students to act promptly.

Talking with disabled students

Staff should not assume that students with the same disability have similar needs. Disabled students can usually advise tutors about the best way to support them. In addition, early communication between disabled students and tutors is likely to lead to positive solutions to assessment issues rather than less satisfactory, reactive solutions. Make links with your institution's disability advisory service to gain practical help and advice in managing the assessment of disabled students.

There may be occasions when offering a disabled student additional time to complete an assignment is a reasonable adjustment. See Chapter 4 for advice on giving coursework extensions.

Identifying reading material

Finding and selecting texts suitable for an assessment may be very difficult for students who have difficulty manoeuvring around a library or speed-reading contents pages in order to check if a text is useful. Tutors can help by identifying key texts (books, articles, web pages, etc.) suitable for an assignment. However, higher education requires students to demonstrate independent research and study skills, including breadth of reading. Tutors can help disabled students by allowing adequate time and encouraging them to make use of support staff in the library.

Assessment venues

Many of the responsibilities for the accessibility and suitability of assessment venues will be not be held by individual tutors. However, you are likely to be able to support your students and avoid problems by alerting the examination office (or equivalent) to the needs of your students.

Understanding and responding to the task

Some disabled students may need to have the assessment task presented to them using alternative means, for example in braille, in large print, on a pre-recorded CD or in sign language. Some disabled students may need to respond to the task in a different way, for example by recording their answers, or by using an amanuensis who will transcribe dictated responses. Your student support service or examinations office should provide support in cases of this nature.

Group-work assessments

Group-work assignments can produce difficulties for students with disabilities. For example, a student with hearing impairment may find it particularly difficult to participate in group discussions where people tend to talk over each other. Tutors should talk through with groups and the disabled person any practical difficulties that may arise because of an individual's disability and plan appropriate adjustments. It is important to consider issues of disclosure – for example, tutors should gain a student's permission before disclosing their disability to other members of the group.

Marking the work of disabled students

Some institutions make allowances in marking for disabled students – for example, providing relevant students with 'dyslexia stickers' which they can attach to examinations to instruct the marker not to deduct marks for technical errors such as spelling, grammar and punctuation.

Our view is that marking of all assessment, including examinations, should reflect the learning outcomes for the work and the assessment criteria and marking scheme. Thus, in order to maintain academic standards, marking should not be adjusted for disabled students. Reasonable adjustments should be made, as necessary, at the stage of setting and completing the assessment task or examination.

This approach does require tutors to work out exactly what the learning outcomes are for each assignment and ensure that the assessment criteria reflect them. For example, when using an examination, you may want to put more emphasis on knowledge and understanding than accurate literacy skills. The latter may be better assessed in coursework which allows disabled students to demonstrate their skills with reasonable adjustments in place. If the ability to demonstrate accuracy in written English under time pressure is a legitimate learning outcome for your course, then an examination with literacy skills as an assessment criterion may be fair and appropriate.

Efforts should be made to ensure that disabled students enjoy the same level of anonymity of marking as other students. This may be difficult if their work is presented in a different format. Tutors should ensure that work of this nature is always blind double marked by a second tutor to reduce the possibility of bias.

Conclusion and further resources

There are many useful resources for helping staff develop accessible assessments such as those provided by the Disability Rights Commission (2002) and South West Academic Network for Disability Support (1999–2002). These summarise issues related to assessing disabled students as well as providing many practical examples to illustrate their advice. An example of guidance from a professional body regarding assessment and disabled students can be found in Teacher Development Agency (2004). Your institution is likely to have dedicated advisers who can provide additional advice and support to both students and staff on this matter.

Assessment and promoting race equality

In the UK, the Race Relations (Amendment) Act 2000 makes it unlawful to discriminate against anyone on grounds of race, colour, nationality (including citizenship), and ethnic or national origin. The law also imposes general duties on many public authorities including HEIs to promote racial equality. This section considers the implications for higher education assessment.

Assessment may involve formal tests and examinations which are externally set. However, it is usually the case in higher education that assessment involves subjective evaluations, and this context makes care with regard to discrimination particularly important. The UK Commission for Racial Equality's Education Code of Practice for Scotland (2005b) states that direct discrimination will occur if students are given lower assessments on racial grounds:

> Such discrimination may arise not just from overt prejudice, but from unconscious assumptions about the relative abilities and characteristics of different racial groups. Indirect discrimination in assessment will occur if the assessment criteria or procedures applied are culturally biased and result in lower assessments being given to a considerably higher proportion of ... students from particular racial groups, and those criteria cannot be justified on educational grounds. Culturally biased assessment criteria are those that assume a uniformity in ... [students'] cultural, linguistic, religious and lifestyle experiences.

Therefore it is important that tutors pay attention to the nature of the assessment methods, but it is also necessary to monitor student outcomes in order to check for unintended racial bias.

A further assessment-related problem faced by minority students is the lack of cultural awareness of staff, which impacts on the consistency of decisions regarding extenuating circumstances and appeals. For example, cultural and religious practices, such as mourning rituals or family demands, may impact on student lives differentially by ethnic group (Dhimar and Ashworth 2005).

International students

International students are an important element of student diversity. While much of the above relates equally to international students, there are several additional factors worth considering in relation to assessment. International students generally have more difficulty adjusting to the demands of university than home students, with academic problems centred on language difficulties and success correlated with better writing skills (Andrade 2006). Studies of international students recommend making tutor expectations clear and providing model answers (Lee 1997). The latter may be particularly important if they are faced with unfamiliar types of assignment. Clear language in assessment questions is very important. In addition, relationships with home students contribute towards higher achievement and better adjustment (Lacina 2002) and therefore mixing international and home students in assessment groups may be helpful. It is important to encourage students to take advantage of any intensive English tuition available in the institution.

Cultural bias in assessment methods

There is limited research on the cultural bias in assessment methods, but there is evidence that different types of assignment or examination differentially impact on international students' ability to demonstrate their learning. De Vita (2002) found that examinations tend to penalise international students beyond differences in their actual ability as shown in other forms of assessment such as coursework assignments or multiple choice tests. International students, in each examination, are faced with a test of their English as well as a test of their ability in the subject. Likewise time limits, for example on multiple choice tests, may disadvantage international students. Their lower marks may not be an indication of ability but merely of difficulty finishing in the specified time. De Vita makes the point that MCQs are not usually piloted on groups that include international students and therefore the times set are too short. In general, he does not recommend assessments completed under timed conditions, certainly as the exclusive form of assessment for a module.

Advice for promoting race equality and countering cultural bias

The Codes of Practice for implementing the Race Relations (Amendment) Act 2000 (CRE 2005a, 2005b) can be viewed at the Commission for Racial Equality's website: www.cre.gov.uk/gdpract/.html. Additional ideas include the following:

- Consider how your assessment methods might disadvantage students from different linguistic and cultural backgrounds. Are you relying heavily on examinations and timed assignments?
- Provide exemplars of different types of assignment and model answers, where appropriate, to help students gain an understanding of expectations. Non-native speakers may need explicit tuition in the nature of the writing that you expect.
- Make sure assessment criteria are clearly published and use activities to help students understand them, particularly concepts such as critical thinking (see Chapter 5 for practical activities).
- Clarify your expectations in the teaching team regarding poor use of English. Include this in published assessment criteria for students.
- Consider how you allocate students to assessment groups. Same-language or same-ethnicity groups may enable them to communicate more effectively as a team, but mixed groups are likely to increase achievement and adjustment to university. You may need to decide what your priority is at any given time in a programme.
- Plagiarism and malpractice advice is very important for students from other education systems (see Chapter 5).
- Take care to demonstrate consistently high expectations of all your students.
- Does your department have a procedure for checking that assessment tasks and methods are not culturally biased? Do you monitor achievement on your modules or programmes to consider whether it is good for all students? If some groups perform less well than others, are you investigating the causes?
- Use responses from students such as course consultative committees and module evaluation to identify the needs of ethnic minority and international students in relation to assessment.
- Ensure that formal assessments (presentations, examinations) do not fall on religious holidays.
- In planning group assessments and peer marking, prepare all the students to take a positive approach to ethnic difference and cultural

diversity. Develop and practise using clear assessment criteria with the students to reduce the risk of discrimination in marking.

Conclusion

This chapter has considered assessment issues from the perspective of widening participation and the diversity of students in higher education. It has examined how principles of equal opportunity should be applied to the assessment process and developed this, in particular, in relation to disability and race. Practical ideas and strategies are presented for working with increasing numbers of students whose prior educational experience has not prepared them fully for the experience of higher education. In general, the chapter has built on other parts of this book in stressing the importance of clear and timely assessment information, the careful preparation and support of students and attention to assessment design.

PART 3
DEVELOPING ASSESSMENT

11 Planning a programme assessment strategy

The importance of a programme approach

Generally, assessment methods have been determined at the **credit level** of module or unit of study, perhaps with an element of overarching guidance regarding factors such as the volume of assessment or the requirement for examinations. This chapter takes as its basic premise that such a fragmented approach will not serve the needs of modern higher education nor provide for the assessment of the broader capabilities expected of the modern graduate. We are using the term 'programme' to refer to 'an approved curriculum followed by a registered student. This will normally be a named award' (Quality Assurance Agency 2006e). The chapter will set out the rationale for a programme approach, followed by comprehensive advice on building a programme assessment strategy.

There are four key motives for a strategic approach across a programme. First, the learning outcomes of undergraduate courses are now more varied (Bowden and Marton 1998), involving not only knowledge and cognitive skills but also practical skills and generic attributes, including a stress on developing employability (see Box 11.1). Many of these are complex achievements (Knight and Yorke 2003) that cannot typically be assessed in one module, but represent a combination of different capabilities. In addition, a demand for reliability requires that repeat assessment of essential components in different contexts is needed in order to have a level of faith in the award. For example, successful application of a key concept in one assignment does not give confidence in students' ability to repeat the achievement in a range of other situations.

Second, a programme approach provides for progression. Students are often asked to do similar assignments at every level without clarity about how they should differ across the programme. What is the difference between a year 1 presentation and a year 3 presentation? How will a laboratory report in year 2 be qualitatively different from a laboratory report in year 1? It is only by surveying the use of assessment across a programme that we can identify how the assessment requires progressively more from students both in terms of breadth and depth, and this is particularly important on modular and **interdisciplinary** programmes.

Third, much of this book has stressed the importance of assessment *for* learning as well as assessment *of* learning. While both demand a stress on valid assessment, the former places greater emphasis on effectiveness, practicability and transparency, whereas the latter accentuates reliability, attribution and comparability (see Chapter 3 for discussion). One cannot expect individual modules to fully embrace all of these principles. Methods such as group, peer and self-assessment will always provoke concerns (perhaps unjustly) about reliability and fairness, and it is impossible to guarantee that some students will not be freeloaders on occasions. However, such approaches can promote learning which is difficult, if not impossible, by other methods. Therefore it is essential that they are used strategically within the overall assessment for a programme. For example, this means designing a programme so that group or peer assessment may provide a significant proportion of the marks for a particular module, but only contributes a small proportion of the marks in any given year.

Lastly, in Chapter 5, we stress the importance of preparing students for assessment. Individual module tutors will always have a role to play in preparing students for specific assignments, but an efficient approach will avoid duplication by identifying particular modules which take responsibility for this general preparation. In addition, a programme approach can ensure that students experience increasingly more demanding opportunities to develop the skills of evaluation and judgement needed for lifelong learning.

In summary, a programme approach is an opportunity to ensure that assessment across the course is fit for purpose in relation to the programme aim and learning outcomes and provides for a reliable and valid grading of the award. Above all, it recognises that assessment is problematic and that a programme-wide approach can draw on different assessment methods to meet different assessment purposes.

Validation

An ideal time to consider the assessment strategy of a programme is when it is introduced or revised. Most English-speaking higher education institutions employ a procedure for the approval of programmes of study which we will refer to here as 'validation'. Indeed, the globalisation of higher education will probably increase pressure for effective and reliable programme validation procedures which provide indicators of quality and standards both nationally and internationally. Although validation of a programme provides an excellent opportunity for academic enhancement, programme teams can be tempted to treat revalidation as merely tinkering with existing practice. Conversely, it can be perceived as a creative opportunity to review practice in the light of evaluation, new developments in the discipline and pedagogical research. Above all, it is a chance to shift the planning of assessment from the module to the programme level. Validation will normally require a description of the programme, including how the learning outcomes will be assessed. In the UK, this document is known as the 'programme specification' (QAA 2006d).

This chapter develops these introductory ideas by providing key prompts and advice to programme leaders and programme teams who are facing course validation. It needs to be read in conjunction with Chapter 13 on diversifying assessment. Whereas this chapter will concentrate on decisions related to the overall assessment strategy for a programme of study, Chapter 12 provides detailed advice to tutors on designing a module for validation purposes.

Six steps to an effective programme assessment strategy

Step 1: Developing programme learning outcomes

Figure 11.1 identifies suggested stages in developing a programme assessment strategy. Central to the whole process is the identification of programme learning outcomes: statements of what you intend students to achieve as a result of the programme of study (see Chapter 2 for a discussion of outcome-based learning). Unlike module-level outcomes, programme learning outcomes are 'of a more strategic nature. They embody the educational purposes and values of the learning experience' (Jackson 2000: 145). Programme outcomes should be informed by a range of internal and external requirements and interests. The development of programme learning outcomes should be an iterative process so that they may be modified as the details of modules emerge.

External requirements and stakeholders
Developments in the last 20 years have generated a range of external reference points that programme teams need to consider in devising programme outcomes and learning, teaching and assessment strategies. In the UK, these include the relevant subject benchmark statements, the national Framework for Higher Education Qualifications (QAA 2006d, see Box 11.3) and, where appropriate, the requirements of professional, statutory and regulatory bodies. They might also include employers and any relevant national legislation or national commitments to European and international processes (QAA 2006e).

Institutional goals and mission
Universities have a range of different goals, often articulated through mission statements, corporate plans and teaching and learning strategies. For example, your institution may have a focus towards the professions and graduate

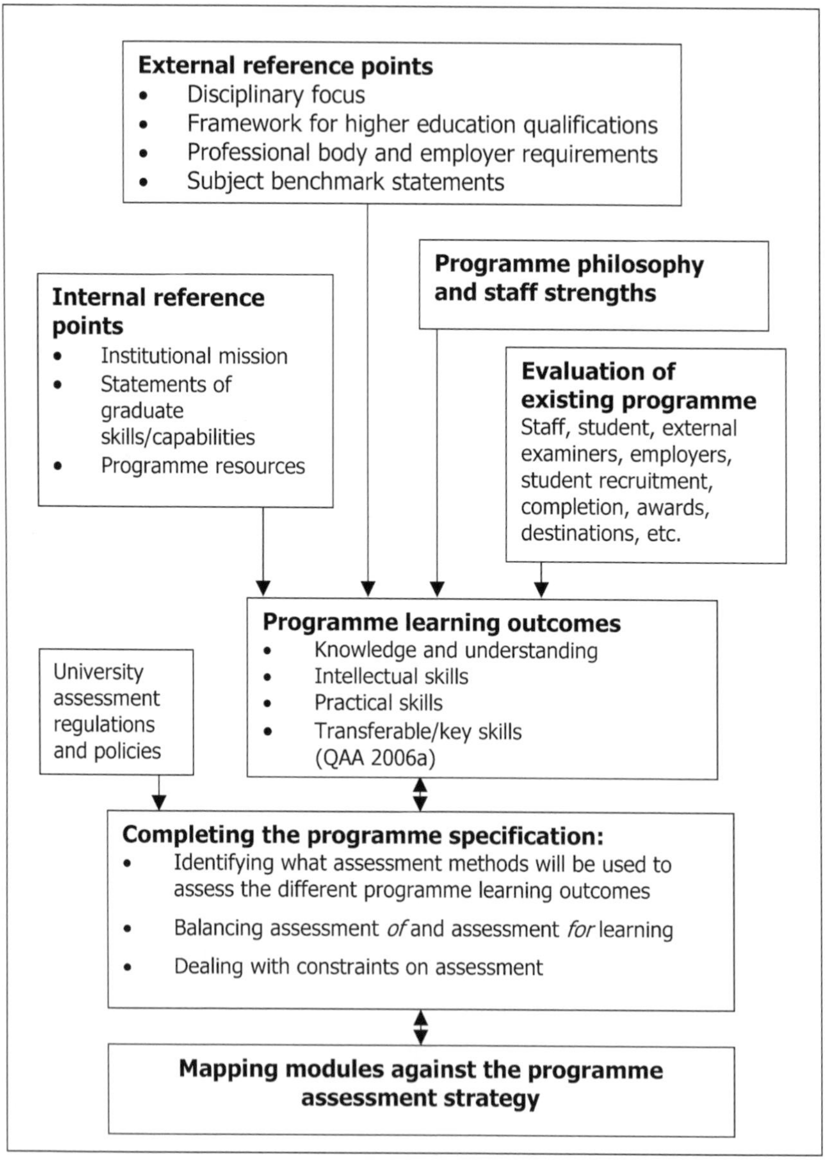

External reference points
- Disciplinary focus
- Framework for higher education qualifications
- Professional body and employer requirements
- Subject benchmark statements

Programme philosophy and staff strengths

Internal reference points
- Institutional mission
- Statements of graduate skills/capabilities
- Programme resources

Evaluation of existing programme
Staff, student, external examiners, employers, student recruitment, completion, awards, destinations, etc.

Programme learning outcomes
- Knowledge and understanding
- Intellectual skills
- Practical skills
- Transferable/key skills
  (QAA 2006a)

University assessment regulations and policies

Completing the programme specification:
- Identifying what assessment methods will be used to assess the different programme learning outcomes
- Balancing assessment *of* and assessment *for* learning
- Dealing with constraints on assessment

Mapping modules against the programme assessment strategy

Figure 11.1 Flow chart for designing a programme assessment strategy

employment, a strong emphasis on developing creative graduates or a commitment to widening participation and retention. These all have implications for programme learning outcomes and, in turn, assessment strategies. For example, promoting research-focused teaching may emphasise the use of inquiry-based assessment, whereas retaining non-traditional students may indicate that the programme should pay particular attention to preparation of students for assessment.

Employability

Universities are under increasing pressure to consider how their programmes prepare students for employment (Knight and Yorke 2003). For example, there may be an institutional statement of graduate skills and capabilities which all programmes are expected to address (Bloxham 2004) or a policy of personal development planning designed to help students monitor, develop and reflect upon their personal development. While many tutors, particularly in non-vocational subject areas, may be resistant to this development (Barrie 2004), it should be recognised that promoting employability is as much about good learning experiences as it is about work placements or careers advice (see Box 11.1). The short shelf life of knowledge (Yorke and Knight 2004) suggests that we should broaden the focus from knowledge acquisition to a wider range of graduate attributes.

Categories of learning outcomes

Learning outcomes may usefully be classified into the following categories:

- knowledge and understanding;
- intellectual skills such as analysis, synthesis, evaluation, and problem solving;
- practical skills;
- transferable/key skills (QAA 2006d).

While Figure 11.1 suggests a largely linear process leading from the programme learning outcomes, it may be more useful to think of it as an iterative development where the outcomes remain mutable while the programme is emerging. Staff ownership of the programme may depend on a significant degree of debate and negotiation in determining the agreed outcomes. Further advice on writing learning outcomes can be found in Gosling and Moon (2002).

Step 2: Mapping learning outcomes across a programme

While we write learning outcomes at the programme level, courses are usually delivered through a series of units or modules with their own learning

Box 11.1 Leads into literature: employability

Higher education has seen a growing emphasis on developing generic attributes in students (Barrie 2004), particularly those designed to enhance their employability. Employability has been defined as 'a set of achievements, understandings and personal attributes that make individuals more likely to gain employment and be successful in their chosen occupation' (Knight and Yorke 2003: 5), including intellectual, subject knowledge and interactive attributes such as team working. Willingness to continue learning, ability to find things out, flexibility and adaptability, risk taking and personal skills such as metacognition and self-management are also elements of employability (Harvey 2004). Above all, employability represents complex learning which is acquired gradually over time (Knight and Yorke 2003). Consequently, if we wish our programmes to enhance students' employability, we need to examine the opportunities we give students to develop these attributes including reflective learning processes.

Traditional approaches to enhancing employability in higher education include work experience (including placements and sandwich courses), entrepreneurship (for example, modules involving the development of business projects), careers education and guidance, and personal development planning. The location of these in specific modules or outside the programme altogether means that they do not necessarily contribute to an overall learning environment designed to foster employability. While work experience can make an important contribution, students need to be helped to learn from that experience and to see it as an integrated part of their programme.

A programme approach to employability might include:

- developing understanding of subject matter with a strong emphasis on students developing the capacity to find things out for themselves and to learn independently;
- opportunity to develop and practice subject-specific and generic skills in challenging situations across the learning environment (classroom, independent learning, student team projects, workplace, etc.);
- embedded and frequent opportunities to reflect on learning and actions;
- work experience;
- creating learning environments and activities that stimulate intrinsic motivation and give students a sense of control over, and relevance in, what they are doing and learning;
- the opportunity for careers education information and guidance;
- close involvement with employers.

See Knight and Yorke (2003) for a full development of these ideas and their implications for assessment. Whatever approach is adopted towards integration of employability, it is likely that self-assessment will play a significant role.

A note on employability for professional courses

Experience suggests that many tutors teaching on professionally accredited programmes conflate professional qualification with employability. While the ticket to practice is a necessary condition of graduate employment in the relevant field, it does not enable students to stand out in a crowd. When a head teacher is making a choice between two well-qualified graduate applicants, it is aspects of their employability that are likely to make the difference. Can they manage their own workload, learn new things independently, instigate change if needed and work effectively with the rest of the team? While meeting professional standards is essential, it should not be done without also developing students' employability, indeed professional bodies are increasingly recognising the value of employability characteristics in their professional standards.

outcomes and assessment. Therefore, in order to deliver the programme outcomes, it is necessary to map the modules against the programme to ensure that all programme outcomes will be assessed (Rust 2002). This is particularly important in terms of outcomes related to developing autonomy, key/transferable skills and employability. Often these outcomes get lost in the translation from a programme to a series of modules. Figure 11.2 is an example of a curriculum map illustrating a method of auditing where programme outcomes are developed and assessed (Jackson 2000).

Curriculum mapping can easily become an administrative procedure: part of validation and not much else. The map needs to be debated, agreed and owned by module tutors and clearly reflected in module learning outcomes. In addition, in order to establish the overall student experience of assessment, including their workload, it is wise to map the use of different methods across the programme (in a similar way to Figure 11.2), including a breakdown of how assessment will be scheduled across the year. The assessment schedule needs to be negotiated among module leaders and then everyone must be required to stick to it.

Step 3: Making assessment fit for purpose

Establishing programme learning outcomes is followed by the production of a learning, teaching and assessment strategy (see Figure 11.1). This identifies the processes by which the learning outcomes are to be attained and demonstrated. Above all, the assignments and examinations of the programme should be designed to match the learning outcomes of the programme; they should be valid indicators of student achievement of those outcomes and thus encourage students to direct their efforts appropriately. In identifying this fitness for purpose, a number of factors need to be taken into account.

Modules	Programme outcome 1	Programme outcome 2	Programme outcome 3	Programme outcome 4	Programme outcome 5	Programme outcome 6
101	D	D				
102		D				
103		D	D	D		
104	DA				D	
105	DA		D			
106		DA	D			D
201					D	
202	DA			D		D
203			D		D	D
204				DA	DA	
205		DA				DA
206			DA			
301			A			DA
302		A		A	DA	
303	A			A		
304			A		A	A

D = developed, A = assessed

Figure 11.2 A curriculum map

Assessment methods have long traditions within different disciplines. For example, it is unimaginable to complete a degree in the humanities without completing many essays or to gain a degree in fine art without producing an exhibition. However, programme validation is a time to test whether you are using those methods because they best serve your needs or because that is what has always taken place. Many traditional methods only assess a limited range of skills, and are not suitable for assessing the broader graduate attributes that programmes aim to produce (Rust, 2002). The subject benchmark statements for disciplines in UK universities list 47 different tools recognised as suitable for assessment purposes in higher education (South West Academic Network for Disability Support 1999–2002), yet many programmes use only a fraction of that number. Timed unseen examinations are still used with enormous frequency despite their limited use in either assessing higher-level learning or predicting future capability (see Box 11.2 for a summary of the evidence). Variety in assessment methods also allows for the measurement of 'process-oriented' outcomes such as communication skills, working

Box 11.2   Leads into literature: examinations

Examinations offer a member of benefits:

- They reduce opportunity for cheating.
- They have good potential for testing knowledge, comprehension and (theoretical) application (Freeman and Lewis 1998).
- They are practicable.
- The revision process can help develop depth of understanding (Entwistle and Entwistle 1997).
- They offer equitable treatment to all students, who have the same time to do the same task.
- They are convenient (Biggs 2003).

On the other hand, they have a number of disadvantages:

- The quality of learning is inferior to that in coursework-assessed modules (Gibbs and Simpson 2004–5), encouraging superficial approaches and memorisation (Entwistle and Entwistle, 1997).
- Question spotting limits how much of the curriculum students pay attention to (Miller and Parlett 1974).
- Unseen examinations are generally only good for assessing declarative knowledge; most questions assess recall of factual knowledge or the 'straightforward application of principles to familiar problems' (Ramsden 2003: 183). They are not suitable for assessing evaluation or synthesis because 'it is difficult to set sufficiently complicated questions with data that is wide-ranging enough in a time-limited examination' (Freeman and Lewis 1998: 178).
- Poor examination technique and writing speed can heavily influence students' marks.
- They provoke anxiety in students which may damage their performance in a way that is unrelated to their ability in the subject.
- They encourage students to put off work until the end of the module (Gibbs 2006b), then 'cram' information which is quickly forgotten (Knight and Yorke 2003).
- Time constraints cannot be justified educationally. They encourage memorisation and limit divergent responses and originality, with students feeling under pressure to reproduce the same material (Biggs, 2003).
- They have little value in predicting students' future achievement or job success (Kvale 1996).
- Choice of questions makes fair comparison between different candidates difficult – it is hard to write equally difficult questions, and some topics may have been dealt with in more depth on the module than others (Biggs 2003).

> - They offer a restricted opportunity for students to learn from their performance.
>
> Contemporary concerns regarding plagiarism will no doubt halt or reverse trends towards fewer examinations. Nevertheless, the considerable list of disadvantages and limitations suggests that examinations should be used with caution and only where the learning outcomes for the module (or some of them) can be effectively assessed by that means. There is evidence that different formats of examination can encourage different approaches to learning (Thomas and Bain 1984), and setting holistic questions rather than ones closely aligned to the teaching is more likely to encourage students to adopt revision techniques which involve looking for connections across the course (Entwistle and Entwistle 1997). Chapter 13 provides examples of how examinations can be enhanced to assess higher-level learning.

effectively with others, critical thinking skills and accessing and evaluating information (Dunn *et al.* 2004).

In addition, a wide range of assessment methods can promote equity and offer an inclusive assessment culture relevant to the needs of a diverse student body (see Chapter 10). Choice and variety in assessment are also associated with intrinsic motivation (Rust 2002). Chapter 13 discusses the issue of diversifying assessment methods in more detail, including suggestions for tackling the assessment challenges faced by different programmes.

Assessment planning at programme level is the opportunity to examine the type and variety of methods used and whether full advantage is being taken of different tools. However, a multiplicity of assessment techniques should be balanced with a recognition that students need to become familiar with different assessment tools in order to demonstrate their learning effectively. Consequently, programme assessment strategies should provide a reasonable variety of assessment methods but schedule their introduction across a programme.

Reconciling the potential conflicts between assessment *of* learning and assessment *for* learning was discussed at some length in Chapters 2 and 3, with the recognition that most quality assurance procedures focus on the assessment *of* learning and neglect its impact on student learning. We recommended the need for balance across a student's programme, recognising that within each assignment or examination, it is not possible to meet all assessment purposes. Different assignments and modules should give prominence to different assessment functions, but the overall assessment strategy will demonstrate valid and sufficiently 'reliable' assessment of programme outcomes. Such an approach is likely to reassure stakeholders about the use of assessment tools which appear less reliable or 'attributable' to individual students.

In summary, assessment *of* learning leads to various qualities in a programme assessment strategy:

- Focus on the programme learning outcomes, and ensure they are summatively assessed by breaking down programme outcomes into component parts which can be assessed at module level. This allows some freedom in relation to assessing all content. For example, if the programme outcome stipulates a detailed knowledge of the discipline with areas of specialisation in depth (SEEC 2003), a sufficient number (but not all) modules need to include assessment of knowledge. Others can focus on assessment, say, of critical thinking skills using disciplinary knowledge as the medium for demonstrating that capacity. However, several final-year modules should include some assessment of specialist knowledge.
- Ensure assessment methods are sufficiently varied to capture the different types of programme outcomes.
- Assess key outcomes using different methods to give greater confidence in the results and to test student capability in different contexts.
- Pay attention to aspects of 'attribution', that is, ensuring that assessments represent the achievement of the individual student. Controlled conditions make this easier but repeat assessments of key outcomes are also effective (Knight and Yorke, 2003).
- Develop programme grade descriptors clearly linked to programme learning outcomes which identify levels of achievement expected in different years of the programme (see Chapter 6).
- Use substantive assignments which allow for demonstration of complex learning.

Assessment *for* learning will require development of other features of the programme assessment strategy:

- Integrate preparation for assessment, particularly understanding of assessment criteria and grade descriptors.
- Plan for progression in the use of peer and self-assessment.
- Schedule assessments part way through modules to allow for formative feedback.
- Allow opportunities to practise new assessment methods in 'low stakes' situations.
- Make allowances for slower learners, for example by deferring summative assessment until the students have had several formative

assessment opportunities. Consider allowing students to submit themselves for some summative assessments when they feel ready, as with a driving test (Boud, 1995).

- Build collaboration into assessment, for example using group assignments.
- Use 'serial' assignments or 'patchwork texts' (see Chapter 13) allowing students to build small regular tasks into a larger assignment for summative assessment. This enables formative feedback and can help breakdown complex achievements into manageable parts.

A programme approach enables you to determine whether there is an appropriate balance in the programme. In general, assessment *for* learning should be given greater emphasis in the early stages and assessment *of* learning in the latter stages. However, both should feature clearly throughout.

Step 4: Provide for progression

Progression in the higher education context is not well researched, and modular programmes allowing choice and cross-discipline studies make it particularly difficult to manage (Gibbs 2006b). Of course, progression can be conceived of in different ways, for example progression in relation to the subject discipline, in terms of becoming a more autonomous learner, or in terms of ethical reasoning. In the UK, the Framework for Higher Education Qualifications (see Box 11.3) demonstrates levels of progression from first-year undergraduate through a series of qualification desciptors. These range from certificate (level 1) to doctoral studies (level 5). These have been translated into **level descriptors** by SEEC (2003). These differ slightly in the Scottish Credit and Qualifications Framework. Taxonomies of thinking (see Chapter 2) can provide another framework for thinking about progression in your programme. Whatever approach is taken, reference to programme learning outcomes should provide the basis for establishing what students are working towards. For example, if you have highlighted developing autonomous and lifelong learners in the outcomes, your assessment should involve progressively more evaluation of students' capacity to learn independently.

An assessment map (Figure 11.2) also allows teams to ensure that programme outcomes are developed and assessed in component parts across the years. For example, students' communications skills may contribute to a programme outcome regarding employability. Such skills cannot be assessed in one module because we expect students to develop greater sophistication, range and confidence over the course of a degree. In addition, although communication is involved in every assessment to some extent, we might wish to foreground it in certain assignments and discount it in the marking criteria for others, such as unseen examinations (see Chapter 10). The assessment strategy set out in Table 11.1 allows for assessment of academic and reflective writing, writing for public audiences and writing using different communication media. Individual assignments combine assessment of subject learning and communication skills and they make progressively more complex demands on the students. Additionally, we can have more confidence in the graduates' communication skills because they have been assessed several times across different contexts (Knight and Yorke 2003). Clearly, programmes will need to prioritise what is assessed in this repetitive way, and programme learning outcomes are a useful basis for working out priorities.

Table 11.1 Assessing written communication skills across a bioscience programme

Level of study	Module assignments assessing written communication
Year 1	1500-word essay, reports on practicals with guided format, information leaflet, group poster
Year 2	3000-word essay, web page, report on experiment via individual poster, lay commentary on journal article
Year 3	6000-word research report written for publication, writing a grant application, project report with executive summary

In addition, programmes will need to identify the composite parts of programme outcomes in order to ensure coverage and progression. For example, an outcome regarding developing independent learners might include assessing information fluency, personal organisation and ability to follow guidance in year 1 as prerequisites for 'critical autonomy' (Ecclestone, 2002) which might be assessed in year 3 through a major independent project or dissertation.

Unfortunately modular programmes which allow diverse combinations of modules present particular difficulty for progression and therefore consideration of compulsory modules is very important (Knight and Yorke 2003). Programmes can also identify 'capstone' modules specifically designed to consolidate and integrate learning across a programme, typically through a major project, dissertation, exhibition or performance (Knight 2006).

Step 5: Match assessment and learning activities

Constructive alignment asserts that assessment tasks, learning activities and teaching should align with learning outcomes, with the potential for problems if this is not the case (see Chapter 2). For example, you may wish to teach a module using problem-based learning methods. Such an approach is valuable for encouraging the student to be active in constructing their own learning. However, if the same module is assessed by an unseen examination, students are unlikely to take a deep and open-minded approach to their exploration of the subject matter. Instead, they are likely to demand information on what they need to 'learn' for the examination. This is not to say that either the assessment method or the teaching method is wrong, merely that they will not work together.

Examinations present particular challenges to alignment (see Box 11.3).

Step 6: Identify constraints on assessment

Institutional regulations and guidance
Programme leaders need to be fully aware of institutional regulations and guidance in determining programme assessment strategies. Examples of ways in which they may influence assessment include:

- requirements to pass all assessment components in modules (that is, students must achieve a pass mark in each component rather than merely achieving a pass mark for their aggregated score);
- requirements to include examinations, a dissertation or other methods;
- requirements regarding assessment workload, or how much assessment should be included in modules of different 'credit' size (often expressed as word equivalence);
- requirements regarding summative assessment of first-year modules;
- requirements to limit the weighting of self- or peer assessment in any module;
- whether all summative assignments must be graded or whether a pass/fail assessment is permitted on some assignments in a module;
- the impact of having large modules (for example 30 or 40 credits). This may be important in the case of reassessment, where marks are held at the pass mark, unduly lowering a student's overall degree classification. Alternatively, you may consider that the benefits of more substantive modules outweigh the disadvantages to a minority of students.

Assessment workload and scheduling
What is a reasonable assessment workload? There is great variation within and across universities regarding the volume of assessment students face (Dunn *et al.* 2004), and this is an area where institutions could be more interventionist in providing some consistency across programmes. A review of 18 UK higher education institutions in 1995 found a wide variation in

to check whether there are any limits of this nature in your institution. In any case, you should consider whether your assessment strategy results in a large number of assignments at the expense of student learning.

Bunching of assessment
It is also worth checking at the programme level whether the assessment strategy is likely to lead to bunching of assessment deadlines and examinations. One programme, in trying to reduce the student workload, limited every module to only one assessment item or examination. While the motive was good, the impact was poor. Staff considered that students would stop attending any module once the assignment was submitted and therefore virtually all deadlines were in the same week at the end of the module. As well as creating a severe assessment pressure point, it meant that students got little feedback on their progress for a whole semester.

Staff workload
Assessment must be practicable in terms of staff workloads. We will not repeat here the discussion in Chapter 3 on this matter except to reiterate that there will always be some trade-off between practicability and other purposes of assessment. Programme assessment strategies need to:

- audit current staff time used for summative assessment, aiming to reduce it in favour of time devoted to formative assessment;
- direct assessment effort of tutors towards assessing elements of the programme learning outcomes rather than every aspect of individual modules;
- provide tutors with clear module assessment workload guidance (see Box 11.3) which limits the volume of assessment;
- use a mixture of graded and pass/fail assignments as appropriate to the purpose;
- sanction and support the use of peer and self-assessment to maintain flow of feedback to students while limiting tutor marking;
- encourage some use of group-based assessments to reduce marking load;
- use mechanised assessment and marking (for example, online MCQs) where it aligns with the learning outcomes and cohort sizes are sufficiently large to justify the initial investment of time;
- carry out assessment in class, such as presentations;
- consider whether module outcomes can be assessed elsewhere, for example on a practice placement, in a portfolio or in a task which draws on the learning from two or three modules such as a substantive project (you need to check whether your institutional regulations require all module outcomes to be assessed within the module before taking this approach);

- use economic moderation methods, for example specifically not requiring feedback comments to be written by second markers (see Chapter 8);
- reduce work generated by 'troubleshooting', student queries and student failure by providing good assessment information for students and preparing them for assessment.

Additional ideas for designing assessments to reduce staff workloads can be found in Chapter 13 on diversifying assessment.

Requirements to pass every element of the module assessment
There may be institutional or professional body rules that require students to pass every element of module assessment, but if not, programmes need to decide at the validation stage whether students must pass each element of assessment. Where marks can be aggregated, students may pass a module with failed elements within their profile so long as the combined weighted marks achieve the minimum pass mark for the module.

Where students are required to pass all elements of assessment, there may be a considerable increase in module failure even for students who have obtained very satisfactory average marks for the module. This approach also works against the benefits of formative assessment if every component carries **high stakes**.

If the aggregated approach is taken, programmes need to show that components of programme learning outcomes are assessed in different modules allowing for students to demonstrate, across their course, that they have met all the outcomes. This needs debate and careful mapping by the programme team.

Involving students
Students have strong views about assessment and may be able to provide important feedback to programme teams regarding the value of existing methods. It is increasingly commonplace to involve students in the design and development of programmes, or at least to draw on their evaluation. However, evaluation may not get at key assessment issues for students, focusing as it does on 'end products' and procedures (Crook *et al.* 2006). Given the central role of assessment in determining students' learning experience, and the difference in staff and student perspectives on assessment (Maclellan 2001), it is worth investigating their experience further. You could invite students or former students on to the programme planning team or use appropriate methods to gather their views.

Conclusion: an iterative process

'Together a regime of assessment needs to address the variety of outcomes being sought and this can only occur if there is a high degree of co-operation between those teaching different parts of the programme' (Boud and Falchikov 2006: 410). Such co-operation is no mean achievement and foregrounds the importance of the programme leader role, not as an organiser and administrator checking that tutors have filled in the forms, complied with regulations and got their marking done on time, but as someone who provides leadership and co-ordination to drive the level of debate which is needed to make a programme assessment strategy a reality. Knight and Yorke (2003: 64) stress the importance of sustained discussion between colleagues regarding assessment 'allied to a pervasive concern with students' learning' as key to building an effective assessment system.

Furthermore, they observe that validation documents do not always reflect actual practice. Thus a programme leader's role in enhancing assessment does not end once a programme is validated satisfactorily. They have an important ongoing role in communicating, promoting and monitoring the chosen assessment strategy, perceiving of it as an iterative process in which information from all elements of assessment is used on a continuous basis to improve student learning.

12 Planning the assessment for a module

Introduction

Writing or revising descriptions of individual modules for course approval (validation) is a key element of a lecturer's role. Writing a module descriptor is often perceived as a bureaucratic exercise, but this obscures the fact that it is the most important opportunity academics have to take greater control of their teaching and assessment. Designing a well-thought-out, constructively aligned module can provide benefits for student learning and achievement, and for your own workload and motivation.

Validation of a module descriptor will normally include verifying that:

- its aims and teaching plan contribute towards the programme level aims and learning outcomes;
- the learning outcomes of a module are broadly pitched at the right level and are feasible in terms of its credit weighting;
- the module's assessment plan is clearly designed to demonstrate that students have met the learning outcomes of the module and complies with the assessment strategy of the programme;
- the module contributes to coherent student progression within the programme.

Validation is seen as an important element of quality assurance and standards, and universities are expected to ensure that courses and modules are delivered *as validated*, including the specified assessment plan. Unfortunately, lecturers do not always pay attention to this at the point of module design and find themselves stuck with an assessment regime that is impracticable or encourages inappropriate student learning. Spending time thinking about the module assessment from the outset can avoid an unsatisfactory course, unhappy students, or an excessive marking load, and can prevent the time-consuming and unnecessary work associated with trying to revalidate at a later stage.

This chapter is designed to assist staff in this process of planning module assessment at the validation stage. While other texts help staff consider the overall process of module design (Moon 2002; Turner 2002), we focus on the decisions that need to be taken in relation to assessment, and provide suggestions for enhancing practice. The chapter will be organised to accompany

- There is greater likelihood of bunching of assessment submission dates, and overloading students with several group assessments or major projects at the same time.
- Modules may unnecessarily duplicate assessment of learning outcomes or preparation for different types of assignment. Not all modules need to include work on 'examination technique' if it is done well in one of them.

See Chapter 11 for advice on constructing a programme assessment strategy.

You will need to be aware of the relationship between your module and any programme learning outcomes. For example, are there any programme level outcomes which your module is responsible for assessing? It is helpful if the programme specification includes a curriculum map (see Figure 11.2 for a template) indicating which programme outcomes are developed and assessed in which modules. Where your module is identified as contributing to the assessment of a programme outcome, it should be reflected in the module learning outcomes and taken into account in the assessment design for the module. Remember, while you may be primarily concerned with your individual module, its main purpose is to contribute to the students' overall learning experience and achievement of the programme learning outcomes.

Assessment regulations

The university's assessment regulations and policies must be taken into account in designing your assessment, otherwise you are likely to find that your module is rejected at the validation stage. This includes matters such as:

- when assessment can take place;
- guidelines (if any) for assessment workload;
- limit on the number of items of assessment per module;
- whether candidates are required to achieve a pass grade in all elements of the assessment for a module or whether it is sufficient to achieve an overall average pass for the module;
- whether some assignments can be graded only as pass/fail;
- whether overlap of assessment items between modules is permitted.

Our experience suggests that many myths circulate around universities regarding what the institution does or does not permit in relation to assessment. For example, 'all final-year undergraduates must do a dissertation', 'at least half the modules must have an examination', 'peer marking is not permitted for summative assignments', or 'students doing group assessments must also do an individual assignment'. On the basis of these myths, lecturers may make assessment choices founded in inaccurate information.

However, there may be assessment regulations and policies such as these operating in your university so find out what they actually are rather than rely on local rumour or tradition. Your programme leader(s), head of department, academic registry or assessment office should be able to provide you with a set of regulations or an assessment guide for staff. We have discussed these issues in some depth in Chapter 11, but the following paragraphs provide some guidance of relevance to module leaders.

When assessment can take place

The academic framework for awards in a university may be more or less rigid in relation to when assessment can take place. For example, many modular schemes require the assessment for each module to take place during or at the end of the module. There may be no freedom, for example, for module learning outcomes to be assessed at a later point or for the learning of two or more modules to be assessed in a joint assignment or examination. Modularisation, as a consequence, has led to a potential increase in the assessment workload for students and staff and less opportunity for students to develop their learning of a subject before they are assessed on it. Some universities are paying particular attention to the latter problem in relation to retaining level 1 undergraduates. Modular frameworks are being redesigned to avoid summative assessment too early in the first year of study before the students have become adjusted to the demands and expectations of higher education learning (see further discussion in Chapter 10 on designing assessment to support widening participation). There may be a good case for using some 'long-thin' or 'short-fat' modules to help spread the student workload.

In response to this issue, within the limitations of your institution's assessment regulations, you should consider when your module's learning outcomes can be most effectively assessed to manage the students' workload, to build coherence into their programme of study and to allow them 'adequate time to reflect on learning before being assessed' (Quality Assurance Agency 2006c: 16). For example, if it is a programme leading to a professional qualification, some learning outcomes might be assessed during a placement or practicum. Alternatively, a project or portfolio might be used to assess learning outcomes from a range of linked modules.

Assessment workload

You should check whether there are any guidelines for the volume of assessment associated with each module. For example, 15-credit modules in the UK are typically associated with assessment 'wordage' of between 3000 and 5000 words or a shorter coursework assignment and an examination. See

Box 12.1   Examples of credit level descriptors

The SEEC level descriptors 'define the level of complexity, relative demand and autonomy expected of a learner on completion of a unit or programme of learning' (SEEC 2003: 3). They are grouped under four headings: knowledge and understanding; cognitive/intellectual skills; key transferable skills; and practical skills.

The following extracts (from SEEC 2003: 12–15) illustrate the progression between the levels. They refer to UK-recognised levels but, in common with the rest of this book, we are using 'years' with year 3 equivalent to final-year honours in order to make it accessible to a wider audience.

Development of knowledge and understanding (subject specific): knowledge base

> Year 1: 'has a given factual and/or conceptual knowledge base with emphasis on the nature of the field of study and appropriate terminology';
> Year 2: 'has a detailed knowledge of major theories of the discipline(s) and an awareness of a variety of ideas, contexts and frameworks;
> Year 3 (honours): 'has a comprehensive/detailed knowledge of a major discipline(s), with areas of specialisation in depth, and an awareness of the provisional nature of knowledge';
> Master's: 'has depth and systematic understanding of knowledge in specialised/ applied areas and/across areas and can work with theoretical/ research-based knowledge at the forefront of their academic discipline'.

Cognitive/intellectual skills (generic): application

> Year 1: 'can apply given tools/methods accurately and carefully to a well defined problem and begin to appreciate the complexity of the issues';
> Year 2: 'can identify key elements of problems and choose appropriate methods for their resolution in a considered manner';
> Year 3 (honours): 'is confident and flexible in identifying and defining complex problems and can apply appropriate knowledge and skills to their solution';
> Master's: 'can demonstrate initiative and originality in problem solving. Can act autonomously in planning and implementing tasks at a professional or equivalent level making decisions in complex and unpredictable situations'.

Key/transferable skills (generic): communications

> Year 1: 'can communicate effectively in a format appropriate to the discipline(s) and report practical procedures in a clear and concise manner';
> Year 2: 'can communicate effectively in a manner appropriate to the discipline(s) and report practical procedures in a clear and concise manner in a variety of formats';

> Year 3 (honours): 'can engage effectively in debate in a professional manner and produce detailed and coherent project reports';
> Master's: 'can engage confidently in academic and professional communication with others, reporting on action clearly, autonomously and competently'.

give useful feedback to students. You will need to balance ideal methods with a level of practicability.

It is also wise to consider your assessment tasks from the point of view of students. Discussion in Chapters 2 and 10 has shown how choice contributes to motivation and a more inclusive educational experience. In particular, allowing students alternative ways of demonstrating their learning helps to provide equity in assessment. Constant use of one method privileges students who thrive on that method.

You can also improve motivation by including assessment tasks that have value in themselves and some level of authenticity. This might include designing learning materials, information leaflets, presenting ideas to other students, application of learning to a professional context and completion of small-scale research. See Chapter 13 for more practical ideas. Consider how your assessment tasks can help to motivate students and develop their employability (see Box 11.1).

How many assessments?

You will need to check whether there are any limits of this nature in your programme and, depending on those limits, you will need to make some decisions. Whereas a programme will normally benefit from using a range of assessments, this does not need to be replicated in each module. Lots of small assignments may limit the chance for reflection and make them 'rather narrow in scope and undemanding in nature' (Gibbs 2006b: 17). Likewise, using too many different assessment methods within a module (for example examination, essay and presentation) may involve double assessment of some outcomes and place too great a workload on students and tutors.

The recommendation to limit the number of summative assignments or examinations should not detract from continuous forms of assessment or regular sub-tasks that might build up to a final summative assignment (for example, a seminar log, laboratory reports or a learning journal). Particularly in year 1, these continuous methods can provide important formative assessment and encourage engagement with the module (see Box 12.2). At higher levels, staff may wish to consider having fewer, larger assignments which encourage more independent working with less tutor intervention.

Box 12.2 Using assessment to improve engagement and attendance

First-year students on a sports science module were asked to submit a reflective log which included description, personal reaction, analysis and evaluation of a range of practical coaching sessions including an action plan for their own development. The log contributed 50% of the module marks. The tutor incorporated an attendance correction factor into the marking such that the grade for the log was weighted in direct correspondence to how many sessions the student had attended. The rationale for this was that students could not reflect on something they hadn't been present for and students were informed of the correction factor at the beginning and part-way through the module. Absences plummeted as a result (T. Barry, personal communication).

A third-year module in youth social policy was structured in the form of a series of formal debates on controversial issues in UK policy for young people. While the students gained the majority of their marks for an individual speech for or against one of the debate motions, they also gained marks for a series of *debate decision reports*. These reports were 500-word summaries of how they had voted in each debate and why. They were only allowed to submit reports on debates that they attended. This approach ensured very high attendance at the course sessions and students listened carefully to each others' speeches to help them write their reports. In order to obtain good marks, they had to explain their viewpoints, drawing on further reading and evidence.

Using formative assessment tasks

In Chapter 4, we discussed the importance of scheduling assessment within a module to capture student study time and to provide formative assessment opportunities. At the planning stage, you need to consider how easy it will be for you and your students to get a sense of how well they are doing on the module. One of the difficulties with using assessment tasks to maintain student engagement and provide feedback throughout the module is the anticipated increase in marking for the staff. However, this does not need to be the case, and Chapters 4 and 13 set out various ways to promote formative assessment.

Assignment weighting

Where a module has more than one element of assessment, tutors need to make a decision at the validation stage regarding their relative weighting and whether students must pass each element of assessment. In relation to weightings, it is usual to assign a proportion of the final mark to each assignment or examination. For example, two coursework assignments and a final examination might be 25% : 25% : 50%. The following points are designed to help in determining weightings:

- If you want early assignments to have a more formative role, then a small weighting is appropriate so that students are not penalised too heavily if they have not grasped the topic or demands of the assignment.
- Weightings should reflect the amount of time students are expected to put into the task.
- Strategic learners may decide that it is not worth attempting assignments with very small weightings.
- Weightings should reflect the difficulty and complexity of the learning outcome(s) being assessed rather than length of examination.

The issue of whether students must pass every assignment is often a matter governed by institutional or programme regulations. If there is no such requirement, you will need to consider whether your module assessment plan would allow students to pass when they have not met some of the module learning outcomes. For example, where two assessments are weighted 30% and 70% respectively, it would be relatively easy for a student to fail the smaller assignment, yet pass the module with a reasonable grade for the larger task. Whereas this may be of limited concern if the smaller assignment had a formative function early in the module, you might feel it was more problematic if the larger assignment was a group task or failed to assess some key module outcomes. Equally weighted assignments reduce the likelihood of students passing a module while carrying a serious failure in an important component of assessment.

Designing tasks to reduce plagiarism

Chapter 3 raised the issue of 'attribution' as increasingly important in higher education. The internet and skilled use of communication and information technology have made it substantially easier for students intentionally or inadvertently to pass off others' work as their own. The opportunity for students to do this can be significantly reduced by the choice and scheduling of assessment tasks. For example, controlled conditions such as examinations make attribution much easier, if not foolproof. Chapter 4 provides advice on designing assessment to reduce plagiarism. In practice, there will need to be a balance between assessment methods which ensure that individual students have completed the work attributed to them and assessing the learning outcomes of higher education, much of which cannot be done in controlled conditions. This balance is primarily a matter for the overall programme assessment strategy, but you may also wish to consider how well your module reduces the opportunity for plagiarism while still assessing the learning outcomes.

Module descriptor template

Each institution has a slightly different process for setting out new course modules. Many use some kind of template that requests information such as:

- module title and number;
- department;
- programmes to which the module contributes;
- level and credit points;
- module leader and other staff contributing to the module;
- mode (full-time, part-time, distance learning) and place of delivery;
- aim and learning outcomes;
- assessment;
- outline content;
- indicative bibliography.

Copies of the blank template should be available from your institution's 'quality' website. In relation to assessment, the form is likely to request information in a tabular format (see Table 12.1).

Table 12.1 Assessment element of a module descriptor

Mode of assessment	Weighting (indicate if formative)	Learning outcomes assessed	Detail
Test	Formative	1–2	Four online multiple choice quizzes on key course content
Coursework	60%	1–5	Project (2500 words)
Examination	40%	3–5	Two-hour short-answer examination

Building in flexibility

There is key challenge in writing the assessment section of your module in relation to the balance between detail and flexibility. However carefully you have considered the assessment plan in advance of validation, it is often difficult to predict exactly how the process will work in practice, particularly if you are trying out a new method of assessment. Staffing changes, student numbers, student feedback and a range of other matters may encourage you to introduce minor changes to your assessment to improve its effectiveness or practicability.

However, if you have completed your module template in great detail, you will find that you have to undergo some form of revalidation process in order to change. Consequently, think very carefully about what detail you provide. Looking at Table 12.1, the descriptor could be completed in a more flexible way. *A series of online quizzes* allows you to change the number and the content focus should you find that the students need this early formative feedback in different aspects of the course. A *Two-hour examination* allows you the freedom to change the format of the examination if you find that the short-answer approach is encouraging lots of regurgitation of facts rather than the application of theory which you intended it to test.

At the validation meeting, you can provide greater detail about your plans if requested, without the strict obligation associated with written information.

Conclusion

This chapter provides tutors with advice on the crucial activity of planning the assessment for a module. The chapter has tackled many of the day-to-day questions facing module designers such as type of assessment, number of tasks, formative versus summative assessment, assignment weighting, and plagiarism prevention. It also considers module assessment design in terms of level and progression. It emphasises the need to articulate the module carefully within the programme and institutional requirements so that it contributes to a coherent student experience.

Challenge 1: Developing authenticity

One aim in diversification of assessment is to increase its authenticity. This describes assessment that 'reflect[s] the ways in which knowledge and skills are used in real world contexts' (Maclellan 2001: 308) and follows from a recognition that learning is 'constructed' in context and is not easily transferred from one setting to another. Thus, being able to reproduce knowledge in a decontexualised examination does not guarantee that the knowledge can be used in a real-life setting. Higher education has a tradition of using authentic assessment, particularly on vocational courses and in work-based settings. However, the focus here is on authentic assessment outside the workplace.

A 'foundation project' (Pickford 2006) in a faculty of information and technology involved over 300 new first-year students working in teams of five as business consultants. They were presented with a chaotic, complex, business scenario of a boarding kennels (cat and dog) business. Their aim was to identify all the business problems and present their findings at points throughout a three-week period. Teams competed to win an imaginary contract for the work which 'was awarded to the team that demonstrated the most enterprise, creativity and originality in their approach as evidenced in their pitch at the end of module showcase' (Pickford 2006: 1). This assignment was particularly aimed at helping students develop enterprise skills, but it also shows how a whole range of benefits can accrue from the effective design of assessment. Pickford suggests that the learning and the assessment were an integrated whole. Working intensively in groups, while useful for developing team-work skills and helping students learn from each other, also probably contributed to their social integration, which is strongly associated with student retention (Tinto 1993). It was authentic in the sense that the students were tackling a real scenario and having to make an immediate impression in their pitch, which reflects the competitive nature of much creative work. However, the author argues that it was not all performance and originality as students had to justify, and thus think about, their business decisions. Students reported enjoying it, which is likely to be motivating, and they had to complete tasks at regular milestones, which helped to maintain engagement. Assessment by staff was efficient and simple as it involved quick recording of impressions against three criteria during the three minutes student had to make their pitch. Multiple assessors, including invited guests and local entrepreneurs, were involved to provide greater validity in the marking. Students were able to see their feedback sheets to gauge the range of opinions on their work.

There are other, perhaps more restrained, approaches to creating authentic assignments such as students writing research bids or responses to invitations to tender. These are complex tasks requiring them to demonstrate understanding of the background, subject knowledge, as well as evaluating potential techniques, risk factors and other elements, depending on the discipline area. While such assignments can replicate authentic tasks, they can also act as valid indicators of higher-level learning. Very tight word limits may help to control staff marking loads.

The creation of web pages for a specific purpose may also form a suitable assessment task, and Knight and Yorke (2003) recommend that this is used as a group task as it involves considerable work, although authoring software is now relatively simple to use and readily available. Web pages allow students to demonstrate the ability to write for different audiences as well as engagement with subject knowledge (see Box 13.1). There is also evidence that students find the task more enjoyable than traditional coursework (Reber 2005).

Box 13.1 Practical examples in authentic assessment

Students in the second year of an English literature degree are asked to visit a cultural heritage site of literary significance. They are asked to examine the way in which the writer and their work are presented for a contemporary audience through analysis of marketing material and through dialogue with staff about curatorial decisions. In the light of this research, students design a web resource for the site aimed at A-level students (university admission level) about a specific element of the author's work (P. Bradshaw personal communication).

A youth and community course used a simulation technique to help students develop the knowledge and skills relevant for their role in recruiting and selecting staff and volunteers. Working independently in groups, with 'knowledge' inputs at regular intervals, the groups had to develop a job description, person specification, application form and advertisement. The jobs were advertised to the rest of the group, with each student required to apply for three jobs. Groups had to shortlist, interview, decide whom to appoint and give feedback. The final assignment was a package of all the documents they had developed plus an evaluation of their work, drawing on the literature provided. The students were highly motivated by the experience, took the interviews very seriously and were well prepared for recruitment and selection in their first appointments. It was a valid and authentic assessment which created limited demands on the tutor in terms of teaching and marking. The main work was in good-quality preparation.

See Box 13.2 for a further example.

Knight and Yorke (2003) report on history students being asked to curate an exhibition, and Vazquez (2003) developed a 'virtual store' simulating the food retail environment. The students worked competitively on this computer programme which integrated both teaching and assessment of the knowledge, skills and personal qualities needed by retail buyers. In general, working with case studies and 'real' problems (Knight and Yorke 2003) has the benefit of mirroring genuine contexts more effectively than traditional essays and examinations. In addition to the potential for motivating students, they also enable a wider range of skills to be assessed.

Challenge 2: Assessing Skills

The alternative assessments described generally allow for the assessment of skills, and discipline areas are increasingly stressing the assessment of both subject-specific and generic skills. Dunn *et al.* (2004) stress the importance of ensuring that assessment takes into account students' mastery of the underpinning knowledge and understanding of a technique or skill as well as its' execution.

Box 13.2 Integrating skills assessment

'An art history module requires students to develop an art exhibition on the Web for summative assessment. It requires them to link "practice" and "theory" by presenting an interpretation through the medium of an exhibition. Students develop their exhibitions with enthusiasm and value the opportunity to choose an artist, period or style that interests them and present their exhibition in their own way. It is the process of learning and communicating understanding rather than the final submission of the Gallery for summative assessment that drives student learning' (Christopher Bailey, reported in McDowell *et al.* 2005: 12).

Implicit in the example in Box 13.2 is the need to develop and demonstrate IT skills in a number of areas in order to produce a visually effective exhibition that communicates well with its audience. Various methods are used to help students gain feedback at draft stages from tutors and peers. This is another assessment which emphasises authenticity and skills assessment as well as an element of student choice, but it is also highly valid in terms of higher level subject-specific skills in the field of art history. The formative feedback opportunities means that it combines assessment *for* learning with assessment *of* learning. Box 13.3 provides an example of an assessment which requires students to use a distinctive medium but which also requires them to demonstrate critical engagement with the underpinning knowledge and understanding. Box 13.4 presents an example of an assessment process which integrates personal development planning into the module.

Challenge 3: Improving the validity of examinations

The discussion in Chapter 3 focuses on the potential lack of validity in many traditional forms of assessment which may have a tendency to concentrate on reproduction of knowledge. Examinations are particularly prone to these

---

Box. 13.3 Integrating skills in social policy

A third-year social policy module asked students to make a half-hour radio documentary designed to provide the public with an understanding of the issues in a specific area of welfare policy. The students were not judged on technical recording expertise, but they were provided with a workshop on sound recording and editing and they had access to media support. They were given stimulus material and worked independently in groups over several weeks researching and developing their programmes. Programmes were submitted together with related documents for summative assessment which was judged on content as well as 'listenability'. The task integrated skills in team work, project management and oral communication into a demanding academic exercise discerning, debating and presenting the evidence on the topic. Students received feedback on the skill elements through peer assessment, and were very motivated by the unusual assessment format.

Box 13.4 Integrating personal development planning into law

A first-year undergraduate law module was redesigned to embed personal development planning, with particular emphasis on career-management skills, legal skills, academic writing and reflective learning. The module is delivered through a combination of classroom and online activities using WebCT™ and involves collaboration between law tutors and careers guidance staff. Assessment has three elements. A reflective practice log includes a quiz on library skills, a court visit report, and reflection on their research skills. A career-management portfolio involves a Power Point™ presentation on the structure of the legal profession and the qualifications, skills and qualities required to work in it, as well as a CV and an initial careers development plan. The third element was an oral presentation on a legal issue. Evaluation indicates that students valued the opportunity to develop their skills, to become more aware of career development issues and to reflect on their learning. See Bloxham *et al.* (2006) for a full description.

---

accusations (see Box 11.2), but current concerns about plagiarism have probably created an imperative to retain them as a major form of assessment and therefore we need to consider how we can improve their validity in assessing higher-level and more complex learning.

An 'interactive examination' (Jonsson and Baartman 2006) in teacher education attempts to improve the professional validity of an examination. Using a computer, students view three short films showing different classroom contexts. They can also access background information and transcripts of the dialogue. They are asked to describe and analyse the situations and recommend how the teachers should act. Once the students have submitted

---

Box 13.6   Using a journal to support extended writing in English literature

'A module on popular writing was summatively assessed by extended essay at the end of Semester two. However, students tended to leave the preparatory research and planning for the extended essay too late, with detrimental effects on their learning and performance. The module was redesigned to include a reading dossier submitted alongside a draft essay proposal. The dossier includes notes made during seminars or for seminar preparation, and notes on primary and secondary reading. It gives students the opportunity to [practise] the analytical skills they need, to discuss their thinking and, through reflection, to identify their own interests. The feedback and dialogue between student and tutor concerning the extended essay has much improved. Formal student feedback consistently comments on the appropriateness of the assessment in helping them to develop' (Mel Gibson, reported in McDowell *et al.* 2005: 8).

Box 13.7   Journal example of first-year engineers

First-year engineering students are required to write twelve 300-word journal entries linked to a series of lectures in a professional practice module. The module tackles topics such as professional ethics, the interdisciplinary nature of engineering, its economic and political context and cultural and intercultural sensitivities. Although resistant at first, students recognised the benefits in terms of writing skills and self-confidence. It also improved their awareness of their 'personal and professional responsibilities (as engineers) on a local and global scale' (Kelly 2002: 1).

(Biggs 2003). Awarding marks for class participation and providing formative feedback at a mid-module point have been shown to encourage active involvement of students (Dancer and Kamvounias 2005). Furthermore, this study recommends both self- and peer assessment using criteria that stress not just attendance but preparation, contribution, group skills and communication skills. These criteria mean that assessing class participation can also contribute to the assessment of important generic skills.

Challenge 5: Linking formative and summative assessment
Assessment *for* learning emphasises the role of formative assessment in improving students' achievement (see Chapter 2). One concern is that students will not produce work for formative assessment alone, and it is worth considering how formative and summative assessment can be made to work in concert by diversifying the assessment methods used.

The 'patchwork text' is an innovation in assessment developed to encourage critical understanding and is particularly suitable for the arts, humanities, social sciences and human service professions (Scoggins and Winter 1999). It might also be used in science disciplines, for example in relation to ethical issues. Students complete several short pieces of writing throughout the module, depending on their discipline – for example, a book review, poem, narrative, portrait, critical incident and a response to a lecture or published document. These might involve different genres or posing different points of view and might include some authentic tasks. In relation to formative development, students share their writing with their peers in order to receive others' responses to it. Students also keep a private reflective diary. At the half-way stage, students review their writing to identify what 'unifying theme' underpins the work. This is also discussed with their peers. The final, summatively assessed assignment is a selection of their earlier writing, which may have been revised, submitted with an 'interpretive reflective framework which brings out and explores the overall theme in relation to the individual pieces of writing' (Scoggins and Winter 1999: 487).

Patchwork texts are designed to tackle the gap between assessment as a fragmentary, formative process (for example, a learning journal or portfolio) and assessment as synthesis, where the learning is brought together in a summative assignment (for example, an end-of-module essay). Whereas essays tend to encourage students to manage their course material and make it coherent, the early writing for patchwork texts allows students to work with course concepts and material in a more exploratory and critical way appropriate to understanding the provisional nature of knowledge and analysing objects (reading, experiences, artefacts) from different perspectives (Parker 2003).

The term 'patchwork' is used to show that it involves bringing disparate items together to form a unifying whole. Scoggins and Winter (1999) make various substantive claims for the power of patchwork texts to extend learning; for our purposes here, it encourages writing for formative assessment because the work contributes to the final assignment.

Challenge 6: Assessing large cohorts

The pressure of large cohorts requires a careful response to avoid retrenching to more cost-effective methods which have poor outcomes for learning. The challenge is to find efficient and economical methods without having an unintended negative backwash on student learning. Merely reducing assessment is not necessarily helpful in encouraging student engagement; however, there are alternatives.

Mechanised assessment, such as online tests, considerably reduce staff time and can give students immediate feedback on performance. As discussed in the section on supporting learning, there are approaches to reducing the surface approach to learning associated with mechanised assessment such as the use of certainty-based marking or by asking students to produce short statements explaining their choice of answers. See Chapter 14 for an extended discussion of multiple choice testing.

Group assignments can help to reduce the marking load on staff particularly in year 1, where formative assessment *for* learning may be as important as reliable indicators of performance (see Box 13.8). Workload can also be managed by assessing students in class time, for example using presentations, debates, posters, and personal response systems.

Consider shorter assignments. Fewer words does always equate with less learning although it does equate with less marking. It is the effort required to produce the work that should be comparable. Potential ideas can be drawn from the type of writing that naturally occurs in your subject or professional discipline. Examples include executive summaries, abstracts, press releases, bids for research grants or contracts, information leaflets, curator's notes, a summary of issues for a campaign group and posters. Care in the choice of assignment can ensure that it does not encourage students to reproduce their lectures or reading, but to draw on them using higher-level skills of application, evaluation, problem solving and creativity. The same issue of the number of words and the learning demonstrated applies to examinations. Short-answer papers are quicker to mark and papers of 1 or 2 hours may be just as effective as a 3-hour examination in terms of assessing learning, particularly if there is no choice of questions.

More generally, it may be worth revisiting your assessment strategy at the programme level to examine the extent to which students are being assessed on similar outcomes across a number of modules. There may be room for reduction. Furthermore, Gibbs (1992) stresses the importance of preparing students well for assessment and carefully scheduling tasks so that there are fewer problems for you and your students to deal with.

Further ideas for assessing large cohorts and reducing assessment workload can be found in Gibbs (1992), Biggs (2003) and Rust (2001).

Assessment methods

Box 13.9 provides a list of different assessment methods drawn from subject benchmark statements, QAA (2006d), Yorke and Knight (2004), Brown *et al.* (1994), Brown (2001) and general experience of the sector. The list is not all-inclusive but is provided as a stimulus for further thinking. Teaching teams may wish to review the list to identify how many methods are currently employed on programmes and to consider whether any new methods are worth further investigation.

Box 13.8   Leads into literature: group assignments

Group assignments are not a type of assessment task but a way of organising them in order to encourage collaboration between students. There is support for the cognitive, motivational and social benefits of group work (Volet and Mansfield 2006). Group assessment has the benefits of helping students see other people's point of view and gain insight into group dynamics, as well as facilitating more substantive tasks than are possible with individual assignments (Mello 1993). Where students work together on a joint assignment, they 'learn from and with each other in pooling not only perspectives and insights but also strategies for tackling such tasks' (Hounsell 2006: 8). In addition, group assignments can provide the opportunity for the development of a range of important employability skills such as working in a team and running meetings (Mello 1993; Brown *et al.* 1994), although Hartley (2005) points out that we have little evidence yet of the transferability of learning in groups to performance in other team settings. Group assessment can reduce tutor marking loads as the number of pieces to be marked is reduced and the marking can sometimes be done in class time, for example with group presentations.

Other advantages of group assignments are that, used early in a programme, they increase the opportunities for social contact among students, which is linked to student satisfaction (Krause *et al.* 2002), retention and enjoyment of study, and they can have a motivational effect as students do not wish to let down other members of their group (Bloxham and Heathfield 1994). There is some evidence that group assignments improve the achievement of lower-ability students on subsequent assignments, although the reverse was found for higher-ability students (Lejk *et al.* 1999).

Group assignments do present potential problems if not handled well, and it is recommended that there should be a limit on the number in any student programme (Falchikov 2005). For further advice on using group assignments and tackling potential difficulties, see

- Chapter 4 on designing and setting up and preparing students for group assignments;
- Chapter 6 on marking group assignments;
- Chapter 11 on considering the place of group assignments in a programme-assessment strategy.

Sources of information

The Higher Education Academy (HEA), based in the UK, has significant resources for assessment available through its website (www.heacademy.ac.uk). In addition, the HEA has 24 subject centres designed to support the

---

Box 13.9   List of assessment methods (not exclusive)

Annotated bibliographies
Essay
Capstone assignment
Completion exercises
Computer-based and online
    assignments
Concept maps
Crits
Data interpretation exercises
Debate speeches
Design tasks (including manufacture)
Direct observation
Dissertation
Electronic presentation, web pages
Evaluation of journal article or other
    paper
Examinations (unseen, seen, open-
book, case study, take-away)
Exchange or sandwich year reports
Exhibitions and displays
Fieldwork reports
Film or radio programmes
Geological mapping
Grant applications
In-class tests
Laboratory examinations and practical
    tests
Laboratory reports
Lay commentary on specialist
    material, e.g. journal article
Making glossaries
Modified essay questions
Multiple choice tests
Objective structured clinical
Examinations

Patchwork texts
Performance and production
Placement reports
Portfolio (written)
Portfolios and sketch books
Poster
Presentation
Problems and case study analysis
Professional tasks*
Project
Reflective journals, diaries and learning
    logs
Reflective learning assignments
Research project
Review of book, article, website, etc.
Short-answer questions
Simulation exercises
Student-led seminar or discussion
Synoptic examinations
Tests
Treatment reports
Viva voce examinations
Work books
Work experience report
Writing tasks: newspaper articles,
    press releases, executive summaries
Writing abstracts

---

*This is a global term to describe a range of assignments which simulate authentic tasks, for example, information leaflet, web page, briefing paper for an official inquiry, newspaper article or press release, tender for a contract.

enhancement of the student learning experience in different subject disciplines. They are accessible through the HEA website, and many offer examples of assessment methods designed for that disciplinary area including resources such as question banks. We strongly recommend making use of this resource when tackling assessment development.

Conclusion

This chapter has discussed the potential reasons for diversifying assessment, followed by practical strategies for addressing particular assessment challenges. These include the general theme of assessing a wider range of learning, and including sections on developing authentic assessments, assessing skills, and improving the validity of examinations. A second theme focused on student learning and involved sections on supporting learning and linking formative and summative assessment. Finally, practical ideas were provided for assessing large cohorts.

It is a matter of professional judgement (Ramsden 2003) what the appropriate assessment methods for your modules are, and it is essential to 'value each assessment method, within the learning environment for which it is intended, and taking its purposes and skills to be assessed into consideration' (Struyven *et al.* 2002: 28). If new techniques are planned, it will be important to help students and staff understand the purpose behind the change. In addition, new assessment techniques will need monitoring to check their effectiveness. This means at least the careful use of existing procedures such as student evaluation, staff discussion, grades achieved, and external examiner responses. New or innovative assignments come under considerably more scrutiny than traditional methods, so it is worth gathering evaluative data when faced with such challenges.

14 Computer-aided assessment

Sarah Chesney and Andrew Ginty

Introduction

There has never been a better time to consider using computer-aided assessment (CAA) in your teaching. The widespread provision of computers across campus and facilities to support learners using their own computers – for example, through wireless access and virtual learning environments (**VLEs**) – has made it an opportune time to reflect on what can be achieved in support of student learning. Furthermore, as assessment in higher education is increasingly focused on summative measurement, the use of computerised diagnostic testing can redress the balance in favour of formative assessment. In this chapter we understand CAA to be 'the application of computer technologies to the assessment process' (Bull and Danson 2004).

This chapter will discuss the advantages of using CAA within your teaching; issues you should be aware of; the current practice of CAA; and advice on effective strategies to support a learner-centred approach to assessment. We shall anticipate future developments within the field of CAA and then look in detail at types of CAA which are commonly available today, such as **objective** tests or multiple choice questions (MCQs) and using discussion tools as a vehicle for assessment purposes.

Peat and Franklin (2002) note that universities are choosing the internet for both delivery of courses for distance learners and to enhance campus-based education. This latter, 'blended' approach in teaching is now commonplace, with courses delivering e-learning via VLEs, departmental web pages, or off-line using CD-Roms or DVDs, to extend teaching beyond face-to-face delivery.

Virtual learning environments

A recent survey found that 95% of UK higher education institutions already use VLEs (Jenkins *et al.* 2005). A VLE such as Blackboard™, WebCT™ or Moodle™ offers a password-secure online environment for learners and staff which aggregates a number of functions, namely:

- communication tools, including e-mail, synchronous and asynchronous discussion boards;
- activities such as online multiple choice tests;
- pages with hyperlinks to external websites;
- areas where documents can be accessed, uploaded, downloaded, saved and printed.

A VLE usually provides you with a range of functionality for assessment, not only being able to produce multiple choice tests, but also using the discussion tools to make judgements and give feedback. The VLE may be used to bring together information and guidance to support the assessment process, including advice on how to undertake assignments, how to seek and critically evaluate learning resources, how to avoid plagiarism, and requirements for submission. When considering how a VLE can be used for CAA, find out how colleagues in your department are using it and what resources are readily available. VLE training is usually locally available for staff. Additional functionality can be added through the use of more sophisticated assessment software such as QuestionMark Perception™. You do not need to possess a high level of technical skill to be able to create and administer basic objective tests.

The online environment provides opportunities to test a student's learning in imaginative ways. The availability of tools such as e-portfolios encourages a style of assessment based upon the personal learning experiences of the student, requiring them to identify and present evidence that they have met learning outcomes and to reflect upon their attainment. An e-portfolio can provide students with more autonomy over their learning and assessment, and some VLEs now have an e-portfolio among their features.

CAA will develop in response to the possibilities of emergent Web 2.0 technologies with their emphasis on sharing, collaboration and social networking. We must take into consideration that many new students will come to higher education with high expectations, having had an increasingly rich user experience in terms of using the web for communication and entertainment. Web 2.0 technologies, including **blogs** and **wikis**, are a means of approaching assessment in which behaviours are perhaps less pre-determined by the tutor, provoking a paradigm shift for some.

CAA can be used to present complex data or scenarios, which would be hard to reproduce in a paper-based assessment. It allows for the inclusion of graphics and multimedia, providing a potentially richer experience and the opportunity to move away from text-based assessments. New kinds of tasks can be introduced (Ridgway and McCusker 2003), for example tasks which ask the learner to analyse or comment upon dynamic visual representations which display complex situations (such as the impact of climate change upon an environment). See Chapter 13 for an example of an interactive

Criteria (include at least one criteria from each section)	Preparation of students	Evidence for assessment	Importance
2. Quality			
Netiquette (online protocols)	Pre-activity group negotiation of what is acceptable; tutor modelling; online guidelines for reference; pre-activity icebreakers	Acknowledgement of others' emotions; courteous language used in contributions; ability to challenge in an inoffensive manner	These generic criteria are examples of how quality of contributions can be assessed. Learners can demonstrate that they can use language appropriate to the discipline, are considerate of others' perspectives and points of view; and are aware of their own learning
Communication	Tutor modelling of exemplar contributions. Emphasis on online socialisation	Clear and appropriate language used; unambiguous contributions; questions and challenges raised when appropriate	
Evaluation of participant's own learning	Pre-activity exemplars of contributions demonstrating this; pre-activity reading about reflection; pre-activity self-assessment tasks, e.g. online quizzes about learning styles	Learner can reflect on their own learning and the course content	
Depth of understanding of subject matter	Exemplar modelling; pre-activity discussion of aims of task	Engagement with relevant literature; Evaluation, analysis as appropriate to level of study	

enormously difficult with large groups and allows for confidentiality if that is preferred. SPARK can be found at www.educ.dab.uts.edu.au/darrall/sparksite/.

Supporting diverse learners

Chapter 10 discusses assessment and student disability in some depth and recommends designing inclusive assessment that allows every learner the opportunity to demonstrate what they have learnt. CAA allows tutors greater flexibility than more traditional methods when addressing individual learner needs. For example, well-designed online assessments allow a student to control how a test is displayed or how data are presented so that it is more accessible to them (colour, audio, text size).

Techdis (www.techdis.ac.uk), an advisory service in the field of accessibility and inclusion, provides a guide to e-assessment which includes useful checklists for measuring the accessibility of online assessments. When designing CAA, be mindful of what you are assessing. One of the challenges is to avoid inadvertently assessing a learner's ICT skills or memorising skills, rather than the learning outcomes of the course. Simply allotting extra time in an assessment for a learner with a disability is not always a panacea, as time spent at a computer screen can be draining. You need to be aware that students with visual impairment, including colour blindness, may be disadvantaged when using specific colours in graphics. Advice and further information are likely to be available from your institution's disability support service.

Advice that can help all learners will particularly benefit a learner with a disability. Provide guidance on how to use the spellcheck tool on the discussion board, or how to write a contribution in Microsoft Word™ which can then be copied and pasted onto the discussion board.

Cheating and plagiarism detection

The ease with which information can be electronically copied from the internet or between learners and pasted into assignments has been blamed for the increase in malpractice in higher education. Strategies to confront cheating should focus on learner support rather than solely on finding punitive measures to deter plagiarism (see Chapter 4 for general advice on designing assessment to reduce plagiarism).

In the CAA environment, randomising online MCQs can prevent learners from cheating and copying from one another. In one engineering course, providing unique tutorial sheets with different sets of data encouraged learners to collaborate, but prevented them from copying answers from one another (Russell and Bullen 2005). Administering this electronically minimised the need for staff time and preparation.

Plagiarism detection software can be used effectively to support learning by allowing students to use it in advance of an assignment submission date and can be an effective means of formative assessment. See Box 14.3. for an example. However, plagiarism detection needs to be addressed with care, and McKeever (2006) provides a useful overview of the issues requiring consideration.

Box 14.3   Formative use of detection software

Engineering students have limited familiarity with extended writing and, despite clear guidance, results can be disappointing. In order to improve performance, formative assessment is provided through use of the JISC Plagiarism Detection Service (www.jiscpas.ac.uk). 'Students write draft essays, which are then submitted to the detection service with the output report returned to individuals and then discussed in class sessions. This has addressed a key problem that students find difficulty in expressing their own understanding without relying too heavily on the sources they use ... Although the focus here is "plagiarism" in fact the tutor and student group discussion on the draft essays and the detection reports have increased students' understanding of the requirements for this kind of writing more broadly' (Roger Penlington, reported in McDowell *et al.* 2005: 6).

Sources of further information

Harnessing Technology (Department for Education and Skills, 2005), a UK government e-learning strategy, outlines priorities that have relevance to tutors wishing to introduce CAA. These include aiming for online personalised support for learners that would include secure access to records including qualifications and online resources. The Higher Education Funding Council for England (2005) envisages a future where tutors have access to tools which enable better communication between them and their learners, thus enhancing feedback and support. These highlight the untapped potential e-learning has to offer and signify a national drive towards a future in which e-learning is accepted and embedded into all aspects of education.

The Higher Education Academy (2005) offers a sector-wide view of CAA in the UK through useful case studies. The Academy's subject centre websites also provide a useful and easily accessible means of keeping up to date with innovations and research within your own specialist discipline.

It is also advisable to search within your own institution to gain an overview of what is happening locally. The university's educational development unit should be able to advise on practice; it may publish guides on implementing CAA or run workshops where you can gain an introduction to the field and share practice with colleagues.

Conclusion

This chapter has provided an overview of CAA, its potential and its challenges. Just as major advances in teaching methods have not been accompanied by a similar development in modes of assessment, so CAA has not always been a focal point of assessment practice despite the exponential growth in the use of computers in university life. While the prospect of computer-based assessment may be disconcerting to many and seem out of place for their discipline area, this chapter has attempted to show that CAA is wide ranging and there are many potential benefits, particularly in providing prompt formative feedback to students.

Training and socialisation of markers

Staff development of new markers is considered important to improve practice and tackle existing dysfunctional approaches (Smith and Coombe 2006). Ecclestone (2001) considers that reliability emerges through a process of staff socialisation, becoming part of an assessment community. Research (Swann and Ecclestone 1999a; Price 2005) suggests that technical changes to practice such as marking grids and assessment criteria are insufficient on their own because application of a marking scheme to a specific assignment is a 'social construct' negotiated between the members of that assessment community and influenced by their tacit knowledge (Baird *et al.* 2004). Discussion of marking schemes, co-ordination meetings and use of exemplar assignments are, therefore, important (Baird *et al.* 2004) although they may be more difficult to organise as module teams grow in size. Research with associate (casual) markers indicated that they were often omitted from such discussions (Smith and Coombe 2006).

Training which is limited to briefings or written guidance is considered to limit the transfer of the tacit knowledge needed (Price 2005). One approach reported in Price (2005) is the concept of a 'marking bee' where markers are brought together to mark in one session. This has the advantage of facilitating inter-marker discussion and, for example with examination scripts, different markers can mark questions in their areas of expertise which is very difficult to organise in any other way.

Role design

The individual work situation of academics will vary considerably, even within one institution or department, and this means that it may be valuable to consider the design of an individual's role carefully. The size, number, professional culture and variety of teaching teams that they are required to join will have a significant bearing on their experience. Membership of too many teaching teams may limit the ability of the staff to participate and contribute fully to any single team and to develop an effective sharing of tacit knowledge regarding the assessment requirements. Perhaps we should also avoid or at least compensate for the opposite experience, a lecturer with membership of only one small team, because this may limit experience in terms of sharing a range of practice.

There is a need to identify potential isolation of new and experienced staff even where they appear to be joining a team of a reasonable size. This isolation may be caused, for example, by geographical location of site, or even simply the design and location of office space and arrangements for coffee breaks, and these may be exacerbated by the busy nature of departmental life.

Both formal and non-formal interventions may be needed to counter these possible issues.

More careful consideration and design of roles may at least highlight the need for the creation of boundary-crossing opportunities when members of staff are firmly located within one teaching team and may not have much chance to gain experience of alternative assessment methods or of bench-marking of standards and assessment practice.

Assessment within subject discipline pedagogy

Lecturers need to be able to contribute to debate on the key principles of pedagogy in their discipline and on the design of assessment within this. In particular, it is important to view events such as comparison and moderation of marks after blind second or double marking as a professional learning opportunity rather than simply a bureaucratic hurdle. In terms of learning and teaching, discussions of subject knowledge, academic writing and asso-ciated assessment requirements during such meetings are likely to be very valuable professional learning events (Rust et al. 2005). Where there is pro-fessional trust and a willingness to engage in critical reflection by all of the participants, these are key professional learning events for experienced aca-demics as well as for those new to the team. These events should be seen as the key to quality assurance and to maintenance of local standards.

Newly appointed staff highlight assessment as a particular area where support is required; many will find it stressful, confusing and time-consuming (Boyd et al. 2006). The basic organisation and administration of assessment and quality assurance processes is a key area of learning for new staff. The public accountability element of assessment and quality assurance procedures is rather threatening and new staff will therefore appreciate careful explana-tion of their role and ongoing support. If newly appointed staff complete a training course then it is important that it engages them in critical con-sideration of generic pedagogical issues in adult and higher education but also in the particular learning, teaching and assessment issues and literature of their discipline. If they do not receive formal training, then the department needs to consider how new staff will be supported in critically engaging with their subject discipline's pedagogy. Generic workshops or guidance from a central learning and teaching unit might be of use in aspects such as design of assessment or marking student work. However, these need to be in addition to individual support on marking and the assessment process within the tutor's subject discipline team.

The development and validation of revised or new programmes is another key opportunity for professional learning focused on assessment. It is important that sufficient time is allocated for this work and that there is activity. Credit is expressed in a quantified form so that learning achievements in different contexts can be broadly compared in terms of intellectual depth (level) and relative volume (number of credits). No additional credit can be awarded for achievement above the threshold level.

credit level – An indicator of the relative demand, complexity, depth of learning and learner autonomy required by a particular unit of study. In the UK, only one credit level can be attributed to any given module.

criterion-referenced marking – This means that student achievement is tested against a set of criteria such as those linked to the learning outcomes for the assignment.

deep learning – An approach to learning where students try to go beyond the surface of the subject matter and understand the underlying meaning. They may not remember all the details, but they will develop an understanding of ideas and concepts, often by linking them to prior knowledge or experience. Students are more likely to retain this type of learning.

diagnostic assessment – assessment designed to identify skills, knowledge and other attributes which can be used to decide on specific pathways of study, or difficulties in learning which require support.

double blind anonymous marking – The situation where students are marking each other's work without knowledge of whose work they are marking or who has marked their work.

double marking – The situation where every piece of assessed work submitted by students is marked separately by two tutors before a final mark is agreed. It is usually reserved for large pieces of assessed work that will make a significant difference to the final grade for an award.

examination – An assessment task undertaken under controlled conditions.

examination board – A meeting which considers and agrees student marks and awards.

exemplar – An example of a completed assignment which is used to illustrate the assessment requirements and marking standards.

extenuating circumstance – A reasonable excuse provided by a student, usually with some kind of proof, for poor performance, or late, or non-submission of assessed work or non-attendance at an examination. It will often be due to illness and is sometimes referred to as a mitigating circumstance.

external examiners – Independent academic experts drawn from other institutions who provide impartial advice on standards and assessment procedures in particular programmes.

feedback – Information about student work and progress provided to students.

Feed-forward – Information about student work and progress which students may use to inform their further learning and tutors may use to modify their teaching plans.

FHEQ – Framework for Higher Education Qualifications. This is a UK framework introduced to provide consistency and transparency in relation to higher education qualifications. It has five levels from undergraduate to doctoral level.

formative assessment – Assessment which is intended to provide feedback to the student such that they can improve their work and to the teacher so that they may adjust their teaching. In practice, much formative assessment in higher education also has a summative function, that is, the marks contribute to the overall grade for the module or course.

grade descriptors – Statements which describe, for each credit level, what a student should demonstrate in order to achieve the various grades in the academic marking scale. They are designed to assist staff in making consistent and reliable marking decisions. They are also designed to help students understand what is required to achieve higher grades. They are generic statements so they should be used in conjunction with the assessment criteria for individual assessment tasks in order to create marking schemes.

Higher Education Academy – A support organisation for higher education institutions, subject discipline groups and individual staff in the UK with a focus on enhancement of the student learning experience.

high stakes – Assessment which contributes significantly to progression on a course or to final grading so that the threat to the student is high.

interdisciplinary – Programmes or studies which encompass more than one academic subject discipline, for example a joint or combined honours degree.

key skills – A broad range of generic skills required for learning and employment. They include communications skills, use of number, information technology, working with others, managing own performance, and problem solving.

learning hours – The notional learning time or study hours that it is expected a learner will need to spend to complete a course including taught sessions, private study and completing assessments.

level descriptor – A statement which describes the characteristics of learning demand which the learner will encounter at a particular level of study.

low stakes – Assessment which does not contribute significantly to progression or final grading so that the threat to the student is low.

malpractice – A term used to mean cheating or somehow breaking the institutional regulations for assessment.

marking scheme – Prepared by applying the grade descriptors for the appropriate level to the specific assessment criteria for an assignment, and usually presented in the form of a matrix.

MCQ – Multiple choice questions.

mitigating circumstance – See *extenuating circumstances*.

moderation – A process for ensuring that grades awarded are fair and reliable and that marking criteria have been applied consistently.

modular – A term referring to programmes of study which are broken up into units which are separately assessed.

module – A specific unit of study or block of learning which is separately assessed. Combinations of modules form a programme of study.

norm-referenced marking – This measures a student's performance in relation to his/her cohort. The grade awarded depends not only on the quality of a student's work but also on the quality of others' performance.

objective test – A test in which there is one defined answer to each question and no expert judgement is required on the part of the marker.

OSCE – Objective Structured Clinical Examination, that is, a form of assessment involving observation of simulated practice used in health professions.

plagiarism – Cheating in assessments by using ideas or words from other authors without explicitly acknowledging the source of the information.

programme – The overall curriculum followed by an individual student, normally comprising a specified set of modules or option choices.

retention – The rate of student progress into the second and further years of a higher education programme.

QAA – Quality Assurance Agency, an external government organization which monitors standards in UK universities.

revision – Preparation by students for an examination.

second marking – Checking of marking by a second tutor, usually involving only a sample of the assessed work.

specific learning difficulties – A range of learning needs, the most frequent among students is dyslexia.

subject benchmark statements – These are used in the UK to set out the expectations associated with degrees in different subjects. They have been published by the QAA (2006d) and 'define what can be expected of a graduate in terms of the techniques and skills needed to develop understanding in the subject'.

subject discipline – A more or less well-defined body of knowledge and its associated community of learners, teachers, researchers and practitioners.

surface learning – An approach to learning where students focus on the details in a lecture or text. They attempt to memorise those details rather than understand the meaning of the topic or concept. Consequently, they can quickly forget the material.

summative assessment – Assessment which counts towards, or constitutes a final grade for, a module or course or where a pass is required for progression by the student.

test – An assessment task taken in semi-controlled conditions such as an in-class or online test, usually of a relatively short duration.

VLE – Virtual Learning Environment, an integrated online course delivery system which provides a consistent user-friendly interface and includes areas for course materials and communications. Examples are Moodle™, WebCT™ and Blackboard™.

wiki – A collaborative website whose content can be amended by anyone who is allowed access to it.

Hyland, P. (2000) Learning from feedback on assessment, in A. Booth and P. Hyland (eds) *The Practice of University History Teaching*. Manchester: Manchester University Press.

Jackson, N. (2000) Programme specification and its role in promoting an outcomes model of learning, *Active Learning in Higher Education*, 1(2): 132–51.

Jacques, D. (2000) *Learning in Groups: A Handbook for Improving Group Work*, 3rd edn. London: Kogan Page.

James, M. and Pedder, D. (2006) Professional learning as a condition for assessment for learning, in J. Gardner (ed.) *Assessment and Learning*. London: Sage.

Jenkins, M., Browne, T. and Walker, R. (2005) *VLE surveys: A longitudinal perspective between March 2001, March 2003 and March 2005 for higher education in the United Kingdom*. www.ucisa.ac.uk/groups/tlig/vle/vle_survey_2005.pdf (accessed 6 December 2006).

Joint Information Systems Committee (2001) *JISC Data Protection Code of Practice for the HE and FE Sectors version 2*. www.jisc.ac.uk/publications/publications/pub_dpacop_0101.aspx (accessed 25 September 2006).

Johnson, J.A. and DeSpain, B.C. (2004) Mentoring the reluctant writer, *Professional Educator*, 26(2): 45–55.

Johnson, V. (2001) Developing strategies to improve student retention: reflections from the work of Napier University's Student Retention Project. Paper presented to the SRHE Conference, Cambridge.

Johnson, V., Macleod, L. and Small, G. (2003) Using a research-led approach to informing retention strategies for students from low income and lower socio-economic groups. Paper presented to the International student retention conference, Amsterdam, 5–7 November.

Jonsson, A. and Baartman, L.K.J. (2006) Estimating the quality of new modes of assessment: the case of the 'interactive examination' for teacher competency. Paper presented to the Northumbria EARLI SIG Assessment Conference, Darlington, 29 August – 1 September.

Juwah, C., Macfarlane-Dick, D., Matthew, B., Nicol, D., Ross, D. and Smith, B. (2004) *Enhancing Student Learning through Effective Formative Feedback*. York: Higher Education Academy.

Kelly, P (2002) First Year Engineers – given half a chance. *Pantaneto forum, 5*. http://pantaneto.co.uk/issue5/kelly.htm (accessed: 24 Oct. 2006).

Kember, D. (2000) *Action Learning and Action Research: Improving the Quality of Teaching and Learning*. London: Kogan Page.

Kilic, G.B. and Cakan, M. (2006) The analysis of the impact of individual weighting factor on individual scores, *Assessment and Evaluation in Higher Education*, 31(6): 639–54.

King, H. (n.d.) *Equal opportunities in assessment*. www.gees.ac.uk/essd/assess.htm#KingH2 (accessed 8 October 2003).

Kirkwood, A and Price, L. (2005) Learners and learning in the twenty-first century:

what do we know about students' attitudes towards and experiences of information and communication technologies that will help us design courses?, *Studies in Higher Education*, 30(3): 257–74.

Klenowski, V. (2002) *Developing Portfolios for Learning and Assessment.* London: RoutledgeFalmer.

Klenowski, V. and Elwood, J. (2002) Creating communities of shared practice: the challenges of assessment use in learning and teaching, *Assessment and Evaluation in Higher Education*, 27(3): 243–56.

Klenowski, V., Askew, S. and Camell, E. (2006) Portfolios for learning, assessment and professional development in higher education, *Assessment and Evaluation in Higher Education*, 31(3): 267–86.

Kneale, P.E. (1997) The rise of the 'strategic student': how can we adapt to cope?, in S. Armstrong, G. Thompson and S. Brown (eds) *Facing up to Radical Changes in Universities and Colleges.* London: Kogan Page.

Knight, P.T. (2000) The value of a programme-wide approach to assessment, *Assessment and Evaluation in Higher Education*, 25(3): 237–51.

Knight, P.T. (2001) *A Briefing on Key Concepts.* York: Learning and Teaching Support Network.

Knight, P.T. (2006) The local practices of assessment, *Assessment and Evaluation in Higher Education*, 31(4): 435–52.

Knight, P.T. and Yorke, M. (2003) *Assessment, Learning and Employability.* Maidenhead: Open University Press.

Kogan, M. (2000) Higher Education communities and academic identity, *Higher Education Quarterly*, 54(3): 207–16.

Kolb, D.A. (1984) *Experiential Learning: Experience as the Source of Learning and Development.* Englewood Cliffs, NJ: Prentice Hall.

Krause, K.L. (2001) The university essay writing experience: a pathway for academic integration during transition, *Higher Education Research and Development*, 20(2): 147–68.

Krause, K.L., McInnis, C. and Welle, C. (2002) Student engagement: the role of peers in undergraduate student experience. Paper presented to the SHRE Annual Conference, Melbourne, 5–7 July. www.cshe.unimelb.edu.au/APFYP/ pdfs/KrauseSRHE.pdf (accessed 14 November 2006).

Kvale, S. (1996) Examinations re-examined: certification of students or certification of Knowledge?, in S. Chaiklin, and J. Lave (eds) *Understanding Practice: Perspectives on Activity and Context.* Cambridge: Cambridge University Press.

Lacina, J.G. (2002) Preparing international students for a successful social experience in higher education, *New Directions for Higher Education*, 117: 21–8.

Land, R. (2004) *Educational Development: Discourse, Identity and Practice.* Maidenhead: Open University Press.

Laurillard, D. (2002) *Rethinking University Teaching: A Conversational Framework for the Effective Use of Learning Technologies*, 2nd edn. London: RoutledgeFalmer.

Lave, J. and Wenger, E. (1991) *Situated Learning*. Cambridge: Cambridge University Press.

Lave, J. and Wenger, E. (1999) Legitimate peripheral participation in communities of practice, in R. McCormick and C. Paechter (eds) *Learning and Knowledge*. London: Paul Chapman.

Lawrence, J. (2005) Re-conceptualising attrition and retention: integrating theoretical, research and student perspectives, *Studies in Learning, Evaluation, Innovation and Development*, 2(3): 16–33.

Lea, M.R. and Street, B.V. (2000) Student writing and staff feedback in higher education: an academic literacies approach, in M.R. Lea and B. Stierer (eds) *Student Writing in Higher Education*. Buckingham: Open University Press.

Leach, L. and Zepke, N. (2005) Integration and adaptation: approaches to the student retention and achievement puzzle, *Active Learning in Higher Education*, 6(1): 46–59.

Lee, D.S. (1997) What teachers can do to relieve problems identified by international students, *New Directions for Teaching and Learning*, 70: 93–100.

Lejk, M. and Wyvill, M. (1996) A survey of methods of deriving individual grades from group assessments, *Assessment and Evaluation in Higher Education*, 21(3): 267–80.

Lejk, M. and Wyvill, M. (2001) The effect of the inclusion of self-assessment with peer assessment of contributions to a group project: a quantitative study of secret and agreed assessments, *Assessment and Evaluation in Higher Education*, 26(6): 551–61.

Lejk, M., Wyvill, M and Farrow, S. (1999) Group assessment in systems analysis and design: a comparison of the performance of streamed and mixed-ability groups, *Assessment and Evaluation in Higher Education*, 24(1): 5–14.

Light, G. and Cox, R. (2001) *Learning and Teaching in Higher Education: The Reflective Professional*. London: Sage.

Lillis, T.M. (2001) *Student Writing: Access, Regulation and Desire*. London: Routledge.

Lillis, T.M. (2003) Student writing as academic literacies: drawing on Bakhtin to move from critique to design, *Language and Education*, 17(3): 192–207.

Lines, D. (2005) Developing a variety of assessment methods including peer and self-assessment: an overview, in Quality Assurance Agency, *Enhancing Practice: Reflections on Assessment, Volume 1*. Gloucester: QAA.

MacDonald, R. and Carroll, J. (2006) Plagiarism: a complex issue requiring a holistic institutional approach, *Assessment and Evaluation in Higher Education*, 31(2): 233–45.

MacKenzie, D. (2004a) *Online Assessment: Quality Production and Delivery for Higher Education*. www.enhancementthemes.ac.uk/documents/events/20040416/ Mackenziepresentation.pdf (accessed 2 April 2007).

MacKenzie, D. (2004b) *Online Assessment: Quality Production and Delivery for Higher Education*. www.enhancementthemes.ac.uk/documents/events/20040416/

Mackenziepaper-revised.pdf (accessed 2 April 2007).

MacKinnon, G. (2000) The dilemma of evaluating electronic discussion groups, *Journal of Research on Computing in Education*, 33(2): 125–32.

Maclellan, E. (2001) Assessment for learning: the differing perceptions of tutors and students, *Assessment and Evaluation in Higher Education*, 26(4): 307–18.

Maclellan, E. (2004a) How convincing is alternative assessment for use in higher education, *Assessment and Evaluation in Higher Education*, 29(3): 311–21.

Maclellan, E. (2004b) How reflective is the academic essay?, *Studies in Higher Education*, 29(1): 75–89.

Maki, P.L. (2004) *Assessing for Learning: Building a Sustainable Commitment across the Institution*. Sterling, VA: Stylus/American Association of Higher Education.

Marton, F. (1976) On non-verbatim learning II: The erosion of a task induced learning algorithm, *Scandinavian Journal of Psychology*, 17: 41–8.

Marton, F. and Saljo, R. (1997) Approaches to learning, in F. Marton, D. Hounsell, and N.J. Entwistle (eds) *The Experience of Learning: Implications for Teaching and Studying in Higher Education*. Edinburgh: Scottish Academic Press.

Mathias, H. (2005) Mentoring on a programme for new university teachers: a partnership in revitalizing and empowering collegiality, *International Journal of Academic Development*, 10(2): 95–106.

McConnell, D. (2000) *Implementing Computer Supported Cooperative Learning*, 2nd edn. London: Kogan Page.

McDowell, L. and Sambell, K. (2005) *Negotiating Academic Assignments: The Experiences of Widening Participation and Traditional Student*. Oxford: OCSLD.

McDowell, L., Sambell, K., Bazin, V. *et al.* (2005) *Assessment for Learning: Current Practice Exemplars from the Centre for Excellence in Learning and Teaching*. Newcastle: Centre for Excellence in Teaching & Learning in Assessment for Learning, University of Northumbria.

McGhee, P. (2003) *The Academic Quality Handbook: Enhancing Higher Education in Universities and Further Education Colleges*. London: Kogan Page.

McGourty, J., Besterfield-Sacre, M. and Shuman, L. (1999) ABET's *eleven student learning outcomes (a–k): have we considered the implications?* www.engrng.pitt. edu/~ec2000/grant_papers/McGourty+ASEE-99.PDF (accessed 28 October 2006).

McKeever, L. (2006) Online plagiarism detection services: saviour or scourge, *Assessment and Evaluation in Higher Education*, 31(2): 155–65.

McLaughlin, S. and Sutton, R. (2005) *The STAR Project: Re-assessment Strategy*. www.ulster.ac.uk/star/curriculum_development/Wolverhampton%20Re-Assessment.pdf (accessed 6 October 2006)

McNiff, J. and Whitehead, J. (2002) *Action Research: Principles and Practice*. London: RoutledgeFalmer.

Mello, J.A. (1993) Improving individual member accountability in small work group settings, *Journal of Management Education*, 17(2): 253–9.

Miller, A.H., Imrie, B.W. and Cox, K. (1998) *Student Assessment in Higher Education*.

London: Kogan Page.

Miller, C.M.I. and Parlett, M. (1974) *Up to the Mark: A Study of the Examination Game*. Guildford: Society for Research into Higher Education.

Moon, J. (1999) *Learning Journals*. London: Kogan Page.

Moon, J. (2002) *The Module and Programme Development Handbook*. London: Kogan Page.

Morgan, A. and Beatty, L. (1997) The world of the learner, in F. Marton, D. Hounsell and N.J. Entwistle (eds) *The Experience of Learning*. Edinburgh: Scottish Academic Press.

Morias, A.M. (1996) Understanding teachers' evaluation criteria: a condition for success in science classes, *Journal of Research in Science Teaching*, 33(6): 601–24.

Moseley, D., Elliott, J., Gregson, M. and Higgins, S. (2005) Thinking skills frameworks for use in education and training, *British Educational Research Journal*, 31(3): 367–90.

Muir, W. (1999) *Report of study visit to Australia and New Zealand*. www.euro-virology. com/services/courtoffice/fellowship/muir.rtf (accessed 20 November 2006).

Murphy, E. (1997) *Constructivism: from philosophy to practice*. www.cdli.ca/ ~elmurphy/emurphy/cle.html (accessed 30 November 2006).

Murphy, R. (2006) Evaluating new priorities for assessment in higher education, in C. Bryan and K. Clegg (eds) *Innovative Assessment in Higher Education*. London: Routledge.

Mutch, A. (2003) Exploring the practice of feedback to students, *Active Learning in Higher Education*, 4(1): 24–38.

Mutch, A. and Brown, G. (2001) *Assessment: A Guide for Heads of Department*. York: Learning and Teaching Support Network.

National Student Survey (2006) *The National Student Survey*. www.thestudent survey.com/ (accessed 15 September 2006).

National Committee of Inquiry into Higher Education (1997) *Higher Education in the Learning Society: Report of the National Committee of Inquiry into Higher Education* (Dearing Report). Leeds: NCIHE Publications.

Newstead, S. and Dennis, I. (1994) Examiners examined: the reliability of exam marking in psychology, *The Psychologist*, 7(5): 216–19.

Nicol, D. and Macfarlane-Dick, D. (2004) *Rethinking formative assessment in HE: a theoretical model and seven principles of good feedback practice*. www.heacademy. ac.uk/assessment/ASS051D_SENLEF_model.doc (accessed 26 September 2006).

Nicol, D. and Macfarlane-Dick, D. (2006) Formative assessment and self-regulated learning: a model and seven principles of good feedback practice, *Studies in Higher Education*, 31(2): 199–218.

Northedge, A. (2003a) Rethinking teaching in the context of diversity, *Teaching in Higher Education*, 8(1): 17–32.

Northedge, A. (2003b) Enabling participation in academic discourse, *Teaching in Higher Education*, 8(2): 169–80.

Norton, L. (2004) Using assessment criteria as learning criteria: a case study in psychology, *Assessment and Evaluation in Higher Education*, 29(6): 687–702.

O'Donovan, B., Price, M. and Rust, C. (2004) Know what I mean? Enhancing student understanding of assessment standards and criteria, *Teaching in Higher Education*, 9(3): 325–35.

Oliver, R. and Omari, A. (1999) Using online technologies to support problem based learning: learners' responses and perceptions, *Australian Journal of Educational Technology* 15(1): 58–79.

Orr, S. (2005) Transparent opacity: assessment in the inclusive academy, in C. Rust (ed.) *Improving Student Learning: Diversity and Inclusivity*. Oxford: OCSLD.

Orrell, J. (2006) Feedback on learning achievement: rhetoric and reality, *Teaching in Higher Education*, 11(4): 441–56.

Orsmond, P., Reiling, K. and Merry, S. (2000) The use of student derived marking criteria in peer and self-assessment, *Assessment and Evaluation in Higher Education*, 25(1): 23–38.

Pajares, F. (2002) *Overview of social cognitive theory and of self efficacy*. www.des.emory.edu/mfp/eff.html (accessed 11 November 2006).

Palloff, R. and Pratt, K. (1999) *Building Learning Communities in Cyberspace: Effective Strategies for the Online Classroom*. San Francisco, CA: Jossey-Bass.

Park, C. (2003) In other (people's) words: plagiarism by university students – literature and lessons, *Assessment and Evaluation in Higher Education*, 28(5): 471–88.

Parker, J. (2003) The patchwork text in teaching Greek tragedy, *Innovations in Education and Teaching International*, 40(2): 180–93.

Partington, J. (1994) Double-marking students work, *Assessment and Evaluation in Higher Education*, 19(1): 57–60.

Peat, M. and Franklin, S. (2002) Supporting student learning: the use of computer-based formative assessment modules, *British Journal of Educational Technology*, 33(5): 515–23.

Pickard, J. (2006) Staff and student attitudes to plagiarism at University College Northampton, *Assessment and Evaluation in Higher Education*, 31(2): 215–32.

Pickford, R. (2006) Assessing enterprise, enterprising assessment. Paper presented to the Northumbria EARLI SIG Assessment Conference, Darlington, 29 August – 1 September.

Pintrich, P.R. (2003) A motivational science perspective on the role of student motivation in learning and teaching contexts, *Journal of Educational Psychology* 95(4): 667–86.

Pitcher, N., Goldfinch, J. and Beevers, C.E. (2002) Aspects of computer-based assessment in mathematics, *Active Learning in Higher Education*, 3(2): 159–76.

Polanyi, M. (1998) The tacit dimension (reprinted), in L. Prusak (ed.) *Knowledge in Organizations*. Boston, MA: Butterworth Heinemann.

Price, M. (2005) Assessment standards: the role of communities of practice and the scholarship of assessment, *Assessment and Evaluation in Higher Education*, 30(3): 215–30.

Price, M. and O'Donovan, B. (2006) Improving performance through enhancing student understanding of criteria and feedback, in C. Bryan and K. Clegg (eds) *Innovative Assessment in Higher Education*. London: Routledge.

Price, M. and Rust, C. (1999) The experience of introducing a common criteria assessment grid across an academic department, *Quality in Higher Education*, 5(2): 133–44.

Prosser, M. and Trigwell, K. (1999) *Understanding Learning and Teaching: The Experience in Higher Education*. Buckingham: Open University Press.

Quality Assurance Agency (1999) *Code of Practice for the Assurance of Academic Quality and Standards in Higher Education. Section 3: Students with Disabilities.* Gloucester: QAA.

Quality Assurance Agency (2004) *Code of Practice for the Assurance of Academic Quality and Standards in Higher Education. Section 4: External Examining*, 2nd edn. Gloucester: QAA.

Quality Assurance Agency (2005) *Outcomes from Institutional Audit: External Examiners and Their Reports*. Gloucester: QAA.

Quality Assurance Agency (2006a) *Outcomes from Institutional Audit: Assessment of Students*. Gloucester: QAA.

Quality Assurance Agency (2006b) *Background Briefing Note: The Classification of Degree Awards*. Gloucester: QAA.

Quality Assurance Agency (2006c) *Code of Practice for the Assurance of Academic Quality and Standards in Higher Education. Section 6: Assessment of students*, 2nd edn. Gloucester: QAA.

Quality Assurance Agency (2006d) *About the academic infrastructure.* www.qaa.ac. uk/academicinfrastructure/default.asp (accessed 28 March 2007).

Quality Assurance Agency (2006e) *Code of Practice for the Assurance of Academic Quality and Standards in Higher Education. Section 7: Programme Design, Approval, Monitoring and Review*. Gloucester: Quality Assurance Agency.

Race, P. (2003) *Designing assessment to improve physical sciences learning*. www. physsci.heacademy.ac.uk/Publications/PracticeGuide/guide4.pdf (accessed 20 October 2006).

Raeside, R. and Goldfinch, J. (1990) Development of a peer assessment technique for obtaining individual marks on a group project, *Assessment and Evaluation in Higher Education*, 15(3): 210–31.

Ramsden, P. (2003) *Learning to Teach in Higher Education*, 2nd edn. London: RoutledgeFalmer.

Randall, M. and Mirador, J. (2003) How well am I doing? Using a corpus-based analysis to investigate tutor and institutional messages in comment sheets, *Assessment and Evaluation in Higher Education*, 28(5): 515–26.

Read, B., Francis, B. and Robson, J. (2005) Gender, bias, assessment and feedback: analyzing the written assessment of undergraduate history essays, *Assessment and Evaluation in Higher Education*, 30(3): 241–60.

Reber, R. (2005) Assessing motivational factors in educational technology: the case of building a web site as course assignment, *British Journal of Educational*

Technology, 36(1): 93–5.

Ridgway, J. and McCusker, S. (2003) Using computers to assess new educational goals, *Assessment in Education: Principles, Policy and Practice,* 10(3): 309–28.

Robson, K. (2005) Assessment – The final frontier – Just how valid, realiable and fair are assessments of disabled students?, in Quality Assurance Agency (ed.) *Enhancing Practice, Reflections on Assessment: Volume II.* Gloucester: Quality Assurance Agency.

Ross, D.A. (2005) Streamlining assessment – how to make assessment more efficient and more effective – an overview, in Quality Assurance Agency (ed.) *Enhancing Practice: reflections on Assessment, Volume 1.* Gloucester: QAA.

Rowland, S. (2001) Surface Learning about teaching in higher education: the need for more critical conversations, *International Journal of Academic Development,* 6(2): 162–7.

Russell, M. and Bullen P. (2005) *Improving student success and retention through greater participation and tackling student unique tutorial sheets.* Higher Education Academy Engineering Subject Centre. www.engsc.ac.uk/resources/wats/downloads/wats_report.pdf (accessed 28 March 2007).

Russell, M., Goldberg, A. and O'Connor, K. (2003) Computer-based testing and validity: a look back into the future, *Assessment in Education: Principles, Policy and Practice,* 10(3): 279–93.

Rust, C. (2001) *A Briefing on Assessment of Large Groups.* York: Learning and Teaching Support Network.

Rust, C. (2002) The impact of assessment on student learning: how can the research literature practically help to inform the development of departmental assessment strategies and learner-centred assessment practices?, *Active Learning in Higher Education,* 3(2): 145–58.

Rust, C., O'Donovan, B. and Price, M. (2003) Improving students' learning by developing their understanding of assessment criteria and processes, *Assessment and Evaluation in Higher Education,* 28(2): 147–64.

Rust, C., O'Donovan, B. and Price, M. (2005) A social constructivist assessment process model: how the research literature shows us this could be best practice, *Assessment and Evaluation in Higher Education,* 30(3): 231–40.

Sadler, D.R. (1989) Formative assessment and the design of instructional systems, *Instructional Science,* 18(2): 119–44.

Sadler, D.R. (1998) Formative assessment: revisiting the territory, *Assessment in Education,* 5(1): 77–84.

Sadler, D.R. (2005) Interpretations of criteria-based assessment and grading in higher education, *Assessment and Evaluation in Higher Education,* 30(2): 175–94.

Salmon, G. (2004) *E-Moderating: The Key to Teaching and Learning Online,* 2nd edn. London: Kogan Page.

Sambell, K., Brown, S. and McDowell, E. (1997) 'But is it fair?': An exploratory study of student perceptions of the consequential validity of assessment,

Studies in Educational Evaluation, 23(4): 349–71.

Sambell, K., McDowell, L. and Sambell, A. (2006) Supporting diverse students: developing learner autonomy via assessment, in C. Bryan and K. Clegg (eds) *Innovative Assessment in Higher Education.* London: Routledge.

Sarros, J.C. and Densten, I.L. (1989) Undergraduate student stress and coping strategies, *Higher Education Research and Development,* 8(1): 47–57.

Scoggins, J. and Winter, R. (1999) The patchwork text: a coursework format for education as critical understanding, *Teaching in Higher Education,* 4(4): 485–99.

Scouller, K.M. and Prosser, M. (1994) Students' experiences in studying for multiple choice question examinations, *Studies in Higher Education,* 19(3): 267–79.

SEEC (2003) *Credit Level Descriptors for Further and Higher Education.* London: SEEC. www.seec-office.org.uk/creditleveldescriptors2003.pdf (accessed 28 March 2007).

Smith, E. and Coombe, K. (2006) Quality and qualms in the marking of university assignments by sessional staff: an exploratory study, *Higher Education,* 51(1): 45–69.

Snyder, B.R. (1971) *The Hidden Curriculum.* New York: Knopf.

South West Academic Network for Disability Support. (1999–2002) *SENDA compliance in higher education.* www.plymouth.ac.uk/assets/SWA/Sendadoc.pdf (accessed 8 October 2006).

Stacey, E. (1999) Collaborative learning in an online environment, *Journal of Distance Education,* 14 (2). http://cade.athabascau.ca/vol14.2/stacey.html (accessed 28 March 2007).

Staniforth, D. and Harland, T. (2006) Contrasting views of induction: the experiences of new academic staff and their heads of department, *Active Learning in Higher Education,* 7(2): 185–96.

Stefani, L.A.J. (1998) Assessment in partnership with learners, *Assessment and Evaluation in Higher Education,* 23(4): 339–50.

Stenhouse, L. (1975) *An Introduction to Curriculum Research and Development.* London: Heinemann.

Stowell, M. (2004) Equity, justice and standards: assessment decision making in higher education, *Assessment and Evaluation in Higher Education,* 29(4): 495–510.

Struyven, K., Dochy, F. and Janssens, S. (2002) Students' perceptions about assessment in higher education: a review. Paper presented at the Joint Northumbria/EARLI SIG Assessment and Evaluation Conference: Learning Communities and Assessment cultures, University of Northumbria, 28–30 August.

Swann, J. and Ecclestone, K. (1999a) Litigation and learning: tensions in improving university lecturers' assessment practice, *Assessment in Education,* 6(3): 357–75.

Swann, J. and Ecclestone, K. (1999b) Improving lecturers' assessment practice in higher education: a problem-based approach, *Educational Action Research,* 7(1): 63–87.

Taras, M. (2001) The use of tutor feedback and student self-assessment in summative assessment tasks: towards transparency for students and for tutors, *Assessment and Evaluation in Higher Education,* 26(6): 605–14.

Taras, M. (2003) To feedback or not to feedback in student self-assessment, *Assessment and Evaluation in Higher Education,* 28(5): 549–65.

Taras, M. (2006) Do unto others or not: equity in feedback for undergraduates, *Assessment and Evaluation in Higher Education,* 31(3): 365–77.

Teacher Development Agency (2004) *Able to Teach: Guidance for Providers of Initial Teacher Training on Disability Discrimination and Fitness to Teach.* London: TDA.

Tenner, E. (2004) The pitfalls of academic mentorships, *Chronicle of Higher Education,* 50(49): B7–B10.

Thelwall, M. (2000) Computer-based assessment: a versatile educational tool, *Computers and Education,* 34: 37–49.

Thomas, E. (2002) *Widening Participation in Post-compulsory Education.* London: Continuum.

Thomas, P.R. and Bain, J.D. (1984) Contextual dependence of learning approaches: the effects of assessments, *Human Learning,* 3: 227–40.

Tierney, W. (2000) Power, identity and the dilemma of college student departure, in J. Braxton (ed.) *Reworking the Student Departure Puzzle.* Nashville, TN: Vanderbilt University Press.

Tinto, V. (1993) *Leaving College: Rethinking the Causes and Cures of Student Attrition,* 2nd edn. Chicago: University of Chicago Press.

Topping, K.J. (2000) Formative peer assessment of academic writing between postgraduate students, *Assessment and Evaluation in Higher Education,* 25(2): 149–69.

Torrance, H. (1993) Formative assessment: some theoretical problems and empirical questions, *Cambridge Journal of Education,* 23(3): 333–43.

Torrance, H. (1995) *Evaluating Authentic Assessment.* Buckingham: Open University Press.

Traub, R.E. and MacRury, K. (1990) Multiple choice versus free response in the testing of scholastic achievement, in K. Ingenkamp and R.S. Jager (eds) *Test und Trends 8: Jahrbuch der pädagogischen Diagnostik.* Weinheim: Beltz Verlag.

Trowler, P. and Knight, P.T. (2000) Coming to know in higher education: theorising faculty entry to new work contexts, *Higher Education Research and Development,* 19(1): 27–42.

Turner, D. (2002) *Designing and Delivering Modules.* Oxford: OCSLD.

Vazquez, D. (2003) *Case study 12, Buying games: business simulations to develop personal and work-related skills.* www.heacademy.ac.uk/profdev/case_study12.pdf (accessed 28 March 2007).

Velenchik, A.D. (1995) The case method as a strategy for teaching policy analysis to undergraduates, *Journal of Economic Education*, 26(1): 29–38.

Volet, S. and Mansfield, C. (2006) Group work at university: significance of personal goals in the regulation strategies of students with positive and negative appraisals, *Higher Education Research and Development*, 25(4): 341–56.

Warren, M. and Cheng, W. (2000) Making a difference: using peers to assess individual students contributions to a group project, *Teaching in Higher Education*, 5(2): 243–55.

Weaver, M.R. (2006) Do students value feedback? Student perceptions of tutors' written responses, *Assessment and Evaluation in Higher Education*, 31(3): 379–94.

Webb, N.M. (1995) Group Collaboration in assessment: multiple objectives, processes, and outcomes, *Educational Evaluation and Policy Analysis*, 17(2):239–61.

Wenger, E. (1998) *Communities of Practice: Learning, Meaning and Identity*. Cambridge: Cambridge University Press.

Wenger, E., McDermott, R. and Snyder, W.M. (2002) *Cultivating Communities of Practice*. Boston, MA: Harvard Business School Press.

Williams, J.B. (2006) Assertion-reasoning multiple-choice testing as a tool for deep learning: a qualitative analysis, *Assessment and Evaluation in Higher Education*, 31(3): 287–301.

Wingate, U. (2006) Doing away with study skills, *Teaching in Higher Education*, 11(4):457–69.

Wolf, A. (1995) *Competence-Based Assessment*. Buckingham: Open University Press.

Woolf, H. (2004) Assessment criteria: reflections on current practices, *Assessment and Evaluation in Higher Education*, 29(4): 479–93.

Yorke, M. (1999) *Leaving Early: Undergraduate Non-completion in Higher Education*. London: Falmer Press.

Yorke, M. (2001a) *Assessment: A Guide for Senior Managers*. York: Learning and Teaching Support Network.

Yorke, M. (2001b) Formative assessment and its relevance to retention, *Higher Education Research and Development*, 20(2): 115–26.

Yorke, M. (2003) Formative assessment in higher education: moves towards theory and the enhancement of pedagogic practice, *Higher Education*, 45(4): 477–501.

Yorke, M. and Knight, P.T. (2004) Self-theories: some implications for teaching and learning in higher education, *Studies in Higher Education*, 29(1): 25–37.

Yorke, M. and Longden, B. (2004) *Retention and Student Success in Higher Education*. Maidenhead: Open University Press.

Yorke, M., Barnett, G., Evanson, P., Haines, C., Jenkins, D., Knight, P., Scurry, D., Stowell, M. and Woolf, H. (2000) Mark distributions and marking practices in UK higher education, *Active Learning in Higher Education*, 1(1): 7–27.

Yorke, M., Barnett, G, Evanson, P. et.al. (2004) Some effects of the award algorithm on honours degree classifications in UK higher education, *Assessment and Evaluation in Higher Education*, 29(4): 401–13.

Zuber-Skerritt, O. (1992) *Action Research in Higher Education: Examples and*

Reflections. London: Kogan Page.

Index